MILWAUKEE ROAD
NARROW GAUGE

NARROW GAUGE

STATION.

RAILWAY
SCENIC·SPEEDY

Daily, and return, from Bellevue to Cascade, Iowa
Leave your team in the barn.
Never a disappointment. Never a schedule missed.
Weather no obstacle now for the traveling man and his lady. Swollen streams no longer a fear.
Sturdy rolling stock for the hauling of freight, grain, coal and other goods. Comfortable coaches.

Overcome the steep grade between Mill Creek and LaMotte.

Bonded by the federal government for the hauling of America's mail!

The gauge has attracted attention far and wide as evidenced by this poster which was created by the *Quad City Times* in 1972 for the cover of its supplement paper *FOCUS*, to accompany a story on *Iowa's Slim Princess-Courtesy of the* Quad City Times.

MILWAUKEE ROAD NARROW GAUGE
The Chicago, Bellevue, Cascade & Western
Iowa's Slim Princess

John Tigges
and
Jon Jacobson

Pruett **P** *Publishing Company*

First Edition

1   2   3   4   5   6   7   8   9

Printed in the United States of America

Library of Congress Cataloging in Publication Data

Tigges, John.
   Milwaukee Road narrow gauge.

   Bibliography: p.
   Includes index.
   1. Jacobson, Jon, 1943-   . II. Title.
TF25. B44T54 1985   385'.52'0977764   85-6502
ISBN 0-87108-694-8

Jacket photo:

Tinder-dry grass spawned a fire that raged through La Motte in July 1910. For whatever reason, since none was ever found, the flames raced uncontrolled toward the little community. The depot above, the railroad's stockyards, two loaded cars of animals, a grain elevator, milk depot and lumber yard were all destroyed before the volunteer fire department could extinguish the fire. In the tranquil scene above, before the buildings were destroyed, No. 1400 is on the point of about a half-dozen freight cars and a combine. The people on the platform seem to be oblivious of the photographer.

To

John Adney and Albin Lee, historians of Iowa's Slim Princess;

John Bradley, former general manager of the Bellevue and Cascade Railroad;

William Cook, former fireman on the C.M.&St.P. narrow gauge branch between Bellevue and Cascade;

Lester Deppe, former engineer and the man who made the last run on the Bellevue and Cascade Railroad;

Ralph Otting, who braked on the Bellevue and Cascade Railroad as a teenager;

and to the memory of Jack Benzer, Richard Bogue, Charles Spielman, Gus Schnee, Richard Sullivan and Frank Widman, all of whom worked on Iowa's Slim Princess *and shared many of their experiences with the author and others.*

Contents

The narrow gauge branch line between Bellevue and Cascade was no different than any other railroad of similar size. Why excavate a cut through a hill if it can be gone around? The scene above illustrates the resulting curved track when a slight rise was avoided between La Motte and Washington Mills.—*K. Leffert*

As for the engine leaving the track, that was a common occurrence on the old Bellevue-Cascade narrow gauge line. We were off the rails almost as much as we were on.

Allen Woodward, engineer of the first train into Cascade, Iowa, in 1879.

While researching this book, two facts presented themselves almost from the outset: First, the Chicago, Bellevue, Cascade & Western Railway, which was the first corporate name for the three-foot gauge tracks that linked Cascade, Iowa, to the outside world, via Bellevue, was maligned virtually from the beginning of its operation. Second, as the history of this railroad had passed down through the years by way of newspapers and word of mouth, it had become a confused tangle that defied analysis. Almost without exception, each fact presented in this book concerning the development of the railroad, its rolling stock and motive power, has been double-checked and in most cases triple-checked. When conflicting bits of information were uncovered, no effort was spared in tracking the truth to it's source. Fortunately, there are men like Albin L. Lee, who first began uncovering the true facts about this railroad, and John Adney, who maintains records of locomotives of many lines, including the "gauge." Both men truly care about the history of railroads, and their cooperation has been much appreciated.

Actually, this is three books in one. First, it traces the history of this narrow gauge line that begins as early as 1847. This story was completed only when the last piece of equipment was disposed of in 1972. Second, it is a picture book, illustrating what is known about the narrow gauge operation that became in time, Iowa's Slim Princess. Third, it contains tidbits of information and anecdotes that would have been distracting had they been incorporated into the history of the line itself. In many ways, the vignetts tell the story of the people involved with the operation of the railroad—their humor, their experiences, their lives.

Although many today look back on the past as being the "good old days," especially when they become frustrated with their day-to-day existence, it might come as a surprise that frustration abounded then, too. Consider Milwaukee Road employee Dick Bogue's statement concerning the narrow gauge branch line between Bellevue and Cascade, "You can describe it as being 36 x 36 x 36—thirty six inches wide, thirty six miles long and sometimes—it can take thirty six hours to get there!"

At least on one occasion, the "gauge" was immortalized in poetry when the exploits of Charlie Spielman, an engineer, were put into rhyme:

A Record Run

Attributed to M.J. Kennedy

Come all you rounders
if you want to hear,
A story about
a brave engineer
who is driving the engine
at the present time;
and had thirty years service
on the narrow gauge line.

It was in September
and the day was fine,
when he got his orders
o'er the telegraph line,
and called for
Engine number "one,"
little thinking he would
make a record run.

He looked at his watch
  and his watch was slow—
When Gongaware yelled,
  "We're r'arin' to go."
They pulled out of Bellevue
  on time to the dot,
ran through Paradise
  and into La Motte.
And Chesterman said when
  he heard the engine yell,
"Old Charlie has the throttle
  and he's coming like hell."
They stopped at La Motte
  with the mail and express,
and the fireman said,
  "I must confess
We are one minute late, but
  I think we'll beat it through;
number 'one's' steaming better
  then I ever seen her do."

Going into Zwingle a car
  jumped the track—
and it took five minutes
  to get it back.
Then Gongaware said, "This is
  going to throw us late,
unless you let her ramble
  at a dangerous rate."
Then Charlie said,
  "I'll bet you a five
we land in Cascade
  at nine twenty five."

Out of Zwingle and
  up the long hill
They ran through Sylvia
  into Washington Mills.
And Joe Thomas said,
  "We are making better time
then ever was made
  on the narrow gauge line."
When they took coal
  at Washington Mills
Charlie said, "Thank God
  We're over the hills!
I'll blow the whistle and
  you ring the bell
and we'll go through Bernard
  like a bat out of hell!"

They stopped at Fillmore
  to unload some freight
and the fireman said, "We're
  two minutes late."
But Charlie said,
  "Number 'one' never fails
and we'll land on time
  if she holds the rails."
Out of Fillmore and
  across the bridge
through Keegan's grove and
  along the ridge,
they passed Kean's crossing
  and hit down the grade,
under the overhead
  and into Cascade.
The fireman said,
  "We made it all right."

When Charlie arrives at
  the pearly gates,
and St. Peter
  his tale relates—
St. Peter will say
  as he strokes his staff,
"When you mention that railroad,
  it makes me laugh!"
Then he'll open the book
  and turn to the page
where it reads: "Employees
  on the narrow gauge."
He'll find in the space
  marked, "ENGINEERS",
that Charlie Spielman
  served thirty years.

And he'll say to Gabriel,
  "Give him a seat
among God's faithful
  and chosen sheep.
On the book of honor
  have his name enrolled.
Crown him with a
  crown of gold.
Bring him a harp
  with a golden string;
have a chorus of angels
  'Allelulia' sing.
Then let him remain
  in joy sublime—
HE HAD HELL ENOUGH ON THE
NARROW GAUGE LINE!"

The employees, like Charlie Spielman and Ed Gongaware, the shippers, the passengers—all had hell in those days but they were a different breed of people. A breed to be admired for their tenacity and drive, their ambitions and accomplishments.

This, then, is the true story of Iowa's Slim Princess.

John Tigges
Jon Jacobson

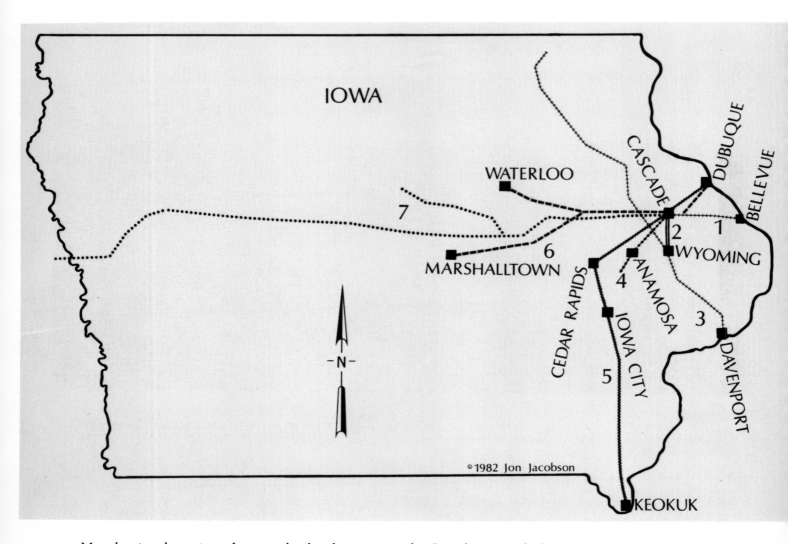

Map showing the variety of proposed railroad connections for Cascade, Iowa. The lines and dates of proposal are as follows: (1) Chicago, Bellevue, Cascade & Western, 1876; (2) the "Plug" from Cascade to Wyoming; (3) Davenport & St. Paul, 1869; (4) Cascade & Anamosa, 1857; (5) the Ram's Horn route, 1848; (6) Chicago, Cascade & Western, 1893; (7) the probable location of the proposed Western extension of the C.B.C.&W.

An 1874 Dubuque County Platt Book, found in an attic in Cascade, has the route of (7) above marked in pencil on the state railroad map. Although the identity of the person who made the markings is unknown, various routes (including the one actually built) for the C.B.C.&W., are marked in pencil on the township maps of the same book.

The above mapping of (7), and 1880 newspaper reports that grading was to be started west of Cascade, led the authors to believe that the person who marked (7) was either involved in planning the C.B.C.&W., or had specific information from the actual planners.

Continuing west from Cascade, (7) is marked the pass between Eldora and Marshalltown, exiting Iowa near Onawa. A branch line at Traer, through Grundy Center and joining the Dubuque & Sioux City near Iowa Falls, is also marked.

1

In the Beginning

An early picture of Cascade, Iowa showing the falls for which the town was named. The large buildings on either side of the river were mills, which drew their power from the flowing waters of the north fork of the Maquoketa River. The dam that formed the walls created a bottleneck for trees and other debris during a severe flood in 1925, and to avoid further damage, the dam was dynamited.—*C. Wyrick*

The biggest railroad construction period the world has ever seen was initiated during the years that followed the Ciil War. When the gold spike was driven in May 10, 1869, at Promontory Point, completing the first transcontinental network of rails, the nation became even more railroad conscious. Railroads—building them, riding them, shipping on them, and investing in them—became an almost fanatical dogma to America of the nineteenth century.

Lines expanded, new lines were developed on paper and on the earth, and lines were consolidated into potential giants. The fact they were needed was not the issue. Railroads in the eastern part of the United States had been, for the most part, built with a purpose in mind. Prosperity belonged to those cities,

towns and villages that clung tenaciously to the rails of some branch line or main line.

The building mania, however, was most predominate west of the Mississippi River, and it was in the wide open spaces that rails were laid from here to there without regard to purpose or reason. The important thing was to get the line in—forget where the rails were going—forget that other lines might connect with it. Thoughts like that were for the thinkers, not the doers. The railroads being built were not looking for business, they were creating it.

A town could survive in the East without rail service. Towns in the western states, however, that depended only on stage companies were suffering from a terminal illness that would eventually result in "ghost-

1

townitis." Rails were needed in the wide open spaces and that thought was not new in the 1850s and 1860s. As early as 1832 an unidentified letter writer in the Ann Arbor, Michigan, *Emigrant*, proposed the idea for a transcontinental network of rails. To this day no one knows for certain the identity of that anonymous writer. There are those midwesterners who believe a man by the name of John Plumbe, Jr. of Dubuque, Iowa, could have penned the idea.

Plumbe's candidacy does have merit. He wrote for many of the leading eastern newspapers and usually under the *nom de plume* "Iowaian." After having served as an assistant to the surveyor who was platting a new line of railroads in Pennsylvania, Plumbe moved to Iowa in 1836. He immediately began talking of a "National Railroad to Oregon Country." Armed with maps and procedural outlines, Plumbe began organizing formal and informal meetings in Galena and Bloomington in Illinois, Burlington in the Iowa Territory and other points in the middle part of the country. Wherever he spoke, resolutions were adopted, supporting *his* "great enterprise." In 1847, at a meeting held in Dubuque, John Plumbe, Jr. was honored as the "Original Projector of the Great Oregon Railroad."

Some of Plumbe's writings still exist, as well as one map dated 1839, showing a portion of his railroad. Although these items are considered rare Americana by the Smithsonian Institution, Plumbe, himself, was destined to be historically insignificant. A goodly portion of the transcontinental line that he envisioned came to fruition when the Union Pacific rails were laid along some of his proposed thoroughfares. Unfortunately, John Plumbe, Jr. did not live to see that road built. When he returned to Dubuque, following a trip to promote his ideas in California, he became distressed upon learning of Asa Whitney's claim of originating the idea of a transcontinental system of rails. He rebutted this claim with letters and pamphlets, but Whitney's gains were too strongly entrenched and Plumbe committed suicide.

One point exists that is irrefutable where Plumbe and his idea are concerned. George Wallace Jones, the Wisconsin territorial representative, presented on May 21, 1838, in the U.S. House of Representatives, a memorial from Plumbe's committee, which had been formed at a meeting shortly after the Welchman's arrival. The petition requested "the survey of a route for a railroad from the Mississippi River, at Dubuque to Milwaukie, Wisconsin Territory." Along with the proposal, Jones displayed maps on which were designated (sic) "the National Rail Road to Milwaukie."

Because of Plumbe and his enthusiasm, the upper Mississippi River valley was very railroad conscious prior to 1850. Cascade, Iowa, a village of less than four hundred people located twenty-five miles south and west of Dubuque and thirty-five miles from the Mississippi itself, was one such place. One year after Iowa's admission to the Union, Cascade was worried about its future as a town without rails. Served by the Western Stage Company, the village wanted to be part of any railroad-building project proposed for the area.

Until 1855, the Old Military Road carried the mainstream of produce, people and packages through Cascade. This road had grown from a one hundred-mile-long furrow plowed in 1939 by a crew of men headed by Lyman Dillon. It connected Dubuque, county seat of Dubuque County, and the then territorial capital, Iowa City. Cascade's population had grown to 450 and the railroading flame of interest was rekindled when the Dubuque Western Railroad was incorporated September 10, 1855. Passing through a series of corporate names, it finally became the Dubuque South Western Rail Road in 1863 and reached Cedar Rapids within the next two years. The rails passed through Farley, Worthington and Monticello, villages of similar size to Cascade and each less than fifteen miles away.

Then, in 1868, the Davenport and Saint Paul Rail Road was incorporated and, once the rails were laid, passed through Monticello, giving it two railroads. By 1872, the tiny town of Delaware which was only twenty miles away, had train service while Cascade had approximately a population of one thousand and still no railroad.

The year 1872 also saw the Iowa Eastern chartered to build its main line from Elkader to Beulah, using iron-plated wooden rails (strap rails). Both towns were north of Dubuque and of a comparable size to Cascade. Still, Cascade

John Plumbe, Jr. (1809-1857) was primarily responsible for arousing interest in railroading throughout the Midwest during the 1830s and 1840s. Before settling in Dubuque (1836), he had assisted in surveying a railroad route across the Alleghenies in Huntington County, Pennsylvania. Realizing the potential of rail travel, he called meetings in various towns in Iowa, Wisconsin and Illinois, gave lectures wherever he could, drafted resolutions, and sent voluminous letters to eastern newspapers. His letters to newspapers were always signed "Iowaian" or were sent. anonomously. In 1838 he succeeded in memorializing the United States Government, through the efforts of his friend, George Wallace Jones the territorial representative, and secured $2,000 for the survey of a route from Milwaukee to Sinipee, Wisconsin, which was on the Mississippi River several miles north of Dubuque. A map, which he produced in 1839 and is also included in this book, showed a portion of this "National Railroad." Several citizens of Dubuque who heard Plumbe speak on the subject of the Pacific Railroad subsequently remarked that his project was "wild and visionary in the extreme" and "the dream of the enthusiast." However, while on tour of the Iowa Territory with Governor Robert Lucas in the fall of 1838, Theodore S. Parvin, the governor's secretary, recorded the following (after a lengthy description of Plumbe, and the topic of his speech): "The young man's name was John Plumbe, Jr. and he, and he alone, is the author, the first promulgator and advocate of a transcontinental line from the lakes to the ocean." While Asa Whitney has been credited with successfully promoting the

George Wallace Jones, while serving as the Wisconsin Territorial Representative, presented, on May 21, 1838, in the United States House of Representatives, a petition requesting (sic) "The survey of a route for a railroad from the Mississippi River, at Dubuque to Milwaukie, Wisconsin Territory." Jones, who had served as territorial representive for Michigan and Wisconsin, named the latter when it became a state, outmaneuvered John C. Calhoun to gain the status of territory for Iowa, and eventually named that state, and served the Hawkeye state as a United States Senator for two terms. He was referred to as General George Wallace Jones, which title superceded all others he ever acquired, including United States Ambassador, when he was appointed surveyor general in 1840 and again in 1844.

---

idea of a transcontinental railroad, he was by no means the first. Whitney did not petition Congress to construct a network of rails across the western portion of the country until after he made a railroad survey from Milwaukee, across Northern Iowa to the Big Sioux River in 1845—SEVEN YEARS after Plumbe had successfully acquired $2,000 from the government for a survey. A quiet man, Plumbe developed a method of producing Daguerreotypes on paper which he called "Plumbeotypes." Unfortunately, he never patented the process but several magazines of the 1840s display his "Plumbeotypes" and still exist in the Library of Congress, Brown University and the American Antiquarian Society.

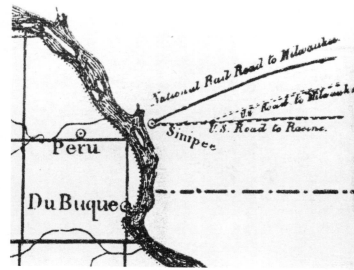

Enlarged portion of Plumbe's map clearly indicating the "National Rail Road to Milwaukie," a proposed "U.S. Road to Milwaukie" as well as a "U.S. Road to Racine." Sinipee was the "paper town" that Plumbe owned. He hoped to recover some of the money he had spent in traveling about the area while promoting his idea for a transcontinental network of rails. Although John Plumbe, Jr. was appointed postmaster at Sinipee, no buildings were ever erected.

This advertisement was placed at the back of John Plumbe, Jr.'s book *Sketches of Iowa and Wisconsin.* It is promoting the map of the Territory of Iowa as it was in 1839. Plumbe's written works are considered rare pieces of Americana today and are to be found in the Library of Congress, Brown University and the American Antiquarian Society.

The above map of the eastern portion of the Iowa Territory, was the first map to indicate the location of the territory's "permanent seat of government" as well as a portion of John Plumbe's "National Rail Road." Plumbe not only executed this map, but wrote many letters to eastern newspapers as well as a book entitled *Sketches of Iowa and Wisconsin,* which is a collector's item today. He also founded a magazine for the sole purpose of promoting his Plumbeotypes (Daguerreotypes produced on paper). He never patented the process.

had nothing and a sense of panic was beginning to build in the townspeople.

And it was not that the citizens were doing nothing about their plight. Concern began to grow when it became evident the rails of the Dubuque South Western Railroad would bypass Cascade. More than concerned, Dr. W.H. Francis gave up his medical practice, closed his drug and general merchandise store and began searching for a railroad to come to his town.

As early as 1848, Cascade had wanted in on the proposed Ram's Horn route from Dubuque to Keokuk, via Cascade, Cedar Rapids and Iowa City. When that plan failed to materialize

George G. Banghart arrived in Cascade in 1841, started a dry goods and general merchandise store, was also a cattle agent and one of the largest shippers using the narrow gauge. Contemporary biographical information indicates he was the largest stockholder in the original Chicago, Bellevue, Cascade & Western, a director from its organization, and was at one time vice-president and treasurer.

anything but talk, two rail lines were proposed in the early 1850's, the tracks of which would run straight across the state of Iowa with Cascade a point on one of the roads.

Articles of incorporation for the Cascade and Anamosa Rail Road Company, were filed on May 26, 1857. The Cascaders were going to be ready for their opportunity with that other rail line. The articles stated that the main line "shall commence on the Great North Western Railroad or near Cascade and run thence South Westerly to intersect with the Iowa Central Air Line Rail Road at or near Anamosa and ultimately thence Southerly to intersect with the ———." The Cascade and Anamosa became as nebulous as the railroad with which it was to intersect beyond the latter town. The most notable thing about this particular endeavor is the signature, S.S. Merrill of Cascade. Could this be the same Merrill who helped establish the Chicago, Milwaukee and St. Paul Railway in Iowa?

Cascade had wanted to be included in the South Western, then the Davenport and St. Paul before the proposed "plug" line from Cascade to Wyoming, Iowa, was examined. All of these ideas and schemes for railroads had failed the determined Cascaders.

At first Dr. Francis advocated the extension of narrow gauge rails from a proposed Milwaukee to Dubuque line, through Cascade and on to Des Moines. Francis kept up a running correspondence with President Benjamin of that company until the entire project fell apart. Then, he wanted to relocate the rails of the then Dubuque South Western Rail Road. Literally, he wanted to move the rails from Farley and Monticello and re-lay them between Dubuque and Cascade. More than one hundred letters passed between Dr. Francis and George Crane, attorney for the South Western road. Twenty visits to the county seat and numerous requests for money from his neighbors and friends brought enough capital to hire the Everts Engineering Corps. Everts was to survey the most plausible route between Cascade and Dubuque. When it seemed as though the impossible scheme might work, it, too, fell apart.

Undaunted, Doctor Francis looked to the east and Bellevue, which hugs the western bank of the Mississippi River. The doctor knew he must accomplish something soon or

Because of John Plumbe, Jr.'s enthusiasm for railroads, the people of Cascade were more than eager to have rails connecting their town with the outside world. The Cascade and Anamosa Rail Road Company was formed in anticipation of connecting with one of two proposed "air lines" which were to cross Iowa to the Missouri River. However, when the two lines produced nothing but air, the C.&A. became just another effort that failed.

Cascade was doomed. He had seen his own town's business fall off, once Monticello had been included on a main line. No longer could the businessmen rely solely on the Old Military Road. Hopefully, his contact in Bellevue, Captain M.R. Brown, would understand the need for a railroad. Bellevue already had a standard gauge railroad rolling trains north to Dubuque and south to Clinton, Iowa. Brown had been instrumental in the Dubuque, Bellevue & Mississippi Rail Way's origin in 1870. That road became the Chicago, Clinton and Dubuque Rail Road in 1871.

The C.C. & D. Rail Road would eventually come under the guidance of James F. Joy who had been president of the Chicago, Burlington and Quincy Rail Road. When Joy left that office in 1871, he wanted to continue dominating the C.B. & Q. but was eventually thwarted in his efforts. Retaining his position as a board member on that road, Joy began looking for other companies in which to invest. One common practice among established railroads of the time was to promote and support indirectly, beginning lines. Once the fledgling company was a proven commodity, the smaller railroad would be added to the larger. It was Joy's intention to pull together several smaller companies and create a salable product. His projects in the upper Mississippi River valley would not come into existence until mid-1877, however.

But time was passing too quickly for Dr. Francis. Although no one in Cascade knew of Joy at the time, Francis felt as though the full responsibility for bringing rails to town fell on him. On October 13, 1876, he wrote Captain Brown concerning the construction of a narrow gauge railroad between their towns. The idea was met with favorable enthusiasm when the citizens of Bellevue determined that relocation of the county seat to their town might be possible if another railroad served them. The following spring, a Eugene Perrin was appointed to explore possible routes. On May 15, 1877, Perrin led a party of Bellevue's leading railroad men on a tour between the river city and Cottonville, which was south and east of La Motte. Potential grades of the proposed route were examined with a more comprehensive survey planned for the near future. Perrin and his crew returned with the report that it did not seem to be a very difficult or expensive route over which to build a railroad. Seven weeks earlier, at the beginning of April, George Wilson, C. Denlinger and

Typical of the terrain encountered when the railroad was constructed, this 1981 photo shows the path of the roadbed. (Dotted line.) Heading west, from left to right, the tracks would climb gradually through this valley toward Bernard, some three miles distant. Although not one of the severe grades on the route, trains would be doubled from this location to Bernard whenever the diminutive locomotives could not handle the tonnage.—*J. Jacobson*

Daniel Cort conducted a similar exploration of their own between La Motte and Garryown by way of Zwingle.

Although the preliminary surveys sounded optimistic, it is almost vital to understand something of the topography through which the railroad was to pass. The northeast corner of Iowa, the northwest corner of Illinois and the southwest corner of Wisconsin were all untouched at least by the last glacier that covered the North American continent. Because of this peculiarity, the terrain is rough, hilly and anything but level. Dubuque and Jackson counties, through which the proposed narrow gauge line would ultimately pass, is representative of this phenomenon. Hills separated by deep gullies and ravines, were initially pushed up by the passing glaciers, giving a wrinkled effect to the land. However, they were never smoothed out by the ice masses. To better illustrate this quirk of nature, river sand was found on the top of a bluff overlooking the Mississippi River when a water stand was erected in Dubuque.

As a result of this inattention by Mother Nature, the little trains would be destined to move over the tops of these hills since there was no reasonably level route between the terminals. Uncompensated grades of up to 2.8 percent and minimum curves of 12½ degrees were the governing factors to be eventually built into the selected route.[1]

Railroad fever was running high. The smaller communities of Jackson County and southern Dubuque County were already anticipating more rapid growth once the rails passed through their corporate limits. The area's population had more than doubled from 3,281 in 1850 to 7,770 in 1860. When the surveys were completed in early summer, the proposed route had the rails heading west from Bellevue to La Motte and Zwingle before cutting back south and east to pass through Cottonville. From Cottonville the trains were to begin angling northwesterly toward Cascade through Otter Creek and Garryown. Bernard, Fillmore and what was to be Washington Mills were to be bypassed in favor of the three communities to the south.

The farmers of the area were equally

Seventy-five percent of the right-of-way would only be thirty-three feet wide. Some stretches would be considerably narrower than that as evidenced by this photo looking east, of one of the many rock cuts at Washington Mills. Ralph Otting, a teen-age brakeman on the narrow gauge in the late twenties and early thirties, is standing on the roadbed.—*Jon Jacobson*

The "Farmer Railroaders" as the backers of the proposed railroad would be referred to, faced the task of overcoming rough terrain such as is shown in the photo above. The picture taken in 1981 demonstrates that the hilly features have not changed in over a hundred years.—*Jon Jacobson*

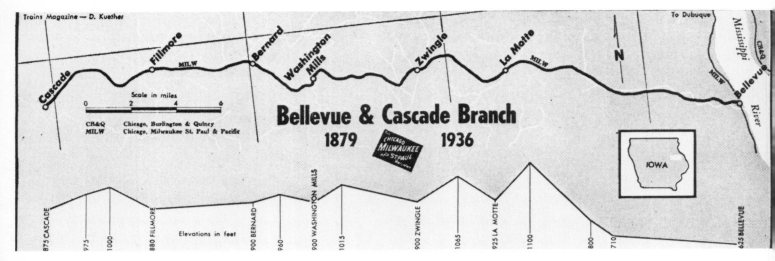

Bellevue & Cascade Branch
1879   1936

Scale in miles
0   2   4   6

CB&Q   Chicago, Burlington & Quincy
MILW   Chicago, Milwaukee St. Paul & Pacific

Elevations in feet

IOWA

875 CASCADE · 975 · 1000 · 880 FILLMORE · 900 BERNARD · 960 · 900 WASHINGTON MILLS · 1015 · 900 ZWINGLE · 1065 · 925 LA MOTTE · 1100 · 800 · 710 · 675 BELLEVUE

The above map shows the type of terrain that had to be overcome to build the Chicago, Bellevue, Cascade & Western Railway. The map was originally drawn to illustrate an article by A.L. Lee that appeared in the April 1954 issue of *Trains*, copyright 1954, Kalmbach Publishing Company.

enthusiastic, ready to lend not only whatever financial aid they could afford but physical labor and animal power for grading the right-of-way. The Dubuque *Herald* published an editorial stating that the farmers should be on the watch for charlatans and opportunists who first might try to convince the population of both terminal towns that such a road was not needed and then try to take over the project. Despite this warning the people involved had such spirit and drive that they felt any adversity could be overcome—somehow.

The Bellevue and Cascade Railroad project was officially born, following the completion of the survey, as the Chicago, Bellevue, Cascade and Western Narrow Gauge Rail Way Company at Bellevue, Iowa, August 4, 1877. A full slate of officers and directors were elected the thirtieth of August at Cascade. Judge Joseph Kelso of Bellevue, who had been involved with incorporating the Dubuque, Bellevue & Mississippi Rail Way, was elected president. G.G. Banghart, the largest cattle producer in the Cascade area, became vice president. Captain M.R. Brown, like Judge Kelso, had previous railroading experience and was chosen treasurer while S.S. Simpson became secretary. Stock worth $200,000 was to be issued for the construction, and the articles of incorporation were filed November 23.

The first opposition to the proposed road came from, of all places, Dubuque. By the end of 1877, interest in the idea of a railroad from Dubuque to Cascade had attracted the attention of several outstanding businessmen of

that city. The newspaper, which had warned the two small communities so explicitly less than ten months before, became involved as well. In an editorial, which appeared in the December 30, 1877, issue of the *Herald*, the Dubuque forces stated that:

> ...citizens in Dubuque have taken hold of the project *we have been so long urging,* [author's italics] of a railroad to Cascade. The matter has been fully talked up, plans projected and an understanding arrived at by which the project is sure to be pushed through to success. A meeting was held on Saturday last, at which articles on incorporation were drawn up, a company formed, and a board of directors chosen. In this list will be recognized some of the best names in Dubuque, men of means, men of enterprise and men who inspire confidence. The name of almost anyone of them alone is sufficient to insure the success of any project they take hold of.

There followed a list of the most influential men of Dubuque and a statement that they could build their proposed railroad for fifty thousand dollars less than the northern extension of the standard gauge River Road, incorporated as the Chicago, Dubuque and Minnesota Railroad in 1871, which had cost $200,000. The Bellevue-to-Cascade route champions must have wondered if the line could be built for $50,000 less than they were anticipating. The barb finished with: "So, make room for the Dubuque, Casade and Western Railroad. We believe it will be built within a year."

The Dubuquers had not reckoned with the

Because of Mother Nature's inattention during the last glacier's passing, the area's topography is hilly with many deep valleys. Ralph Otting who worked on occasion for the narrow gauge while a youth, stands just to the side of the roadbed in 1981. Behind him, to the east, is the entrance to the cut at the "summit," the highest point on the line.—*Jon Jacobson*

indomitable spirit of the Cascaders, which had grown and toughened by each rejection over the years.

Ten days later, the *Herald* ran the following letter and resolution, which had been drafted by Dr. Francis:

> The board of directors of the Dubuque, Cascade and Western Railroad have invited a committee of directors and citizens of Cascade to hold a conference with the members of the company at Dubuque. Assurance is given that Dubuque is in earnest. Dr. Francis, the assistant secretary of the C.B.C.&W. Railroad, called a meeting at his office on Thursday evening. The invitation of the directors of the Dubuque, Cascade and Western Railroad was discussed and the following resolution was offered and adopted.
>
> *Resolved:* That whilst we, the people of Cascade and vicinity, are not insensible to the great advantages to be derived by railroad connections with the city of Dubuque; and whilst we have been long and earnestly desirious that such connection should be

completed, and whilst we appreciate the seemingly earnest efforts that are now being at the city of Dubuque, to complete so desireable an enterprise, yet we are now earnestly and actively engaged in a project to construct a railroad from Bellevue to Cascade, with every reasonable prospect of success, and sincerely regret our inability to give assistance to the Dubuque, Cascade and Western project, until we have completed the railroad from Cascade to Bellevue, or demonstrated the fact that such a railroad cannot be constructed.

> Dr. W. H. Francis, (assistant) Sec.

Without crying foul, the Dubuque paper pointed out the fact that the people of Cascade were doing their darndest to get away from the county seat in supporting the Bellevue and Cascade Railroad project. Not all of them, mind you, just some of them. Why alienate an entire community? Nor had the Dubuque *Herald* published the letter with the intention of discouraging those involved in this new railroad project. Apparently, the editors just wanted to point out how the successful businessmen of Dubuque had been snubbed by the Bellevue and Cascade leaders. More complaining followed in the editorial but to no avail. The Dubuque, Cascade and Western Rail Road died an appropriate death in the minds of the ambitious few who could not follow their own advice.

Before the Bellevue-to-Cascade route champions could move, legally or physically, toward beginning their railroad, another voice of dissension was heard. John Burk wrote to the Dubuque *Herald*, reflecting the Garryown farmers' reluctance to give land for the right-of-way, by supporting the idea of a road connecting Cascade to the county seat. He applauded the efforts of the "men of wealth and influence" who were behind the Dubuque, Cascade and Western, by cutting down the efforts of his neighbors who were involved in the original proposition. Burk further claimed to "know that no township along that route will vote a tax, and it is obvious that no company will build such a road." Dubbing the proposed line as a "worthless company," Burk called for the repeal of the law granting the C.B.C.&.W.'s existence.

Undaunted by the flagrant name-calling, the railroad entrepreneurs of Bellevue and Cascade forged ahead with their plans. By January 30, 1878, the state had approved their company. The route would include Bellevue,

La Motte, Zwingle, Washington Mills, Bernard, Fillmore and Cascade. The station at Paradise Valley would be added shortly thereafter as well as the siding at Sylva Switch.[2] Because the towns of Cottonville, Otter Creek and Garryown as well as the farmers in that area refused to cooperate by deeding land to the proposed railroad, they were excluded from immediate service. If they wanted to use the railroad facilities, they would have to go to some neighboring town on the mainline.

In June 1878, a change in the officers took place when John W. Tripp was made president and Dr. Francis took over as secretary. At the first annual meeting, September 4, 1878, Tripp and Francis were reelected to their respective posts. The Reverend James Hill, who was from Cascade and had won fame as the "fighting chaplain" during the Civil War, became vice president. G.G. Banghart assisted Judge Joseph Kelso who was elected treasurer. A.J. Dorchester acting as Dr. Francis's assistant, rounded out the slate of officers. Several prominent citizens from each township were named to serve along with the elected officers as board of directors. Capital and labor of $200,000 seemed assured and on September 19, 1878, President Tripp turned the first shovelful of dirt to inaugurate the Chicago, Bellevue, Cascade & Western Railway.

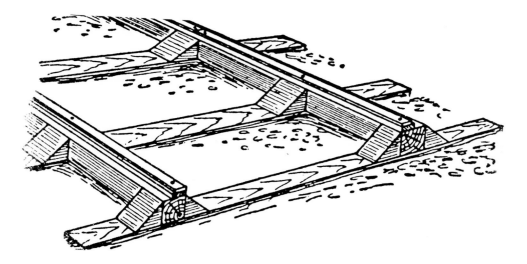

When the communities of Elkader and Beulah, Iowa had train service in 1875, the people of Cascade realized they had to do something soon or their town would not survive. Elkader and Beulah were similar to Cascade in size and the rails linking them were made of wood plated with iron (strap rails). Eventually, iron rails replaced the strap rails.

In those days:

Riding a stagecoach as depicted in the movies usually appears to be a rather enjoyable experience. However such was not the case—especially in the hilly regions around the northeastern parts of Iowa. Since there were no facilities on board and since the distances traveled took the coach past many farms, it was not uncommon for enterprising farmers to set up a tavernlike arrangement in their home's living room. The stage would stop whenever someone had a need for such of various reasons at the nearest farm that acted as a way station. If it was close to meal time, food and drink would be available. A glass of beer, large enough to hold twenty ounces, could be had for five cents.

incorporated: *August 4, 1877*

Chicago, Bellevue, Cascade, & Western Railway Co.

IOWA

Dubuque and Minnesota R.R.

WISCONSIN

ILLINOIS

DUBUQUE

DUNLEITH (East Dubuque)

Illinois Central R.R.

Dubuque and Sioux City R.R.

Farley   Epworth   Peosta

Dubuque, Bellevue and Mississippi R.R.

MISSISSIPPI RIVER

CHICAGO MILWAUKEE ST. PAUL AND PACIFIC

Dubuque Co.

Jackson Co.

[Hempstead] FILLMORE

Lytle's Creek   WASHINGTON MILLS

SYLVA

LAMOTTE

Whitewater Creek   BERNARD

-N-

CASCADE

GARRYOWEN   line of original survey   ZWINGLE

"The Summit"

PARADISE

Operated as:

- *Chicago, Clinton, Dubuque, & Minnesota Railroad Co., 1879-1880*

OTTER CREEK

COTTONVILLE

BELLEVUE

- Chicago, Milwaukee, & St. Paul Railway Co., 1880-1927
Chicago, Milwaukee, St. Paul & Pacific Railway Co., 1927-1933

- **BELLEVUE and CASCADE RAILROAD CO., 1933-1936**

Length of line 35.72 miles

BELLEVUE-CASCADE NARROW GAUGE

The map above illustrates the route of the narrow gauge rails that connected Cascade to Bellevue and the outside world. It also depicts the immediate routes of several other railroads, most notably the Dubuque and Minnesota RR (1869) and the Dubuque and Mississippi RR (actually the proper corporate title was Dubuque, Bellevue and Mississippi RR) that came into being in 1870. These two roads formed the Chicago, Clinton, Dubuque and Minnesota RR, which controlled the gauge when the River Road was sold to the Milwaukee.

14

2

1878 - 1879 "At Last We Have It!"

The locomotive above was one of two similar engines owned by the Iowa Eastern. These 2-6-0 Grant Moguls are said to be the first locomotives of this design delivered west of the Mississippi. Builder's number 885 was erected in 1872, the same year the Iowa Eastern was chartered. The Iowa Eastern came under the ownership of the Milwaukee Railroad in 1881 and was widened to standard gauge the next year. One of the Grant Moguls went to the Waukon and Mississippi narrow gauge branch of the Milwaukee and was numbered 64. While on the Iowa Eastern the locomotives did not carry numbers but were named "Diamond Joe" and "Pathfinder." Note the unusual wheel arrangement under the tender. It is obviously a builder's photo since the headlight has not been put in place.

In the nineteenth century narrow gauge railroads were the salvation of many small communities, which otherwise might never have had the benefit of rail transportation. The nation's first narrow gauge locomotive, a Baldwin 2-4-0 type named the "Montezuma," arrived on the Denver and Rio Grande railroad property in 1872. Within ten years there were innumerable slim gauge lines all over the West, crisscrossing each other. In Iowa seven, three-foot roads plus a twenty-four-mile branch line, would be operating within the state by the end of 1879. Compiled from the 1879-1880 Board of Railroad Commissioners reports, the seven roads were:

1. Burlington & Northwestern Railway
2. Chicago, Bellevue, Cascade & Western Railway
3. Crooked Creek Railway
4. Des Moines, Adel & Western Railroad
5. Fort Madison & Northwestern
6. Iowa Eastern Railroad
7. Waukon & Mississippi Railroad

A logical question at this point is, Why were these little railroads built in the first place if the standard gauge of 4 foot 8½ inches was being built elsewhere?

There were several reasons for choosing a narrow gauge line. First, economics. The rail

15

normally used for narrow gauge track could be very light, such as thirty pounds-to-the-yard. The motive power was much lower in cost than standard size locomotives and the same was true for the smaller rolling stock. Second, feasibility. The rails could be laid on poorly graded right-of-ways since the trains would not weigh as much. Ready-to-build-and-run railroads could be ordered from manufacturers' catalogs. Then, too, the curves could be much tighter than the long gentle ones that were preferred for the faster moving standard gauge trains. Since the track could be laid without the extreme care and dedication required by the larger rails, a railroad could be built much more quickly. As a result, the three-foot width became the standard of mountain railroading in the West, and the only way towns such as Cascade, Iowa, could get railroad service.

The ultimate hope, which these small towns held, was that a "standard" railroad would acquire their slim gauge line. Then, the tracks to their town would be widened and further prosperity could be enjoyed.

Cascade was desperate for the trains to come to town. The Iowa roads of the 1870's were terrible at best. Impassable in the winter, muddy bogs during the inclement seasons and rough to traverse when it wasn't snowing or raining. Horses, horse-drawn wagons and walking were the only modes of transportation for people and produce over land, outside of the railroad.

But the year 1878 saw the hopes of Cascade's citizens soar. They were finally going to have their own railroad. Following the ground breaking ceremony at Cascade, grading work was begun at several locations by the fifth of November. Hills were being leveled and valleys smoothed near Zwingle, following an inauguration ceremony there, which was presided over by President Tripp and Dr. Francis. At La Motte, which was east of both Cascade and Zwingle, a mile of main line grade was prepared within days.

With one or two exceptions the entire right-of-way between La Motte and Cascade had been secured without cost to the company. While stock subscriptions were worked out instead of a cash purchase by many of the stockholders, there were those who had feelings of apprehension about the dollar cost

at first. Would there be more labor available than cash? Predictions of higher costs involved when "amateur railroaders" did the work, failed to materialize. C.H. Brown, who managed the grading operation at La Motte saw that no waste happened under his guiding hand. To prove his point, the engineer quickly estimated that 2,000 cubic yards of earth had been moved at an expense of $50 while a regular contractor would have charged $200. The "farmer railroaders" were going to prove the impossible could be done.

So much enthusiasm pervaded the area, that the people of La Motte had a grand railroad "bee" on November 5, 1878. Participation involved a gift of labor on the road. Now, how could this venture meet with anything but success with that type of spirit?

The question of tax bond issues had been settled and all the railroad company had to do was get their rails to the towns along the planned right-of-way to collect $65,000. If all it had taken was spirit and labor, nothing would have stopped the line from being completed in record time. Unfortunately, such would not be the case. To complicate matters, President Tripp chose to resign on January 7, 1879. Suddenly the thin finances appeared to be more than just shaky when the question of stocks purchased by work consignments was taken into consideration. G.G. Banghart, who had been the vice president at the road's inception, had been elected to assist Judge Kelso, who was treasurer. The largest stockholder in the company, Banghart, must have had feelings of anxiety. His chief interest in the road lay in being able to ship his livestock by rail to market and at the same time utilizing the easier mode for bringing merchandise in to his general store.

However, the Reverend James Hill, exercising his new duties as president of the line, did not waste time. He quickly invited F.O. Wyatt, general superintendent of the Chicago, Clinton, Dubuque and Minnesota Rail Road, to tour the proposed line, which was already being graded in several places. Wyatt had been engaged in railroading since 1852, working for various lines in the East and South. In 1869, he built, under the direction of James F. Joy, the Wisconsin Valley Railroad and had been transferred to the River Road in 1877. Hill felt the railroad man would be able to offer some fresh insight into their problems. Wyatt's most notable suggestion, once he had examined the terrain, was that a tunnel should be bored upward to La Motte from the Mississippi River Valley. Apparently, he felt this was wiser than building a grade on the surface to the summit, which was over five hundred feet above Bellevue.[3]

When Wyatt returned to Dubuque on the twenty-fifth of January, rumors began circulating that the River Road was about to extend material aid to the narrow gauge

James Hill

CASCADE.

An early Dubuque and Cascade resident, the Reverend James Hill gained fame during the Civil War as the "Fighting Chaplain." One of the original incorporators of the C.B.C.&W., Hill served as president of the line in 1879, but resigned before completion.

undertaking. However, the *Herald* saw fit to squelch such ideas by saying the River Road probably did not see much future profit in the branch line should it be completed. Specifically, it stated that most of the trade of the country through which the road will pass, is already gobbled by competing lines and Mr. Wyatt is too good a manager to involve the trunk line in the expense of maintaining feeders that would eventually operate upon the treasury."

The C.C.D.&M. was then currently offering to its stockholders an issue of $400,000, five-year two-percent bonds. These were to be available at par and accrued interest February 1. The proceeds of this bond sale were to be used to meet expenditures involving the purchase and building of extensions. The River Road was in good financial shape and had no bonded debts at this point.

While nothing happened immediately following Wyatt's inspection trip of the C.B.C.&W. property, the people along the proposed main line were patiently waiting for spring. The citizens of Bellevue were more interested than ever in the project and the opinion was that the line would be completed by late summer, early autumn at the latest. Feelings that the year's produce would be sent to market by rail, were in the majority. The Dubuque *Herald* persisted in reporting the fact that "Chronic growlers who have and will continue to predict all kinds of disaster—will find fault with this and that thing, and will be dissatisfied under all circumstances." The fickleness of the contemporary journalists can be seen in the article's next paragraph when they encouraged the farmers to prepare timber for use as ties along the right-of-way.

On May 16, 1879, Ike Baldwin, an ardent supporter of the road from the beginning, ran headlines in his Cascade *Pioneer* that read:

SCREAM OUT OLD BIRD! HURRAH FOR THE NARROW GAUGE! DAYLIGHT AT LAST! THE MANNA THAT LEADS US OUT OF THE WILDERNESS RISES FROM THE BULLRUSHES OF DETROIT AND THE ST. CLAIR FLATS. J.F. JOY, THE RAILROAD CAPITALIST COMES TO THE RESCUE. THE STOCK AND FRANCHISE OF THE C.B.C.&W. RAILROAD TO BE TRANSFERRED TO J.F. JOY, PRESIDENT OF THE C.C.D.&M. R.R. AND THE

CORPORATION TO BE CONTROLLED BY THE C.C.D.&M. RAILROAD COMPANY! GOOD NEWS FOR THE RURAL DISTRICTS! HOW ARE YOU, METROPOLIS OF IOWA?

Joy, who had been president of the Chicago, Burlington and Quincy Railroad from July 12, 1865, to July 11, 1871, and had headed the Burlington and Missouri River Railroad prior to that, operated out of Detroit, Michigan. In 1879, James F. Joy was president of the Chicago, Clinton, Dubuque and Minnesota

James F. Joy, who had been president of the Chicago, Burlington and Quincy Railroad from July 12, 1865 to July 11, 1871 and had headed the Burlington and Missouri River Railroad prior to that, operated out of Detroit, Michigan. After his tenure as president of the C.B.&Q., he remained with that road as a member of the board of directors. By 1879, he had taken over the financially troubled Chicago, Clinton and Dubuque Railroad and the Chicago, Dubuque and Minnesota Railroad, and forged them into the Chicago, Clinton, Dubuque and Minnesota—"The River Road." He not only served as president of the C.C.D.&M. but of the Wisconsin Valley Railroad as well. Serving as officer or director of several other roads, the financier usually seemed to favor the smaller road over the larger. Once he sold his interests in the River Road to Milwaukee, he withdrew from the railroad scene in the area.

Rail Road, and the Wisconsin Valley Railroad. He also served in like capacity or as a director for several other roads.

George Runkle of Tomah, Wisconsin, who was associated with the Wisconsin Valley Railroad, was appointed as Joy's accredited agent. Through Runkle, Joy sent the following proposition to President Hill and the other officers of the C.B.C.&W. Railroad:

J. F. Joy agrees to build the C.B.C.&W. Railroad by furnishing the necessary capital, iron and rolling stock, if the people along the line will comply with the following conditions, viz: To guarantee that the right of way between Cascade and Bellevue shall be accrued without lessening the present aid subscribed; to secure the depot grounds selected by the general manager of the C.C.D.&M. Railroad; to guarantee the subscription along the line to be good for ninety (90) cents on the dollar and to be paid in labor or money to aid in the construction or building of the road; the present officers to step down and out and the corporation to be controlled hereafter by J.F. Joy and the new officers elect.

After considering the proprosition, preliminary steps were taken to turn over the stock. There were two meetings held, one in Cascade on Thursday May 15, another in Zwingle on May 17. F.O. Wyatt, general manager of the River Road, was elected president of the C.B.C.&W. and George Runkle was appointed general manager. A series of meetings were then held in which questions of the stockholders were answered. When the issue was voted on July 12, 1879, the C.B.C.&W. came under the control but not ownership of the Chicago, Clinton, Dubuque and Minnesota Rail Road.

James F. Joy, who at one time had been president of the C.B.&Q., had always favored small roads over the larger, believing that if the small one prospered, the larger one would reap proportionally greater profits without additional investment. For this reason, he expected the larger road to serve the smaller company in different ways, expecting in time to absorb the lesser road into the greater one. As president of the C.C.D.&M., his orders to Runkle were simple—finish the road to Cascade. He felt this little line would in time benefit the larger one, which he controlled.

Engraved photo of E.G. Potter's Paradise Valley Farm from the 1875 Iowa Atlas. Potter, an early Bellevue settler, owned extensive property and business holdings. He was instrumental in the formation of the Dubuque, Bellevue and Mississippi Railway, which ultimately evolved into the C.C.D.&M. After his death, the narrow gauge branch passed through the farm and the unofficial station of Paradise was established as a right of way concession to

Potter's son, Byron. Much of the area along Mill Creek, which is west of Bellevue and offered the only access to the higher inland communities to be served by the narrow gauge line, was known to the railroad men as Potter's Flats and/or Paradise Flats.

Captain Eldridge G. Potter, settled in Bellevue, Iowa in 1842 and became one of the area's most wealthy and influential residents. After his death, the negotiations for right of way for the C.B.C.&W. through his farm, resulted in the unofficial Paradise station as seen above.

Thirty-pound rail was laid out of Bellevue toward Paradise Valley, which was four miles to the west. This valley represented the only feasible entrance to the higher ground inland from the river. According to his descendants who still own Paradise Valley, Byron Potter had inherited one thousand acres of choice farmland from his father, Captain E.G. Potter who had made his money farming and in the riverboat trade on the Mississippi. The family was not unfamiliar with railroading. E.G. Potter had been instrumental in organizing the Dubuque, Bellevue and Mississippi Rail Way Company, which was the first road to hug the bank of the Mississippi River between Dubuque and Bellevue. Consequently, Byron Potter graciously donated the land necessary for the right-of-way across his property in exchange for a "personal" station. The little depot was for the exclusive use of his family, guests and employees as a means of transportation to Bellevue or inland, if they so chose. In time, the railroad built a small structure, which became a "flag stop" of sorts to pick up anyone at Paradise Valley who signaled a passing train. However, it was never a scheduled stop.[4]

Beyond this lush area stood the most challenging terrain of the entire route—the "summit" as it would become known. Today, it is still referred to by that name by some of the local citizens. Choosing to ignore F.O. Wyatt's suggestion of boring a tunnel, Runkle built a 2.8 percent uncompensated grade through and over the hills.[5]

By August 1, 1879, the road's first locomotive was being prepared at the C.C.D.&M. shops in Dubuque. When it was ready, the locomotive was transported on a flatcar equipped with rails, to Bellevue and transferred to the three-foot gauge track. A straight-stacked, trim little Pittsburgh 4-4-0 American type, this first steam engine was destined to perform heroic service while the first twenty miles of track were being constructed.

With his one locomotive and necessary railroad cars plus a wealth of knowledge, Runkle attacked his task as though he was possessed. It took twenty-four carloads of material, exclusive of bridge-building supplies, to complete one mile of track. In time, one hundred thousand ties would be laid, and over three million feet of bridge timber cut and

fitted in place. Not counting the pile bridges, there would be fifteen trestle spans, one of which was four hundred feet long and thirty-five feet high.[6] Runkle closely followed each step of the construction particularly the building of the bridges. When the specified requirements called for ten-by-ten-inch timbers, Runkle installed twelve-by-twelve-inch and cut every single one himself.

When the first train entered Zwingle, October 29, 1879, a gala celebration was held. Speeches, baseball games, brass bands and a sumptious feast prepared by the town's women all took place out-of-doors, despite the cool weather. Located in the extreme southeast corner of Dubuque County,

CASCADE.

An early vocal supporter of Cascade's efforts to secure a railroad, owner and editor of the Cascade *Pioneer* Isaac W. Baldwin later became one of the B&C's most severe critics when equipment and weather difficulties caused service problems normal to that era of railroading.

Zwingle was only three and one-half miles west of La Motte. Founded in 1846 by Daniel Cort, the town already boasted a doctor, two churches and businesses vital to the small community's survival. Now that "Runkle's road," as the gauge was affectionately called, was there, additional lots were platted for buildings that could be erected the following spring.

By the time track had been laid to Washington Mills and the end-of-track was twenty-three miles from Bellevue, a second locomotive, a twin to the first, became available. As the distance increased, the locomotives were operated late into the night to insure sufficient building materials for the workers. It seemed as though the trains never stopped their run to Bellevue for supplies. When one engineer tired out, another took his place and the work continued.

Runkle worked long hours into the night, getting to know every square inch of the road. One newspaper account stated that he claimed he could walk a trestle with his eyes shut and come out on the opposite end unharmed.

Construction continued at a furious pace and the only negative aspect the crews encountered was the grading completed by the farmer railroaders. Unfortunately, only five of the fourteen miles of right-of-way, which had been graded, could be used.

When the four hundred-foot curved trestle at Washington Mills had been finished, the rails were laid hastily in an effort to beat the deadline of "a train in Cascade by January 1," imposed by the bond issue. Sixty-five thousand dollars was at stake. Once the trains were running on a regular basis, the trackwork could be done properly at a more leisurely pace. The difficult terrain was behind Runkle and his men. Ahead lay gently rolling terrain with two hills of four hundred feet of 3 percent grade between Bernard and Fillmore, and a four hundred foot grade of 2.75 percent. Although the one between Bernard and Fillmore was actually steeper than the 2.85 percent grade to the summit east of La Motte, it was only four hundred feet long as opposed to the three-mile length of the latter.

On Wednesday, December 31, 1879, the Cascaders' hopes and dreams came true. Their railroad, such as it was at that time, was finished. Seventy-five percent of the right-of-way was only thirty-three feet wide;[7] there were many grades exceeding 2 percent besides the summit's 2.8 percent climb. The turntables and water towers weren't built yet but a train was ready to enter Cascade. While the last rail was laid in place, Engineer Allen Woodward, his fireman, Sam Elmer and Webb Smith, the brakeman, waited patiently in engine number "two." A huge crowd of men and boys climbed aboard the locomotive and flatcars, filling every available space, so they could brag later that they had been on the first train into Cascade.

The echoing ring of the sledge driving home the last spike was lost among the cheers. The engine backed out of town and, with steam up and whistle screaming, sped toward the almost completed depot. The day after Christmas had been the starting time for the new facility, and the twenty-four-by-fifty-foot building was finished the day after the first locomotive arrived in town.

Hundreds of people from Cascade and other surrounding communities pressed forward to see the embodiment of power and prestige as represented by the small locomotive. It seemed like a dream come true to the people of Cascade. After thirty-one years, they actually had a railroad.

Ike Baldwin, who had encouraged the community with hopeful words in his Cascade *Pioneer*, when the going seemed impossible, summed it up with his headline, "AT LAST WE HAVE IT!" Another editor from a neighboring community was heard to mumble under his breath: "By jing! It ain't no pippin after all!" But it was the irrepressible Baldwin who dashed about the throng, grasping friends and strangers alike. He stated profoundly to each, "Lord, let thine servant depart, now that his eyes have seen the salvation of Cascade." (*Pioneer Press,* 1st Chapter, any verse.)

The next day, January 1, the first regularly scheduled train carried the initial shipment when C.C. Little sent four thousand pounds of poultry on its way across the hills toward Bellevue. Within several days, stockcars were brought in to ship G.G. Banghart's larger livestock to market. The bulk of the grain crop along with herds of pigs had been held to utilize the new mode of transportation and the future looked bright for the little railroad.

When Tom Duffy, the *Herald* reporter, rode over the narrow gauge line with George Runkle in the cab of a 4-4-0 locomotive, his heart must have been in his mouth when he saw the steep fall to Lytle's creek 150 feet below. Ralph Otting stands on the remaining roadbed at the east end of Washington Mills in 1981.—*Jon Jacobson*

What looks to be a natural wash is in reality the roadbed on the highest point of the branch line, which was known as the "summit." Although overgrown with brush, the memory of the diminutive trains is evident to an active imagination even in 1981. Standing perfectly still, one can almost hear and smell one of the Pittsburgh 4-4-0 locomotives as it doubles the hill.—*Jon Jacobson*

Tight curves were not unknown on the Chicago, Bellevue, Cascade and Western. The minimum curve was 12½ degrees, which translates into a circle of track 918.56 feet across. The above roadbed, still readily visible in 1981, led to the west approach of the longest bridge at Washington Mills. The man is Ralph Otting who worked on the narrow gauge as a teenager.—*Jon Jacobson*

George Runkle, who was hired by Joy to complete the narrow gauge branch line, kept his personal attention on every operation but most especially on the building of the bridges. When the specifications called for ten-inch-by-ten-inch timbers, Runkle installed twelve-by-twelve and according to records, cut every single one himself.—*L. Deppe*

Passenger service was inaugurated the same day that a combine was coupled to the freight train. The first train was scheduled to leave Bellevue following the arrival of the southbound standard passenger train. Three hours and fifteen minutes were allowed for the trip to Cascade.

Obviously, there are no people living today who actually road on the C.B.C.&W. when it was under the jurisdiction of the Chicago, Clinton, Dubuque and Minnesota Rail Road. A ride then, as seen through the eyes of Thomas Duffy, a reporter working for the Dubuque *Herald*, might be in order. The following is taken verbatim from a larger article that reported the first train's arrival in Cascade. The date of the newspaper was January 1, 1880:

> For the purpose of gathering information as to the character of the road and its conditions for the benefit of the *Herald* readers, we mounted the engine with Mr. Runkle, vice president of the road, who had had general supervision of the construction and took a run over it. The newness of course requires careful hands at the throttle valve and in Mr. Hammer and his brother engineers, it has them. Since the work of construction commenced but one jump from the track has occurred and that was "pure cussedness" on the part of the little engine, which had got tired and wanted to rest. At Bellevue, the tracks are so arranged that the transferring of stock and grain to the broad gauge cars will be done with such facility that the cost of stock will be but twenty-five cents per car and on grain but eight. The stock car on the narrow gauge is run up a drive way which connects on the opposite side of the pens with one entering the broad gauge car, and but a few seconds is required to drive the stock from one into the other. For the transferring of grain, the narrow gauge track is on elevated ground, several feet above the broad gauge. A schute will connect the cars and in a few minutes the contents of the narrow gauge car will light into the one below. It is no trick at all. The ground is ready for the round table which will be put in immediately and then Bellevue will begin to feel as if she reaches out over a pretty extensive country. Charley Herron is as proud over the prospect of his hands being kept full of business as men generally are over their seventh baby (if it is a boy), although he seems to have his hands full

enough now to satisfy any moderate railroad agent.

> Going out of Bellevue the track ascends very gradually as far as Paradise, the elysian name that has been given to the first station and embryo town on the road, four miles distant. The name was probably donated by some young Bellevue lover who wandered out that way picnicing with his dulcina during the balmy days of summer, when a green carpet instead of a white mantle invited poetic visions and love sang dulcet songs into happy ears. Runkle says it is a lovely place and we are too willing to admit that he ought to get to Paradise sometime to say anything that might look like envying him the pleasure of going by his own narrow gauge. It is located on land belonging to a public spirited old settler named Byron Potter, who owns two thousand acres stretching four miles up the valley and through the entire length of which he gave the right of way to the company.

> From this point the grade begins to increase very perceptibly until it reaches what is called the La Motte "summit" twelve miles, through which there is a rock cut thirty five feet deep and one thousand feet long. The elevation is five hundred feet above Bellevue. . . . Approaching the summit near La Motte, the last mile is made up a grade of one hundred and thirty two feet which is the steepest, that at Washington Mills being the next highest, one hundred twenty feet. Before reaching the summit above named a four hundred foot tressle work spans a forty foot ravine where there is quite a curve.[8] Looking on it as the engine approaches, one would almost hesitate to believe that any engine could climb it with heavy loads behind, but the feat is accomplished with certainty and with unaffected ease. From there to Washington Mills is an easy run. At the latter place there was some hard work both in cutting and spanning chasms to get around and over the winding water courses. Part of the road runs through solid rock and along rocky bluffs where there is not soil enough to fill a clay pipe. Runkle must have felt that this was Paradise Lost if hard work could affect his temper any. It is nothing here for two miles but rock cuts and tressel works. The only truss bridge on the line—a forty foot span, with three hundred feet of spilling approaches—crosses the stream at this place twenty five feet above the water. From this point twenty three miles from Bellevue, the

This is the trestle as indicated in previous photo. Poised almost thirty feet above the ground, engine No. 417 pauses while its crew has its picture taken. At least fourteen bents supported the track between the two hills.

While it took twenty-four carloads of material to complete a mile of track, nothing but bridge building supplies were needed to span the distance between two hills such as in the photo above. This 1981 photo looks easterly at the site (dotted line) of one of the Washington Mills trestles .—*Jon Jacobson*

running is comparatively to Cascade, thirty six miles. As far as Washington Mills the road is pretty compact, but from that point onward it will require considerable work to give it permanency. At this place town lots have been surveyed and the name of Clifton given to this embryo city. The people there are going to reap the benefits of the railroad by moving early. One cannot help thinking after riding over the road that wonders have been accomplished in a short time, and when the difficulties of the undertaking are considered, he feels disposed to grant deserved credit to those who did the work. . . .

On the last visit of the eastern directors to Dubuque they rode over the narrow gauge and were so well pleased that they declared in favor of pushing it westward. The present objective point is Troy Mills, Linn County, fifty miles from Cascade, by way of Bowen's Prairie and Nugent's Grove. Mr. Young, the engineer will enter upon the survey next week and a force of men will be put to work on a heavy cut near Cascade at once. One hundred thousand dollars aid have been promised along the extension already, and all that is asked is said to be forthcoming in due time. As the thing now looks Wyatt and Runkle seem to have the dead wood on a fine scope of country lying between the Illinois Central and Northwestern roads with the Missouri River in the not far future. More power to their elbows. Pluck and perseverence ought to win and seem deemed so in this case. [sic]

In a day when the meaning of the printed word was more flexible than it currently is, flamboyant statements were the rule. Washington Mills, for example, would never be known as Clifton. It would remain the home of a flour mill and several minor businesses plus a few houses. The railroad station would be a small, a *very* small structure . . . and Washington Mills could boast of being the only place on the gauge where mail was picked up "on the fly" if there was no other reason for the train to stop.[9] The closing paragraph is perhaps more wishful thinking on the part of the *Herald* reporter since the rails were laid as far as they would ever be on the gauge. The idea was nice, though. Imagine. Beyond the Missouri River, just over the hill, is the Pacific Ocean.

RAILROAD DIRECTORY.

Chicago, Clinton, Dubuque
and Minnesota Railroad Company.

GOING NORTH.

Chicago (C. & N.W.)...Lve 9:15 p m	Ar. 10:30 a m
St. Louis (C. B. & Q.). " 8:00 a m	8:45 p m
R'k Isl'd (C. B. & Q.). " 9:40 p m	8:55 a m
Clinton............ 3:17 a m	4:12 p m
Sebula............ 4:22 a m	5:09 p m
Bellevue.......... .. 5:27 a m	6:24 p m
Dubuque { .... Arr. 6:45 a m	
...........Lve 8:00 a m	Ar. 7:32 p m
Guttenburg........... 10:05 a m	
McGregor............ 11:03 a m	
Waukon Junction.... 11:40 a m	
Lansing............ 1:12 p m	
Brownsville........... 2:40 p m	
LaCrosse............Arr. 3:45 p m	

GOING SOUTH.

LaCrosse,............Lve 12:48 p m	
Brownsville .... 1:50 p m	
Lansing............. 3:15 p m	
Waukon Junction. ... 1:21 p m	
McGregor............ 5:00 p m	
Guttenburg .... 5:58 p m	
Dubuque { ....Arr. 7:47 p m	
..........Lve 9:10 p m	Lve. 6:15 a m
Bellevue............ 10:25 p m	7:26 a m
Sabula............. 11:30 p m	6:25 a m
Clinton............Ar. 12:40 a m	Arr. 9:27 a m
R'k Isl'd (C. B. & Q.). " 5:00 p m	7:00 p m
St. Louis (C. B. & Q.). " 6:00 p m	7:15 a m
Chicago (C. & N.W.). " 7:15 a m	3:40 p m

Turkey River Branch.
Train leaves Wadena, 6:00 a. m.; Turkey River, 10:50 a. m.; arrives at Dubuque, 1:20 p. m. Leaves Dubuque, 3:40 p. m.; Turkey River, 5:10 p. m.; arrives at Wadena, 9:40 p. m.

Waukon & Mississippi Railroad.
Trains leave Waukon at 8:00 a. m. and 2:15 p. m.; arrive at Waukon Junction at 10:25 a. m. and 4:20 p. m. Leave Waukon Junction at 11:45 a. m. and 5:00 p. m.; arrive at Waukon at 12:40 p. m. and 7:20 p. m.

☞ Pullman Palace Cars are run between McGregor and Chicago, and between Dubuque and Rock Island, via this line.
P. O. WYATT, Gen. Manager.

Once the small trains were running, their schedules were coordinated with those of the standard gauge C.C.D.&M. Railroad. The above timetable dates from the late 1870s. The long layover in Dubuque allowed passengers time to eat while the train and motive power were serviced.

Once a train left La Motte, bound for Cascade, there were still grades to be conquered but none so steep as the 2.8% climb to the "summit." Of the thirty-six miles of main line, the longest and most seemingly level stretch

was west of Fillmore. What appears to be level track in the photo above, is actually a slight grade between La Motte and Washington Mills. With the advent of the steam locomotive in the hinterlands of Iowa, grade crossing signs became necessary to warn farmers who might be traversing the track with their teams of horses, to be prepared for the possible approach of a smoke breathing, puffing and clanging engine traveling at the then unheard of speed of ten or twenty miles per hour.

Allen Woodward (left) began his railroading career in Minnesota as an engine wiper for the Chicago, Dubuque and Minnesota Rail Road. After a few years service as fireman, he was assigned to a narrow gauge locomotive as engineer and worked on the Caledonia Junction to Preston branch of the C.C.D.&M. and then both he and it were transferred to the new narrow gauge railroad being built west of Bellevue. Woodward was the engineer of the first train to pull into Cascade, December 31, 1879. (1933 photo.)

27

The first locomotive on the C.B.C.&W. was the straight stacked Pittsburgh engine above. Builder's No. 393, it was referred to as number "one" after Allen Woodward and his engine arrived to help construct the narrow gauge railroad. When the Milwaukee bought the River Road, it was numbered 413 but because of its smaller cylinders (eleven-by-sixteen) it was replaced within a year by locomotives No. 416 and No. 419. No. 413 went to the Milwaukee Shops where it powered a transfer table. In 1899 it was renumbered 1401 and was scrapped in 1905.

Once the freight consist was ready, the last bit of work to perform before leaving one of the terminals, was coupling the combine to the rear of the train. In a scene probably not too far removed from the first day of full operation, Pittsburgh built No. 416 gently nudges car No. 7 ahead. There is a bit of a resemblance to a Chicago, Burlington and Quincy Railroad combine of the time in the car above. It has been suggested that James F. Joy used his position of power with the Burlington to have rolling stock built at the C.B.&Q. shops for the Chicago, Bellevue, Cascade and Western. Photo dates sometime between 1880 and 1899.

C. B. & W. R. R. Tax of 1878

1882				1882			
~~any~~ 2	To Balance Delinquent	11550			Balance Delinquent		11550
		11550					11550
~~1884~~ 8	To Balance Delinquent	11550		1885 Dec 31	By Balance Delinquent		11550
		11550					11550
86 1	To Bal. Delinquent	11550		1888 Apr 11	By Declared Unavailable		11550

C. B. & N. R. R. Tax of 1880

1882				1882			
~~any~~ 2	To Balance Delinquent	11115		Jany 31	By Collections		— —
				Feby 28	" "		75
				1884 Jany 7	" Errors &c		3840
					" Balance Delinquent		7200
		11115					11115
1884 8	To Balance Delinquent	7200		1885 Dec 31	By Balance Delinquent		72
86 1	To Bal Delinquent	72		1887 Dec 31	By Errors &c		2170
				Dec 31	" Bal Delinquent		5025
		72					72
88 any 1	To Bal Delinquent	5025		1888 Apr 11	By Declared Unavailable		5025

In addition to stock subscriptions, local taxes were voted to help finance construction. According to contemporary newspaper accounts, 68 percent of the residents of Bellevue voted in favor of a 5 percent property tax in late October 1877. Earlier that month over 72 percent of the voters in Cascade and Whitewater townships (near the eventual western terminus) approved a 3 percent property tax, in part due to the newspaper plea made by the Rev. James Hill (see appendix).

The above recapitulation of unpaid railroad taxes in 1882, tends to indicate that at least three taxes were accessed on the western end. A "C.B.&W.R.R. Tax" for both 1878 and 1880 and a "Whitewater R.R. Expense Tax of 1878" show unpaid balances due of $115.50, $50.25, and 88¢, respectively.

Early Dubuque County tax records are incomplete so the total fund generated by the above taxes is unavailable. As the line had to be finished by the C.C.D.&M., we know that the total original financing was insufficient.

Whitewater R. R. Expense Tax of 1878

1882				1882			
Jany 2	To Balance Delinquent	88			Balance Delinquent		88
		88					88
~~1884~~ 8	To Balance Delinquent	88		1885 Dec 31	By Balance Delinquent		88
		88					88
1885 1	To Bal. Delinquent	88		1888 Apr 11	By Declared Unavailable		88

S. B. Rollin

Freight Office C. C. D. & M. R. R. Company,

Destination _____

May 17 18 80

To CHICAGO, CLINTON, DUBUQUE & MINNESOTA R. R. CO., Dr.

Where From.	For Charges on	Weight.	Amount.
Clinton	1 Barb Machine	130	60
Consignor Marshall 483	1 Box Barbs		
No. of Car 576 F		170	80
Date of W. B. 15			
No. of Way-Bill 48		Advanced Charges.	1 20
Station Pro. No. 79			2 00

Received Charges _____ Agent.

All Charges payable on delivery. Property to be removed within twenty-four hours after arrival. Part of Consignment will not be delivered, unless payment is made on the whole

The above freight bill is for one barb machine and one box of barbs. The individual farmer had to attach the pointed pieces of wire to the fencing himself. The two dollar total charges for transporting the items represented a lot of money for the day and the C.B.C.&W. was ready to start receiving freight as well as the money involved for handling it.

A few days after the narrow gauge C.B.C.&W. began operations, a string of stock cars, similar to those in the latter day photo above, was brought to Cascade to ship G.G. Banghart's larger livestock to market.

Once the narrow gauge railroad was completed, the citizens of Bellevue hoped the county seat would be relocated there. With two railroads serving it plus the steam boats on the Mississippi stopping at its shore, the town began booming. In the above view, all of the narrow gauge facilities are built and those marked are: (1) two-stall roundhouse; (2) twenty-four-foot diameter water tank and depot; (3) stockyard and animal transfer station. The standard gauge tracks run north to Dubuque and south to Savanna. Today, all the narrow gauge track and buildings are gone and diesel powered freight trains traverse the middle of Second Street. Northerly view from bluff south of Bellevue.

In those days:

When Doctor William H. Francis gave up his medical practice and closed the doors on his drug and general merchandise store to promote the building of a railroad to Cascade, he demonstrated an unconquerable faith in his adopted town. Born in County Armagh, Ireland, he arrived in New York in 1847 and settled, after several moves around the country, in Cascade in 1862. His efforts on behalf of the Chicago, Bellevue, Cascade & Western Railway cost him a total of $3,000 in lost income but the townspeople demonstrated their gratitude once the rails reached Cascade. They presented Dr. Francis with a team of horses and a buggy that cost $1,000 dollars. When the railroad was in safe hands, Francis resumed his practice.

Allen Woodward began his fifty-nine-year career as a railroad man with the Chicago, Dubuque and Minnesota and was with the C.C.D.&M. when Joy agreed to finish the gauge. After five years of working as an engine wiper and fireman, he moved to the right hand side of the cab on a narrow gauge locomotive. From September 25, 1877, until more motive power was needed in finishing the construction of the line to Cascade, Woodward operated his steam engine on the Caledonia Junction to Preston branch of the C.C.D.&M. in Minnesota. When he and number "two" reached Bellevue in November 1879, Woodward's engine was put on the track and was to work west of Washington Mills. Number "one" brought trainloads of building material to Washington Mills where the freight was transferred to the cars coupled to the new engine. The locomotive's numbers reflected their position in hauling the construction material. In the race to beat the deadline of January 1 imposed by the bond issues, tracks were laid across "picked" cornfields, the ties resting on corn stubbles. The order of the day was, "Get those rails down some way, any way, so that we can get a train into Cascade before January first." Once Woodward had piloted his locomotive and four flatcars up to the depot in Cascade, he spent the next several hours backing up and coming into town with different loads of people.

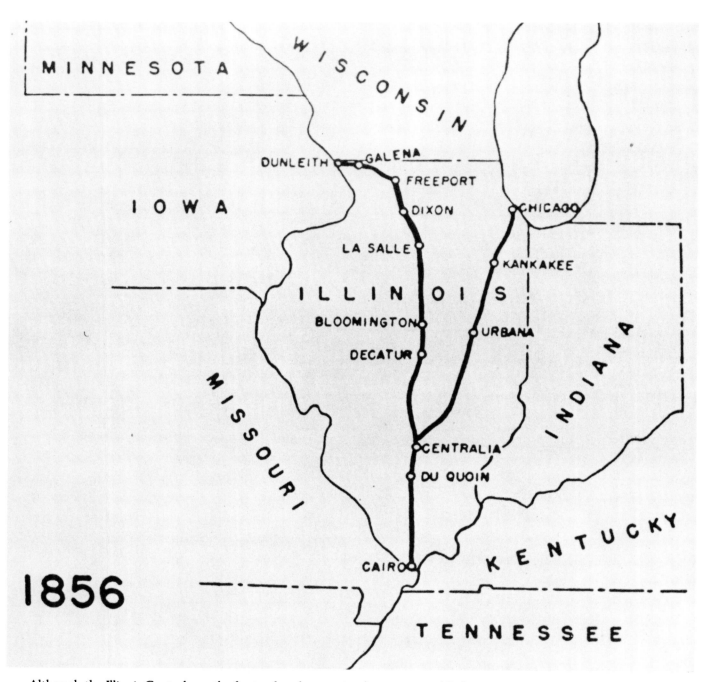

MINNESOTA

WISCONSIN

IOWA

DUNLEITH   GALENA
            FREEPORT

            DIXON   CHICAGO

LA SALLE
                             KANKAKEE

ILLINOIS

BLOOMINGTON   URBANA

DECATUR   INDIANA

                         CENTRALIA

MISSOURI   DU QUOIN

                                           KENTUCKY

                    CAIRO

1856

TENNESSEE

Although the Illinois Central was the first railroad to service the river city of Dubuque, it would not avail the people of Belleue or Cascade. In time the I.C. purchased the Dubuque and Sioux City right-of-way across northern Iowa.

3

1838-1880 The River Road

Snake-like, the rails of the Chicago, Dubuque and Minnesota Railroad wound northward, hugging the west bank of the Mississippi River. This view of the River Road, looking north from Point Ann to McGregor, Iowa is circa 1900 after the Chicago, Milwaukee and St. Paul Railway had purchased the C.C.D.&M.

The ribbons of rails that hugged the western bank of the Mississippi River carried people and produce north and south. The company owning this road at the time of the narrow gauge's inception, watched, knowing that the produce from Cascade and the other towns, would have to be transported on its trains once the little railroad was operating. As we have seen James F. Joy, president of the River Road as the north/south standard gauge line was called then, was largely responsible for the completion of the three foot gauge line to Cascade. For the rest of its existence, Iowa's Slim Princess would be tied physically and financially to the River Road.

Roads such as the River Road could trace their ancestry to the enthusiasm of John Plumbe, Jr. By 1838, this little Welshman had excited enough people and attracted enough attention to have the Iowa Territory's congressional representative, George Wallace Jones, make a plea for funds to be used to conduct a survey of a railroad from Milwaukee to the Mississippi River. Jones recounted later in his autobiography that his fellow U.S. congressmen gave him a "great laugh and hurrah in the house" when he requested the aid. Nevertheless, two thousand dollars was allocated when the Senate passed the bill July 7, 1838.

Ten years later, Lucius H. Langworthy of Dubuque was elected president of a railroad that projected a line from Dubuque to Keokuk by way of Cascade and Iowa City. This, the Ram's Horn route, never got beyond the talking stages.

The next year, 1849, Lyman Dillon, who had marked the route of the Old Military Road with a one hundred-mile-long plowed furrow, sought but never received a congressional grant of land for the construction of a railroad from the Mississippi River at Dubuque to the Missouri River at or near Council Bluffs. A further action taking place across the Mississippi River formed the Illinois Central Railroad Company on February 10, 1851. This latter network of rails was designed to reach Dunleith, Illinois (opposite Dubuque), from Cairo, Illinois, with a branch line from Centralia to Chicago.

Then on May 19, 1853, the Dubuque and Pacific Rail Road Company was incorporated in Iowa to construct a line from Dubuque westward to the Missouri River or beyond using the land Dillon had sought in 1849. This road was to be developed as a natural extension of the Illinois Central rails when they reached Dunleith (now East Dubuque, Illinois). On June 12, 1855, the first locomotive officially steamed up to the banks of the Mississippi River at Dunleith on the Illinois Central.

On December 16, 1867, a group of Dubuque businessmen headed by an attorney, Platt Smith, incorporated the Dubuque and MacGregor Railway Company. In 1869, the name was changed to the Dubuque and Minnesota Railway and the articles of incorporation amended to enable an extension of rails to Winona, Minnesota. As head of the D. and M., Smith ordered the construction to begin northward along the river. This was the first portion of the River Road.

About this time it became ideal to include the growing rail center of Chicago in the titles of railroads with the hope that one day a company's rails would reach the Windy City. By 1872, the Dubuque and Minnesota Railway, the north "River Road," had over one hundred miles of track hugging the western bank of the river, extending from Dubuque to La Crescent, Minnesota. That same year, the

J.K. Graves, a prominent Dubuque Banker and politician, was active in the formation and construction of the Chicago, Dubuque & Minnesota and the Chicago, Clinton and Dubuque which were ultimately combined to form the Chicago, Clinton, Dubuque & Minnesota. Earlier, he had been president of the Dubuque & Pacific which was completed as the Dubuque and Sioux City Railroad. The D.&S.C. became part of the Illinois Central.

name of the company was changed to the Chicago, Dubuque and Minnesota Railroad.

While those rails were reaching northward from Dubuque, another tentacle of steel was snaking along the western bank to the south through Bellevue. Organized to begin business on January 1, 1870, the Dubuque, Bellevue & Mississippi Rail Way began building shortly thereafter. It came as no surprise that the "south" River Road also had dreams of reaching Chicago to make connections with Lake Michigan and the East Coast.

As a result, this company also retitled itself as the Chicago, Clinton and Dubuque Rail Road in October 1871. That same year, the new road's rails reached Sabula Junction, forty-four miles to the south. There it gained running rights over the Sabula, Ackley & Dakota for some five miles. Two more miles of its own rails brought it to the "Midland Road" (now the Chicago and North Western) over which it operated into Clinton.

The road to the north and the one to the south were eventually affiliated and many officers of one company held identical positions in the other. In addition to sharing officers, the two "river roads" erected extensive shops in Dubuque to build, service and repair equipment. At the peak of employment under dual ownership, one hundred men worked full time. Eventually, the two companies consolidated their lines, equipment and offices in Dubuque.

Continuing inflation, high costs of construction, fuel for the locomotives, maintenance of the right-of-way and labor costs matched the frenzy of the 1873 financial panic. Both the Chicago, Dubuque and Minnesota and the Chicago, Clinton and Dubuque railroads found themselves in receivership. This situation resulted in a merry-go-round of name changes, corporate restructuring, reorganizations and consolidations. Emerging from the debris of meetings, agreements and concessions on February 22, 1878, was the new Chicago, Clinton, Dubuque and Minnesota Rail Road, which embraced the properties of the two predecessor lines.[10]

While the two River Roads were consolidated into one with James F. Joy as president, other construction was moving forward and away from the Mississippi River into the hinterlands. The Waukon and Mississippi, which had been organized April 15, 1875,

Before consolidating with the Chicago, Dubuque, and Minnesota, the Chicago, Clinton and Dubuque Railroad was the only road servicing Bellevue. The large building to the left of the railroad bridge is a mill, which was originally owned by E.G. Potter. Potter had been instrumental in building the C.C.&D.'s predecessor line, the Dubuque, Bellevue and Mississippi Railway.

finished its twenty-three-mile line between Waukon Junction on the Mississippi and Waukon in 1877. That line's first narrow gauge train arrived in Waukon on October 27, 1877, to the accompanying cheers of a large crowd. Shortly thereafter, the company came under the guidance of the River Road and the tracks were laid several miles beyond Waukon, with Decorah as its ultimate goal. Thirty-four miles further south, the Turkey River Branch had been extended to Wadena by 1878 while the Chicago, Bellevue, Cascade & Western Railway was being organized and the first shovel of dirt turned.

In 1880, the River Road was, counting all its branches, a two hundred-mile entity. Connecting with the Chicago, Milwaukee and St. Paul's Iowa and Dakota Division at McGregor, it continued north to La Crescent, Minnesota. At the latter town, it made connections with the C.M.&St.P.'s main line to Madison, South Dakota, and its Milwaukee-Twin Cities main line. To the south of Dubuque, the C.C.D.&M. connected with the main line of the Chicago and North Western at Clinton, Iowa.

Because of its association with James F. Joy and his eastern financial people, the River Road remained independent of the C.B.&Q. and was rapidly becoming an attractive piece of property. Before the year 1880 was half over, the C.&N.W. and the C.M.&St.P. stepped int ᴗ the picture, looking at the River Road with a desire to own the choice little railroad. A conflict seemed unavoidable between the two companies if both wanted the River Road.

However, when the Milwaukee people made their intentions clearly known, the North Western never tried to compete. The latter road had been bested by the combination of Alexander Mitchell and S.S. Merrill, president and general manager respectively, of the Chicago, Milwaukee and St. Paul Railway at every confrontation for the right-of-way in the Hawkeye state. Time after time, the Milwaukee had invaded the North Western's territory to win trackage rights in different parts of Iowa and South Dakota as well, much to the frustration of the Chicago and North Western officials.

Once they had determined to acquire the River Road, the C.M.&St.P. people set up a series of meetings with the stockholders of the

C.C.D.&M. On August 28, 1880, in compliance with a published call to those holding stock, the final meeting was held in Dubuque at the River Road's main offices. On the agenda was the vote for ratification or disapproval of the purchase of two narrow gauge railroads. Since the Chicago, Clinton, Dubuque and Minnesota had taken over the completion of the narrow gauge to Cascade without an exchange of cash, the board of directors had to decide whether or not to buy it outright. The Caledonia and Preston

A prominent Dubuque attorney, Platt Smith was the driving force behind the Dubuque & Pacific by writing the articles of incorporation, obtaining stock subscriptions, and purchasing much of the right-of-way in person. He remained with the above road until it reached Iowa Falls, then organized the Iowa Falls & Sioux City Co., directing until the road was completed to Sioux City in 1870.

(Minnesota) narrow gauge found itself in a similar situation and both roads were to be voted on at the Dubuque meeting.

Armed with the proxy votes of more than 56,000 shares out of the total of 61,894, the board of directors unanimously voted to purchase the narrow gauge lines. When other negotiations were completed, the Chicago, Clinton, Dubuque and Minnesota Rail Road would be able to sell the entire system to the C.M.&St.P. The stipulations of the agreement were that the Chicago, Milwaukee and St. Paul Railway Company would own outright the C.C.D.&M. railroad and its branches. This involved giving the stockholders of the latter road, a mortgaged bond dated July 1, 1880, on the Milwaukee itself, which was for 6 percent for forty years. In turn, the stock of the C.C.D.&M. was to be exchanged for 80 percent of the face value with the new owner paying all current expenses. Stock that was not turned by October 1, 1880, was to be made available to the Milwaukee at the rate of 75 percent.

Whatever the circumstances of the transaction, the Chicago, Milwaukee and St. Paul Railway took title to the Chicago, Clinton, Dubuque and Minnesota Rail Road, tie, rail and equipment on October 19, 1880, when the negotiations were completed.

Once they sold out to the Chicago, Milwaukee and St. Paul Railway, the shops would top their employment at two thousand and continue operation well into the twentieth century. By 1929, the Dubuque shops closed only to reopen five years later to serve as a facility for dismantling and burning wooden cars, which had become obsolete. A "rip track" operation lasted until 1954. Today, the buildings of the River Road's shops still stand, some of which are rented out as warehouse space.

Thus, the little line, whose rails reached from Bellevue to Cascade and which would become known to many lovers of rail lore as Iowa's Slim Princess, came under the ownership of the Chicago, Milwaukee and St. Paul Railway.

Catfish Creek was first spanned by the Dubuque, Bellevue and Mississippi Railway in 1870. To the right of the bridge is the Mississippi River and looking through the right side of the structure, Dubuque is just visible. The limestone monument on the promontory was erected in 1897 when the bones of Julien DuBuque for whom the city is named, were reinterred. Alexander Simplot designed the tower.

The extensive car shops and roundhouse, which the Milwaukee acquired when it purchased the C.C.D.&M. in 1880 were used until 1929 when they were closed down. Many of the Milwaukee cars in the above picture were probably built in the shops in the background. Today, the buildings are rented out as warehouses for the most part.

While the shops and yards at Dubuque were the focal point of the C.C.D.&M.R.R., they were used extensively for many years by the Milwaukee after the property changed hands in 1880. In this photo there are well over a dozen steam locomotives visible but there is no way of knowing how many of the twenty-two stalls in the roundhouse were occupied.

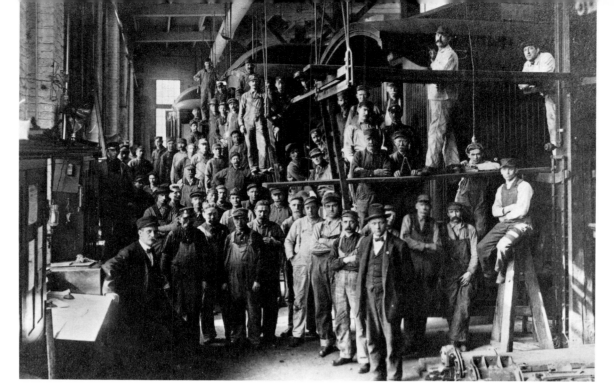

Some of the employees in the car shops pause for the benefit of the photographer. Passenger cars and freight cars of all types were built in Dubuque until 1929 when the shops closed. There were nineteen stalls bordering the transfer table that separated the two buildings. This photo dates from after the turn of the century.

At their peak, the Dubuque Shops of the Milwaukee Railroad employed 2,000 men. Although the passenger cars look dark in the above photo, the color the workman is applying is really orange. Rumors began circulating in 1887 that the Dubuque Shops were to be closed. Locomotives and cars of the gauge were maintained in Dubuque until 1929.

Probably one of the rarest photos in this book, the above locomotive was originally owned by the Chicago, Dubuque and Minnesota. While all of the locomotives that the Milwaukee acquired when it purchased the River Road, were either numbered and/or named, this particular engine was neither named nor numbered. The Milwaukee numbered it 412 in 1880 and 1419 in 1899. In 1901 the C.M.&St.P. Railway sold this, the only standard gauge Pittsburgh locomotive to ever operate on the C.C.D.&M. Bedecked with American flags as it is, could only mean that an excursion train, possibly on the Fourth of July, was or is about to be dispatched someplace. In the above photo, which was taken in Dubuque, the 1871 built locomotive is shown heading south. It is either going to someplace such as Bellevue or has returned from upriver, possibly from Guttenberg or McGregor.

If the shops in Dubuque were closed as the rumors circulating in 1887 stated, the locomotives of the narrow gauge line between Bellevue and Cascade would have to be serviced at North McGregor (Marquette). The distance was some fifty miles further from Dubuque and if the Pittsburgh 4-4-0s had to be serviced farther away, the inland towns would be affected by the longer time a locomotive would be absent. The rumors proved to be just that and nothing more. The locomotive and car shops remained in Dubuque until 1929. The scene above is the rip track which was north of the car shops. The flatcar in the center of the photo is jacked up on the one end (right side) while the truck is removed and work is performed on the underside.

In those days:

The *Palimpsest*, the Iowa state historical publication, in May 1964 recounts an interesting, albeit romantic account of how the Milwaukee "stole" the River Road away from the North Western. In an issue devoted solely to the Milwaukee Road in Iowa the following appeared:

> The River Road, while associated with J.F. Joy, was still independently operated and never made a part of the Burlington Railroad, which the Joy interests dominated. As a consequence, the North Western and the Milwaukee looked with envy at the River Road. A clash soon resulted between the two trunk lines when both sought control. The North Western officials, a contemporary account records, were riding over the line in their business car and were getting ready to buy the River Road. Unfortunately for them, the Milwaukee officials got wind of the negotiations. While the North Western Car was tied up for the evening at Lansing, the Milwaukee beat them to it by purchasing the road that night! At any rate, the Milwaukee took title to the Chicago, Clinton, Dubuque and Minnesota on October 19, 1880.

Pictured above in Minnesota, No. 418 was delivered in October 1880 along with a companion engine which was to be numbered 419. Respectively, the two identical pieces of motive power carried Pittsburgh builders numbers of 401 and 402. While No. 419 went to the Bellevue-Cascade branch, No. 418 went to the Preston, Minnesota branch line. No. 418 was scrapped in 1901.

4

1880-1890 The Good Years

The above receipt from the Dubuque County Treasurer shows that one Jacob Schneider paid $18.75 on March 8, 1880 to "aid in the construction of the C.B.C.&W. Railroad." Using the accessment rate of 3 percent determines that Mr. Schneider's property in Cascade township was valued at $625.

With the narrow gauge tracks linking it to the outside world by way of Bellevue, Cascade moved from the village status to that of "town" when it incorporated in 1880. The trains, all of which carried passengers, were scheduled to run in conjunction with the standard gauge arrivals and departures and would fluctuate accordingly during the branch line's existence. At first, the C.B.C.&W. ran two mixed trains each way six days a week. Only extras, which were unscheduled, ran on Sundays.

The two locomotives in use at the beginning of operations made two round-trips per day, usually pulling ten to twelve, twenty-four-foot freight cars and one passenger car. Longer trains were permitted on the eastbound trains since the grades were not as severe as those faced by those heading west.

The initial schedule of trains lasted only a

few weeks. In February 1880, Allen Woodward and his engine were transferred to the Waukon & Mississippi narrow gauge branch line north of Dubuque. Later that year, after the road changed owners, another locomotive was brought in from a Milwaukee three-foot line in Minnesota to help out. Eventually two locomotives, a little bigger than the first engine used on the gauge, were brought in and would operate well into the twentieth century. The first locomotive went to the Milwaukee shops where it powered a transfer table.

A leisurely schedule was employed and the two Pittsburgh locomotives averaged less than twelve miles an hour in meeting their requirements. The only delay, and it was built into the timetable, was doubling the summit. When it was reached, the train would be split into two sections and the first half hauled to the top and set out on a siding. Then the engine

Once water tanks were erected at La Motte and Washington Mills, the practice of utilizing a syphon hose to water the engines enroute from the creeks over which the slim rails passed, was abandoned. In the photo above, the water tank at Cascade is guarded by its windmill.

would back down and bring up the second half. Once the train was recoupled, it continued on its way to La Motte.[11]

Until the turntables were constructed at Bellevue and Cascade, it was necessary to back the train from the inland town to the river town. By the end of January, the two devices were operating and the dangerous practice of backing an engine thirty-six miles was abandoned. At first, a syphon hose was utilized to water the engine en route from the meandering creeks the track criss-crossed. Once water tanks were erected at La Motte and Washington Mills, the locomotives were given water in a more normal manner. Loading the tenders with coal was done a little more unconventionally. Instead of coal chutes, a winch-operated scoop, capable of handling one-half ton of fuel at a time, was used. Eventually, the winch was rigged to allow air pressure from the locomotives to operate it, doing away with the backbreaking job of cranking it by hand.

While a two-stall roundhouse was constructed in Bellevue for the Slim Princess' steam power, a single-stall unit was built at Cascade along with the turntable. Little by little, the narrow gauge branch line was assuming the attitude of a real railroad, much to the delight of the shippers, customers and passengers.

A relaxed atmosphere filled the countryside and the trains, as though not wanting to upset this delicate balance of calm, trundled its passengers and freight amiably but slowly. It was more than common to pick up passengers between stations and carry them close to their destination, which might only be the next farm or intersecting dirt road. At three (later two) cents a mile for fare, a farmer or his wife felt they could afford the luxury of riding instead of walking. Often, a wolf could be seen slinking behind a stand of trees as a puffing 4-4-0 eased to a stop to pick up or discharge a passenger in the middle of nowhere.

Schoolteachers began using the gauge to get to work and set their school hours in compliance with the schedule of the train. Housewives from Bellevue would ride as far as Mill Creek and get off to pick watercress, catching the eastbound a few hours later to return home. While the passenger business was a minor item on the bookkeeper's ledger, it was an important part of good will and public relations with the population of the area. And in the early years, until the twentieth century, the passenger operation would make money.

Although the small trains hauled passengers, the real money was in freight business and Iowa's Slim Princess had almost more than it could handle. The above way bill predates the ownership of the Chicago, Milwaukee and St. Paul Railway. Dated March 12, 1880, the Chicago, Clinton, Dubuque, & Minnesota Railroad charged $6.66 to ship 8,000 pounds of hogs to the stockyards in Chicago.

However, the real money was in freight business and the gauge had almost more than it could handle. In fact, it did. In anticipation of a booming growth, Bernard in the early 1880s, for example, boasted of a new store that would handle not only groceries but clothing, hardware, boots and shoes, and lager beer, all of which would be shipped inland on the gauge. A new grain elevator was built along railroad property and a blacksmith shop opened. La Motte, Zwingle and Fillmore followed suit, ready to go into business and let the gauge take care of the hauling.

By 1881, shipments of grain and livestock were greater than the small trains could handle. When peak prices were missed because of delays in shipping, farmers and businessmen alike began to grumble. On January 28, 1881, the honeymoon was over between the narrow gauge and the citizens of Cascade. Ike Baldwin, genial editor and publisher of the Cascade *Pioneer*, was also the town's new mayor. Speaking out on the subject, Baldwin stated:

> The narrow gauge is unable to meet the demands made upon it by shippers. No less than 1,000 hogs have been awaiting shipment at one time and more constantly coming in and no cars to move them. Shippers have been compelled on account of the overflow, to drive their hogs to Monticello and Onslow for shipment. Every station on the line seems to be jammed full of stock and grain. At Bernard, Burke Brothers claim that they could receive 2,000 bushels of oats daily if they could get it out of the way. We fear our railroad friends have underestimated the products of this section or else they would have prepared to haul it out. Now a large portion has to go to the North Western at Onslow or to Monticello. One thing is certain, there is an overflow of shipments that cannot be handled by the n.g.

Baldwin, who had vigorously backed the Chicago, Bellevue, Cascade & Western Railway, was now disgruntled with the road's lack of capabilities. It was as though he were opening the door to have Old Nick step in and attack the untoward gauge.

Less then forty days later, on March 2, 1881, it began to snow and didn't stop until the fourth. Blowing and drifting snow brought Iowa and much of the Midwest to a complete halt. Four feet of the stuff covered the entire area with drifts as high as fifteen feet peaking here and there. Trains on all roads ground to a halt. Some were even derailed and many passenger trains were stranded for days, with some passengers sustaining themselves in one instance, on peanuts and apples from the baggage car. Fences buried in snow were easily crossed over by horse-drawn sleighs.

Naturally, the narrow gauge running to Cascade fell in line with the other railroads out of no choice of its own. Railroad cuts that had been hacked out of limestone bluffs just three years prior, were hopelessly drifted full. Forty-five mile-an-hour winds filled them in before they were half shoveled out. One drift was two miles long and had depths ranging from two feet to eight. For weeks the Chicago, Milwaukee and St. Paul didn't deliver the mail until it was forced to do so by order of the then governor of Iowa, John H. Gear.

Larger towns such as Dubuque were isolated like the tiny towns along the gauge. But after a week of no train service and cold temperatures, another concern began eating at the people along the hilly branch line. Coal and wood supplies were beginning to dwindle. Before a crisis arose, the storm was gone, and the track was opened, allowing fresh reserves of coal, wood and food to be brought in.

Once winter passed, and the snow melted into the ground, the gripes voiced by Baldwin and the businessmen dissipated with the coming of spring. The gauge people ran extras to keep up as best they could with the "bumper" crops and large shipments of animals. To help the situation, a third 4-4-0 American type locomotive was brought in from another Milwaukee narrow gauge branch line. Business along the line continued to boom, and three new stock dealers set up operations in Bernard to compete with the Banghart Company in Cascade. G.G. Banghart, the largest stockholder in the C.B.C.&W., had desperately wanted the railroad to ship his large herds of cattle to market. He died in August 1881 without ever getting his full share of usage.

On September 13, 1881, the board of directors of the C.B.C.&W. amended their articles of incorporation, moving the principal place of business to Dubuque and the offices of the Chicago, Milwaukee and St. Paul Railway.

While some standard gauge trains were stranded for days because of the blizzards in the 1880s, and some were even derailed because of obstructing drifts, the gauge merely ground to a halt. Unable to cope with drifts as high as ten and fifteen feet, the locomotives sat in Bellevue and Cascade while produce and passengers alike were snowbound. Although the snow in the above picture is not that deep and the right-of-way is clear, it didn't take too much of it being blown about by strong winds to clog the narrow cuts along the main line.—*L. Deppe*

The trains on the Milwaukee narrow gauge branch line, all of which carried passengers, were scheduled to run in conjunction with the standard gauge arrivals and departures at Bellevue. In the photo above, the eastbound or down train has been turned and is ready to depart from Cascade for the eastern terminal, Bellevue.

The locomotive above was identical to No. 416 and No. 419, the two Pittsburgh 4-4-0s that would serve a combined total of eighty-five years on the gauge. Although there is no record of No. 417 having ever operated on the Cascade branch line, the photo in chapter three, of which the above is a close up of the locomotive, has been correctly identified as having been taken on the gauge. It has been concluded that No. 417 was probably pressed into service to help the new railroad operate until October 1880 when No. 419 was delivered. An alternate thought is that it might have been brought to Iowa from Minnesota to help during a rush of business or while one of the other Pittsburgh engines was being serviced in Dubuque. Many narrow gauge locomotives carried a pilot on the rear of the tender for reverse running. Turntables were a luxury that most small railroad companies could not afford. However, the gauge eventually had a turntable in both Cascade and Bellevue for the small locomotives.

The scenery along the narrow gauge branch line was ruggedly beautiful. Deep gullies and ravines were crossed many times by trestles such as the one above and offered more than one thrill for those fortunate enough to have ridden Iowa's Slim Princess in the days of steam power.—*L. Deppe*

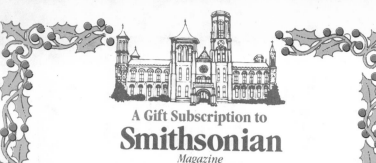

A Gift Subscription to

Smithsonian
Magazine

Including Membership in the Smithsonian National Associates

is a thoughtful, year-long expression of your affection and esteem for friends, relatives, or colleagues.

12 issues of Smithsonian Magazine

… the colorful, exciting monthly publication of the Smithsonian Institution that covers virtually every field of human awareness—the arts, the sciences, the environment, man: past, present, and future.

Travel Benefits

eligibility for Smithsonian trips and tours both foreign and domestic.

Discounts

10% to 20% members' discounts on purchases from Smithsonian shops or catalogs, books from Smithsonian Press and other publishers, superb record collections like the unique Smithsonian collection of Classic Jazz—either in person or by mail.

Special Reception

an attractive area in the Smithsonian "Castle" is set aside and staffed to assist members visiting Washington, D.C. Dining privileges in the Associates Court reserved for members and staff only.

To enroll your gift recipients, fill in the convenient order form envelope attached.

Smithsonian Institution

Service Center, P.O. Box 2954, Boulder, Colorado 80322

Give the gift
everyone loves
to open twelve
times a year

Smithsonian

One of its last functions as a railroad company was voting for, along with other lines that had been acquired by the Milwaukee, Alexander Mitchell as company president and P.M. Myers as secretary on November 23, 1881.

While the towns of La Motte, Bernard, Zwingle, Fillmore, Washington Mills, and Cascade began prospering because of the small trains, Bellevue on the other hand was reaping a different type of bonanza. With the Chicago, Milwaukee and St. Paul standard gauge railway passing through from north to south, Bellevue already was a railroad town. When the narrow gauge line terminated its tracks there, railroading became its biggest industry and hope for a relocation of the county seat to the river town prevailed.

Cattle were transferred from the little cars to the standard ones and shipped out. Coal and lumber were transferred to the gauge for shipment inland. Freight handlers alone were paid $1,620 in wages each month while four train crews on the narrow gauge branch line, who lived in Bellevue, took home an additional $1,100. The branch was making money, paying their bills and except for the rash of complaints earlier in the year, just about everyone was happy with the little railroad.

While the passenger trains had hauled the mail in and out of the towns along the branch line, the new mail contract the Milwaukee received in 1882 garnered an additional $1,521.90 in revenue for the narrow gauge. The contract stipulated $42.75 per mile per annum.

For the next six years, operations went relatively smoothly for the branch line. Gradually, the train crews were becoming cagey about handling little problems that arose while they were en route. For instance, the journals on the inside-framed 4-4-0s were difficult at best to maintain without a pit of some sort. So, several of the pile bridges along the route had one tie removed and when a journal would begin running hot and was in need of lubrication, the engine would be stopped with the overheated bearing spanning the opening of the bridge. Ducking underneath it, the engineer or fireman would be able to get at the job of lubricating without much effort. Within minutes, the train would be on its way.

Each winter, however, rumblings of discontent could be heard emanating from around potbellied stoves as people bemoaned the inefficiency of their railroad during the winter months. By the time the news from the outside world receached them by way of newspapers brought in on the gauge, they didn't care to read old news. If they had, they would have realized that others were in the same situation regardless of the type or size of railroad service. February 1887, brought along with winter snows, disaster after disaster, for all railroads. A quick thaw managed to undermine many roadbeds and the Chicago, Burlington and Quincy Railroad faced washouts south of East Dubuque, Illinois. The passengers on a standard Milwaukee train found themselves stranded between an unsafe bridge in front and a washout behind them. The Illinois Central had two bridges washed out in Illinois and the Minnesota and Northern had many weakened bridges.

For once the gauge wasn't affected as badly, probably because of George Runkle's fastidious bridge building. But the people seemed not to notice, even though their railroad was operating as well as it ever had in the winter months.

Rumors began circulating among the Milwaukee employees in December 1887 that the Dubuque shops were to be closed. The locomotives of the narrow gauge line were hauled on a flatcar equipped with rails to the Dubuque shops for maintenance and repairs that couldn't be made in Bellevue or Cascade. If the 4-4-0s had to be serviced farther away, the inland towns could be affected by the longer distance. The rumors soon proved to be just that and those thoughts were destined to become a dim memory when winter struck.

The blizzard of '81 had been considered the worst since the white man had crossed the Mississippi to settle. However, the one gathering in the Far West was soon to replace it in the memories of those who had lived through the storm of 1881. It began snowing on January 12, 1888, and the resulting blizzard is still considered the worst ever to hit the United States. This was not an isolated storm. Snow fell from the Rocky Mountains to Lake Michigan, stopping *all* trains within twenty-four hours. Drifts ranging in heights to eighteen feet burdened the countryside. By Sunday the fifteenth, trains were running again but 150 people had died—for the most part in South Dakota and Minnesota.

Skies were clear on the sixteenth and it got cold. By the nineteenth of January, the storm was a bad memory until some sadistic weather prophet announced another blizzard was building in the West. It, fortunately, failed to materialize. But the temperature began dropping until Chippewa Falls, Wisconsin, recorded sixty-eight degrees below zero on the twenty-second.

Winter could not last and spring eventually arrived, once more doing away with the grumbles of discontent heard along the narrow gauge. The eighties were to finish with normal winters, closing the gauge every once in a while because of snow. Not until the new decade, would the disgruntled city fathers of Cascade move to act against the Slim Princess.

Anticipating an economic boom, Bernard in the early 1880s had a new store that sold just about everything from books to lager beer. Horse-drawn buggies and wagons line the street of Bernard's business district. At the right-hand edge of the photo above, the corner of the railroad depot with a kerosene lantern on a post are visible. A new grain elevator was soon operating after the tracks were laid and a blacksmith shop opened. All of the towns along the gauge were proud of their railroad.—*Higbe*

Loading the locomotive tenders with coal was done just as unconventionally as syphoning water for the enroute engines from creeks. A coal bucket with a capacity of one-half ton was lifted above the tender by means of a winch, and emptied. After the rolling stock and motive power were equipped with air brakes, the lifting mechanism was modified to operate by air pressure generated by the locomotives' pumps. In the photo above, which was taken at Washington Mills, there are three buckets visible.

The humpbacked or overhead bridge which carried traffic above the branch line just east of Cascade. During heavy snow falls, the deep cut beneath the bridge was frequently blocked.—R. Otting

Once the Milwaukee owned the River Road, it had to cope with the problems along the gauge. Because of the tremendous amount of business it was generating, the railroad was forced to build another siding to help double longer trains and store extra cars when not in use. Sylva Switch was installed shortly after the C.M.&St.P. took over but it was seldom used. In the picture above, believed to have been taken at Sylva Switch, the section gang poses in front of its work train. The caboose's cupola was later rebuilt in the Dubuque Shops and an unusual cat walk was added to either side of the cupola. The No. 55 is the original number for the caboose and was used until sometime in the 1920s when it was renumbered 055. Dick Sullivan, who worked for many years on the narrow gauge stated, "It was 55 not 055. The zero in front would have designated a main line caboose and the 'gauge' was not a main line. In the late twenties, it was given the number, 055. Why? I don't know. But it only carried that number for about seven or eight years."

The rope seen draping from the end of the boxcar and across the flatcar in the photo above is the front view of the communications system in use on Iowa's Slim Princess during its early days. A code of tugs on the rope informed the engineer of the conductor's orders. The rope is visible in several of the earlier photos in this book. The small door at the end of boxcar No. 287 was common to narrow gauge stockcars and boxcars. With doors at each end, longer commodities such as poles for use on telegraph lines and later telephone lines, could be hauled without fear of being dumped. Flatcars coupled at either end served as idler cars and insured clearances with the next loaded car.

Its consist made up of two stock cars, seven boxcars and passenger combine No. 7, the eastbound or downtrain is about ready to whistle clear of the Cascade yards. Although it is December, the weather is mild and the crew has mounted their annual Christmas tree on the rear platform. (See **In Those Days**, Chapter Four.) The drum above the platform holds the signal rope that was stretched the full length of the train to the engine's cab. Most roads using this primitive communication system, implemented it during darkness. However, the gauge apparently used it both day and night.

In those days:

> I can recall one incident that almost caused my hair to turn gray. I was pulling 14 cars of hogs and a passenger coach. There is a hill between La Motte and Bellevue we called "summit." We were descending this hill at a rapid clip. All the hand brakes had not been set tight and the train was literally running away. We came to a trestle over a creek at what we called Paradise and there was a number of horses on the trestle, some of them with their legs already caught. There was no way of stopping the train and it plowed into the horses, killing six of them and injuring two others so severely that they were shot to put them out of their misery.

> —Allan Woodward, March 1933 interview

Two incidents occurred in April and May 1880 that could have been interpreted as portents of things to come. On April 16, one of the seventy-one employees working for the Chicago, Bellevue, Cascade & Western Railway, H. Basel, was killed. Aligning the link at the rear of the tender, while the engine was moving backward, Basel, a brakeman, stumbled and fell between the rails. His feet and legs were crushed by the tender brake and he died from his injuries a few hours later. The accident report read in part, "Occasioned by want of care on his part." Then, on May 24, Peter Cana, an itinerant deaf mute, was run over and killed while walking on the track. Because of Horseshoe Bend, a sharp curve one mile west of Zwingle, the engineer and fireman of the locomotive pulling a heavy gravel train, were not able to see him in time to stop.

Before the advent of air brakes and such "Buck Rogers" inventions as radio, the gauge used a simple device for communications between the conductor and engineer. A rope was draped over the full length of the train from locomotive to passenger car or caboose on the rear. If for some reason the conductor wanted the train stopped, he pulled the rope, giving the appropriate signal. The rope is visible in several of the earlier photographs in this book.[12]

It didn't take long for the people along the gauge or the railroad people themselves to discover the good thing they had going. Since only extras ran on Sunday and were unscheduled as such, trains seemed to operate strictly for the convenience of the paying passengers. La Motte was and still is a delightfully serene pocket of quietude and people from the other towns quickly selected it as "the" picnic spot for the area. Young couples, families with children in tow and members of social organizations could be found armed with picnic baskets every Sunday of the summer, taking the train to La Motte. The train crew members would give approximate time of return but would wait for any stragglers who might have encountered a delay of some type.

Although the people of Cascade and the businessmen along the branch line were basically unhappy with the service they were receiving from the gauge, the farmers on the other hand, along with many of the area people were not. They remembered the men who operated the trains at Christmas time. On Christmas Eve, the trip from one terminal to the other usually took longer, since the train had to stop at virtually every farm. Ladened with edible gifts, people would flag the train to a stop and present each member of the crew with a smoked ham or several freshly dressed chickens or a couple of dozen eggs or three or four jars of home canned beef. To show their gratitude and holiday spirit, the railroad men in turn would decorate the last car of each train with a small evergreen tree. Usually the tree rode the rails during the week between Christmas and New Year's Eve.

The Milwaukee Road, known as the best railroad for passenger service, continued to promote its trains. In the photo above, which was taken after the turn of the century, a shoppers' special flying the white flags of an extra, is arriving in Bellevue. Those people who lived in the inland towns along the gauge would transfer to the small train and be taken home. Begun in the 1890s, the shoppers' special continued well into the twentieth century until better roads were achieved for automobiles. Despite such service, the gauge was still under attack.

5

1891-1900 Enter the Chicago, Cascade & Western

An early way-bill on the C.M.&St.P. for a shipment of unknown articles from Clinton to Zwingle dated June 3 with the year torn off at upper right. The total listed weight is 150 pounds with a charge of 25¢ plus 42¢ in back charges totaling 67¢.

In his usually lavish style, Isaac "Ike" Baldwin had been instrumental in buoying up sagging spirits when the going got rough before the gauge was completed. One of his more sweeping statements in the Cascade *Pioneer* had been, "The population and business of Cascade will more than double once we have rails to the outside world." However, after 1880, the population of Cascade remained static and when the next decade began, there were 955 people living in the small town. By the end of the century, it would increase by 32 percent, which was a far cry from the instantaneous 100 percent predicted.

It had been Baldwin. who first lodged a formal complaint against the railroad in 1881 when he ran an editorial in his paper, concerning the poor service. Having survived the two horrendous blizzards of '81 and '88,

the newspaper entrepreneur, along with the other townspeople, felt that nothing but good times were coming in the future for them and their railroad.

Many, including Baldwin, believed the past problems of slow service and no service during heavy snows, could be solved with a new and more direct route to the outside world—a standard gauge route. Dubuque, with its teeming thousands, was the population center of the area, and it was to this city that the people of Cascade naturally looked with yearning eyes.

When service had not improved on the narrow gauge by 1893, a meeting was called on February 22, for the sole purpose of securing better railroad facilities at Cascade. H.L. Dehner was temporary chairman and Ike Baldwin recorded the minutes. The first item

The mill house from which the small community of Washington Mills derived it's name. This photo, looking from east to west was taken near or from the B.&C. right-of-way in the 1880s or 1890s. Traces on the mill race (lower right) and the foundation can still be seen in 1982.

George Runkle, who according to one newspaper account, was credited with cutting every upright timber for the many bridges would have argued strongly for *his* railroad. The bridge above at Washington Mills included a ten span trestle (foreground), a sixty-five-foot steel girder, a sixty-foot steel girder and a seven-span trestle leading to solid ground in the distance.—*L. Deppe*

Looking northwest at the water tank in the Cascade yards. A portion of the stockyards can be seen at the far left.

Although the population had remained static after the three-foot rails reached Cascade, the business men and farmers of the community wanted more and better service from the gauge. They wanted the yards at the western terminal full of cars for their use, not just a few cars as depicted above.

on the agenda was an address by the local newspaper editor.

Noting that the winter they found themselves experiencing was "an unusual winter and that it had affected all railroads more or less, the narrow gauge particularly," Baldwin warmed up to the subject. Not since 1888 had the gauge been so snowbound with blockades. He admitted that "the narrow gauge had been of great benefit to Cascade, has built up the town and farm property at least 50 percent and in view of these facts, I'm not the man to kick the little railroad." Baldwin did, however, believe the time had come when Cascade should have better facilities and favored the construction of a railroad from Cascade to Dubuque. He felt this could be done on "a very easy line."

Feeling he had been led to believe the Milwaukee people themselves contemplated such a move, Baldwin had investigated the procedure for abandonment of part of the narrow gauge line. The alternate route he supported was a wide gauge line running southwest from Dubuque through Rockdale to New Mellary Monastery before entering Bernard and then operating over the narrow gauge grade into Cascade. From Cascade, the proposed tracks would run westerly toward Monticello where it would intersect with another main line of the Milwaukee at Switch Junction.

Former Mayor Schaffer and the chairman pro tem, Dehner, followed Baldwin with similar thoughts before the meeting was exposed to the acerbic wit of Robert Quirk who declared, "The narrow gauge is a crime against modern civilization and the men who constructed it were the silliest people on earth." He cited the difficulties in shipping stock to Chicago and getting there in time for the early market. When he reiterated his earlier blasts, a defense of the narrow gauge was voiced by Baldwin and Schaffer.

Various schemes were discussed and a committee of three appointed by the chair to open correspondence with different railroad companies who might be interested. The indomitable Baldwin was one of the three men chosen.

The railroad building craze was over for the most part in the United States, but a new interest was shown by many in the area who heard of the new plan. Surprisingly, people came to Cascade from the western part of the state where the narrow gauge had been proposed to run at one time, wanting "in" on the new project. Eldora, Iowa, was one hundred miles west of Cascade and that town was definitely intrigued.

But the one element the Cascaders needed most, was the city of Dubuque and its interest. Speculative figures were bantered about by exponents of the new company, suggesting the area of broadened business ventures open to the oldest city in Iowa. The Cascaders openly offered that the Milwaukee should be more than interested in such an endeavor. When no takers appeared immediately, the same overtures were made for the benefit of the Chicago Great Western and the Chicago and North Western.

None of these new suggestions met with much favor by the people of Zwingle, La Motte or Bellevue as might be expected, since they were being excluded. When Cascade had needed help in getting a railroad built, these communities had pitched in totally. Now that the little road was under attack by the citizens of the western terminal, the eastern towns and their people were obviously not needed in the new venture and could go jump in the Mississippi. At least that was the opinion of an anonymous writer from Zwingle who stated that small town's case in an article in the *Dubuque Daily Herald*. The reporter wrote:

> Judging from the amount of stock and produce shipped over the road, it pays the company fully as well as any other road they own of the same length and cost. Zwingle is perhaps not the best station on the road but the books show a respectable amount of business done here. In 1892 there were 55,000 bushel of oats besides other grain shipped from here; 4,900 hogs and 926 head of cattle. There was 1,099,289 pounds of freight received and 3,365,620 pounds forwarded.

The cash receipts for the year 1892 were $6,250.96 from Zwingle alone.

The Zwingle reporter continued,

> I understand the Chicago, Milwaukee and St. Paul Company intends to and are putting

Even though No. 416, would serve gallantly for thirty-nine years on the gauge, the citizens of Cascade, led by Ike Baldwin felt the little trains had served their purpose and it was time for a wide gauge operation to serve them.—*Streuser*

Undaunted, Baldwin's followers formed their own corporation, the Chicago, Cascade and Western Railroad Company filing the papers April 13, 1893. The capital stock was set at $1,000,000 when interest from as far away as Eldora, Iowa was expressed.

heavy iron rails and new heavy engines on the road, which will enable them to haul all the freight offered along the line. Perhaps if Cascade people would furnish the hatful of money proposed at their second meeting the company would make a standard gauge of it.

Accusations were then made that the Cascaders wanted selfishly to be the only rail outlet in the area. Surprisingly, no rebuttal was issued from the westernmost point on the branch line.

Without the business acumen necessary for beginning a railroad, the Cascaders were not apparently aware of the clouds of panic gathering on the national financial horizon. It was an election year, monies from the eastern part of the United States were being pulled back from outlying regions, and there were other, more newsworthy items flitting about in the newspapers of the day. The World Columbian Exposition was slated for opening in Chicago; Lizzie Borden's antics were being reported; and there was talk about a great cowboy race from someplace in Nebraska to Buffalo Bill Cody's Wild West tent at the Exposition. In addition, the election news was gaining space in the papers, and the Cascaders had little chance of attracting attention their way.

Undaunted, they formed their own corporation, signing articles of incorporation April 10, 1893. The new line's name was to be the Chicago, Cascade and Western Railroad Company, with business headquarters in Cascade. The provisional board of directors

were to be among others, I.W. Baldwin and the Reverend James Hill. Hill, who had been responsible for James Joy's interest in completing the narrow gauge in the first place, never did sign the articles. However, the capital stock was set at $1,000,000 and it was Article II of their corporate papers that summed up their bitterness and frustrations with Dubuque's disinterest:

The objects of this corporation are to construct, operate and maintain a line of railroad in and through the town of Cascade, Iowa and between a point on the Mississippi River in Iowa and the towns or cities of either Waterloo, Iowa [sixty miles to the west] or Marshalltown, Iowa [ninety plus miles to the west] and on such other lines and to such other points or places as the Directors may from time to time determine.

They hadn't shut out the possibility of having Dubuque join them, but that "point on the Mississippi River in Iowa" was nebulous enough to include the full eastern border of the state. Still, when a newspaper article appeared shortly after the filing of the articles, Dubuque was still mentioned as being the eastern terminal.

But the clouds of financial panic were gathering faster than anyone wanted. By June a large financial lending institution in Sioux City, Iowa, failed when money invested from outside the state was withdrawn suddenly. A bank in Cedar Falls, Iowa, followed suit within a few days. Banks in Milwaukee, Wisconsin,

Once freight reached Cascade, the only motive power to deliver commodities were teams of horses or mules such as the one above. Waiting for the train from Bellevue (the up train), the men on the flatbed wagon pose for the photographer. Stock No. 153 is in the background.

The shortcomings of the narrow gauge branch line were clearly evident when rolling stock was compared with wide gauge equipment. Four small cars equalled one standard gauge boxcar. The photo above clearly illustrates this point. Such drawbacks irritated the customers along Iowa's Slim Princess.—*L. Deppe*

With a headlight almost as big across as the boiler face, No. 1405, before leaving Cascade, strikes a pose for the photographer with its crew and depot agent. Left to right: Phil Webber, brakeman; John Dunn, conductor; O.E. Winter, depot agent; Ed Butler, engineer; John Theilin, fireman. By 1899 when this picture was made, the assault on the gauge was only a memory and No. 1405 (416) would operate for nineteen years before being scrapped.—*Streuser.*

Cascade Branch—(Narrow Gauge). (Table 49)

			103	Mls.	STATIONS.	126				
			AM			PM				
----	----	----	†8.50	0.	Lv. **Bellevue**(k)Ar	4 30	----	----	----	----
----	----	----	10.05	11.4	" ...La Motte...Lv	3 05	----	----	----	----
----	----	----	10.30	15.7	" .....Zwingle.....\"	2 35	----	----	----	----
----	----	----	11.00	22.0	"Washingt'n Mills\"	1 55	----	----	----	----
----	----	----	11.20	25.2	" .....Bernard.....\"	1 35	----	----	----	----
----	----	----	11.35	29.7	" .....Fillmore ....\"	1 10	----	----	----	----
----	----	----	11.55	35.6	Ar... Cascade ...Lv	†1245	----	----	----	----

The gauge employed a leisurely schedule between terminals during all of its existence. Even though the toughest grade to climb, the "summit," required doubling many times, it took ten minutes longer to go down the grade since the brakes on each car had to be set at the top and released at the bottom. Naturally, time was allowed at each station for cutting out cars and spotting them at the appropriate sidings since there were no switch engines. The above timetable was in use in 1899.

and Denver, Colorado, would go under before the panic subsided.

Before any banks failed, however, the Chicago, Milwaukee and St. Paul Company issued a retrenching order in May 1893, which commanded the "stoppage of all improvements on the company's lines; the lopping off heads in all departments; the discharge of every employee whose service is not an absolute necessity; and the curtailment of expenses in every manner possible." In late 1893, the Chicago Great Western announced a 10 percent cut of wages across the board—a cut the employees accepted to insure their jobs.

On the other hand, Dubuque had managed to stay clear of "foreign" money, and the banks were controlled by local people who had the business expertise necessary to weather the panic. They were *not* about to invest in as shaky a venture as a new railroad, despite the wooings of Cascade. Questions such as, "Does Dubuque want to add 3,000 square miles to its trade territory?" were asked. The citizens of Cascade even suggested possible answers, "If so, it should do something in behalf of the Chicago, Cascade and Western Railway." But Dubuque had its own unspoken answer.

While political issues were sweeping the pages of every newspaper, the cowboys finished their great race from Nebraska to Chicago in June and Ike Baldwin decided, with proper urging, to run again for public office as he had done successfully in 1884. When the

votes were tallied, the newspaper editor was once more state senator but only by sixteen votes. Most Democrats were swept out of office and the Republicans who replaced them promised an economic resurgence.

At best, 1893 could be called a year of depression for the railroads, although none of those operating in Iowa went into receivership. When the Burlington, Cedar Rapids and Northern Railroad declared a 1.5 percent dividend, newspapers heralded the fact.

Because of the panic, the Milwaukee was not able to fulfill their intentions of "heavy iron rails and new heavy engines" if indeed they had made any such suggestion at all. The little Pittsburgh 4-4-0s would continue pulling their trains over the hills between Bellevue and Cascade, until additional motive power was acquired. Quite a few years would pass before another attack as formidable as the C.C.&W. was made on the gauge. But it would come. It was inevitable.

And what of the Chicago, Cascade and Western Railroad Company? Ike Baldwin went to Des Moines as a state senator and with his immediate drive and initiative removed from the scene, the C.C.&W. Railway died a premature albeit appropriate death. The annual meeting to be held in January 1894 was announced in May 1893 when the articles of incorporation notice was run. However, no mention of the meeting appeared in the newspapers again.

Eastbound train No. 126 is being detained by (from left to right): Ed Gongaware, conductor; Henry Goodsell, station agent at La Motte; Willie Cannon, brakeman (and subject of several anecdotes in **In Those Days**); James Fonda, mail clerk (who was pinned inside the wreckage of combine No. 6 in the 1907 wreck); Arnie Stark, fireman; Frank Leffert, brakeman, who are having their picture taken. The engineer, who is not present, is probably in the cab of the locomotive patiently waiting to be on his way.

Frustrated by Dubuque's lack of interest in the C.C.&W., the directors of the fledgling railroad set the eastern terminus of their new rail system at "a point on the Mississippi River in Iowa." That was just nebulous enough to include the entire eastern border of the Hawkeye state. Other than Dubuque, the eastern terminal could have logically been, Bellevue, Clinton or Davenport. All were serviced by steam boats such as the *Albatross* in the picture above, which was taken at Bellevue.

Looking north across Locust Street (behind picket fence) at the Cascade depot. The Hamilton and Kearney Grain and Lumber elevator dominated the small town's skyline. The western terminus of Iowa's Slim Princess generated much business for the narrow-gauge branch. Photo above dates from around the turn of the century.

The Hamilton and Kearney grain and lumber business held sway on the north side of the tracks in Cascade. Beyond the elevator (right background), lay the stockyards. Photo dates from about 1900.

Setting a standard of rail travel opulence never to be outdone on the gauge, passenger coach No. 12 and combine No. 8 follow one of the Pittsburgh 4-4-0s beneath a plume of smoke. It's wintertime; there's snow on the ground; it's cold. But not too cold to have your picture taken before the train, No. 103, clears the Bellevue yards. The unidentified men are only too happy to be traveling inland on Iowa's Slim Princess, which has withstood the attack of the Chicago, Cascade and Western Railroad.

In those days:

Cascade began holding a fair in September 1891. Since there was no official Dubuque County Fair, the Cascaders delighted in their fall extravaganza. Growing each year, the fair was able to draw as many as 5,000 per day in 1897. Special excursion trains were run from Dubuque to Bellevue on the standard gauge and inland on the narrow gauge to the fair site. The train left Dubuque at 8:00 A.M. and arrived in Cascade at 10:30 A.M. The distance of fifty-six miles by rail covered in two and one-half hours is not that bad when the normal running time of three hours between Bellevue and Cascade is taken into consideration. Naturally, the regular schedule included switching duties at each town and doubling the summit. The excursion train left Cascade at 5:30 P.M. and arrived back in Dubuque at 7:50 in the evening. The round trip cost $1.75 or about one and half cents per mile.

William Cook, when interviewed in March 1981, at the age of eighty-four, was the only surviving crewman of the steam days on the gauge. Bill came from a railroad family. His father bossed a section gang when he lived in La Motte; his brother-in-law was a freight handler in Bellevue and Bill "fired" on the branch between the years 1912 and 1920. Bill Cook stated, "The Milwaukee Road superintendent told my father that the Bellevue [to Cascade] line was the best paying thirty-six miles the Milwaukee owned." That more or less confirms the anonymous Zwingle reporter's statement. Later, the gauge would start showing deficits.

One afternoon or evening, before the installation of air brakes, an eastbound mixed train was leaving Bernard. Ed Gongaware, the conductor, was standing on the rear platform of the combine and spotted, as the train passed over a grade crossing, a fight taking place in the street in front of a tavern. Reaching up, Gongaware pulled the rope to the cab of the engine and stopped the train. He threw open the door to the passenger compartment and shouted, "Come on boys! There's a fight!" Everyone— the passengers and the crew—got off the train and went up the street to watch the fight. When the differences of opinion had been settled, Gongaware shouted, "Come on! Let's go!" Everyone returned to the train and the eastbound pulled into Bellevue a little behind schedule that night. Several years later, Jerry Reynolds who was from Bernard, was Dubuque-bound on the Milwaukee wide gauge from Bellevue. The man sitting next to him shot a covert look when he sat down in the last available seat in the crowded coach, and then persisted in examining his seatmate. Finally, Reynolds asked, "What's the matter?"
   "You got on in Bellevue. Right?"
   Reynolds nodded.
   "Did you come down on the narrow gauge?"
   "Yes, I did."
   "Do you live up there?"
   Another nod.
   "You're the guy, all right. I'm a traveling man out of Chicago and I was traveling the narrow gauge when the conductor stopped the train for a fight in Bernard. You're one of the guys who was fighting. I never saw a railroad like that!" [Gerald Feeney, 1980 interview.]

Train crew and bystanders, including a boy dressed in a suit carrying a baseball bat, pose on the platform in front of the Cascade depot. In this 1880s view showing the freight door on the east side of the depot, a large, barnlike storage building can be seen behind the post with the kerosene lantern. The ownership and use of this building remain somewhat of a mystery as other photos show it to have been replaced with lumber and coal storage sheds by the middle to late 1890s. The combine is No. 12.

6

1901-1907 The Disastrous Years

		GOING WEST.			STATIONS. U. S. Express Co. Dec. 6, 1903.		GOING EAST.			
		No109 Mix'd	No103 Mix'd	Mls		Popu lation	No104 Mix'd	No110 Mix'd		
		P M	A.M.				P.M.	A.M.		
----	----	b 6 55	b 9 30	----	lv......*Bellevue ....ar	1607	b4 30	b 8 40	----	
----	----	7 35	10 30	11	........La Motte........	272	3 15	8 05	----	
----	----	7 50	10 50	16	.........Zwingle	241	2 40	7 53	----	
----	----	8 10	11 15	22	...Washington Mills ..	112	2 00	7 37	----	
----	----	8 20	11 30	25	.........Bernard........	113	1 45	7 27	----	
----	----	8 33	11 45	30	.........Fillmore	115	1 25	7 15	----	
----	----	8 50	12 05	36	ar.......Cascade lv	1266	1 00	7 00	----	
		P.M.	P.M.				P.M.	A.M.		

CHICAGO, MILWAUKEE & ST. PAUL RAILWAY. Cascade Branch.

In effect December 6, 1903, this schedule shows two mixed trains each way on a daily basis. The population of each stop on the line is listed under "going east."

Crying their same chant of inadequate service, the shippers and businessmen of Cascade girded themselves for another winter's battle. Each year about December, the Milwaukee people were reminded by their customers along the branch line, of their inadequacies: poor service—even though there were as many as four and sometimes five trains per day using only the two locomotives for motive power; the complete inability to handle the immense increase of the stock shippers' business at each depot; the monetary loss sustained by the local businessmen when peak market prices were missed and the fact that the railroad could not make amends in this area.

But each winter passed and the diminutive trains scurried over the hills and through the valleys, never exceeding the twenty miles-per-hour speed limit, trying to catch up with their work. Once the twentieth century was begun and the lingering effects of the 1893 panic finally disappeared, the small railroad equipment was updated with modern devices. Carbide lamps were installed on the

locomotives and by 1903, the link and pin couplings were replaced with drawbars and knuckle couplers, air brakes eased the job of slowing for curves and stopping the trains.

The two Pittsburgh 4-4-0s had done yeoman service in keeping the trains operating and were twenty-six years old in 1905. Additional motive power was needed. A third-handed, sixteen-year-old Brooks 2-6-0 was purchased from Ausable and North Western in Michigan for $2,000. The added muscle of this Mogul-type locomotive would take some pressure off the two American engines. Now, when repairs or backshopping were needed, the branch line would not be operating only with one locomotive. Naturally, the businessmen and shippers welcomed the new 2-6-0 as an indication of new and better operating conditions on the gauge.

After twenty-eight years of operation, two fatalities had occurred by 1907. There had been the normal derailments and smashed fingers and hands that went along with link and pin couplers but no passenger deaths were attributable to the railroad and its operation.

The year 1905 was a banner year for the Milwaukee Road as far as the shippers were concerned. No. 1400, a Brooks Mogul which was built in 1889, was put to work on the gauge. Larger, heavier and more powerful than the Pittsburgh 4-4-0s, the Mogul began showing the embittered Cascade business men that trains, regardless of gauge, were capable of performing to the customer's satisfaction. In the photo above, taken shortly after its arrival on the C.M.&St.P. property, No. 1400 poses for what could almost be a builder's photo, except for the men and boys who are admiring the new locomotive. The spoked lead wheels on the engine were replaced with solid ones in one of the 2-6-0s back shoppings.

Over ten thousand people climbed the steps leading to the flat car so they could walk past the Liberty Bell and touch it when the special Milwaukee Road train, which was transporting it, stopped for an hour in Dubuque. Enroute to the 1904 St. Louis World's Fair, the symbol of the United States' independence would pass through Bellevue some twenty miles to the south. The C.M.&St.P. depot is on the right and the Burlington depot is behind the light pole in the center of the picture.

Narrow Gauge, Cascade, Ia.

By 1905-06, most of the gauge's motive power and rolling stock had been equipped with the latest appliances such as knuckle couplers and air brakes. The Pittsburgh 4-4-0s were outfitted with carbide headlights to match the newly acquired Brooks 2-6-0. Ed Horning, Sr., the man on the left was the engineer of this crew. Other than Ed Gongaware who is on the extreme right, the other four men are unidentified.

The first six months of business in 1880 had resulted in more than 25,000 passenger miles. With almost one and a half million passenger miles under its wheels, the Slim Princess had not had a single fatality.

The winter of 1906-1907 had been unusual when past years were taken into consideration. Not much snow had fallen and the trains were not under their normal, weather-inspired attack. At least the railroad was operating without the complication of snow blockades.

Then the only fatal wreck to take place on the narrow gauge branch line occurred February 22. The following excerpts are taken word for word from the Cascade *Pioneer-Advertiser*. Writing with total abandon, the editor did not have to worry about lawsuits since that fine line every newspaper traverses today, did not exist then. Libel was in vogue but take note that the only thing attacked is the inaminate corporation.

The accident that had been feared for years on the Narrow Gauge Branch of the C.M. and St. Paul railroad, between Cascade and Bellevue has occurred, and one life lost and nine maimed and wounded is the grim and tragic results.

About 11:35 a.m. last Friday the combination coach in the rear of the train No. 103, west bound, was derailed about fifty feet from the east end of the trestle across a deep ravine near Washington Mills, and while the train was moving at a moderate speed when the derailment took place, the coach apparently slowed around and as it approached the trestle dropped off on the south side of the tracks and was draped along the edge of the works for some distance, as shown by the battered condition of the timbers, and then plunged downward into the gulch forty feet below carrying with it a box car loaded with way freight.

75

The wagon loaded with Prairie Queen flour, four Zwingle dandies pose with the station agent. Automobiles were not totally unknown in the area at the time but the "new fangled contraptions" were not as dependable as a good team of draft horses. In the background, a plume of steam rises from one of the locomotives, which is hidden behind the far boxcar.

The coach, which was a combination baggage, mail and passenger car [number six] turned completely over and struck flat on its side the rear end no doubt, striking the ground first, the freight car followed, falling down end ways at the west end of the coach and remained in that position.

The standing order when approaching this portion of the track is slow speed and application of the air. Engineer John Hanlon was strictly observing the rule and all the air was applied necessary to hold the moving train as it emerged from the rock cut and moved toward the trestle. There were no indications of unusual character apparent until the engine at the head of the train of five freights and coach had traveled nearly the length of the trestle, when a quick movement of the air gauge indicated that something was wrong. Fireman J.J. Eitel glanced quickly out of his window and saw Conductor Martin hanging onto the hand rails on the side of the way freight car and the next instant the car dropped off the trestle to the bottom, striking endways, carrying the man with it. Neither Eital nor Hanlon saw the coach fall. The movement of the air gauge indicated the sudden release of the coach as it became

detached from the train. Leaving the engine, the two men and Brakeman, Louis Ernst, who had left the rear end only a moment before and had stepped into the cab as the accident happened, hastened to the wreck, and to the rescue of the passengers, not a few of whom they knew were aboard. Mr. Hanlon climbed over the mangled coach, its sides slammed together, not unlike the covers of a closed book and looking down through the window of the mail apartment shouted, "Is there anyone alive in here?" From the depths of the broken fragments of the mail furniture and the mail, J.M. Fonda, the clerk responded, and said that he was alive but was pinned down. In a short time he was rescued, but while the work of taking him out was in progress, a man shot up out of an opening in the shattered roof and cleared himself of the wreckage. This was D.M. Auten of Oelwein (Iowa). He was somewhat dazed at first and although bruised and sore, he aided the trainmen in the rescue of the wounded passengers and his timely call for water prevented the additional horror of fire being added to the fearful disaster, as coals from the stove in the rear of the passenger apartment had already started a blaze.

With the safety valve squirting excess steam into the ether, No. 1400 stands impatiently while the photographer takes its picture with some of La Motte's finest posing with the crew. As soon as the formalities are completed, the passengers will climb aboard the combine at the rear of the train, the hogger will mount the steps to the cab, there will be an ear-splitting double scream of the whistle, and the air brakes will be released. Then there will be a soft chug-chug-chug as the Mogul builds momentum and heads east toward the down grade side of the "summit." Shortly after its acquisition, the spoked lead wheels on the locomotive were replaced with solid ones at the Dubuque shops. Photo dates from about 1906.

This was the view of the track engineer John Hanlon saw as he eased his train onto the trestle. By the time the last two cars were on the bridge, the wheels were off the track as can be seen in the photo above. Although the ties were chewed up some, there was no substantial damage to the bridge and the trains continued running without interruption. The school house (right background) was used as an emergency medical facility until the injured could be transported to hospitals.

There had been job related accidents in the past and two men had died when injured by trains on the narrow gauge. With approximately one and one-half million accident free passenger miles in its twenty-seven year existence, the railroad company, its employees and customers were shaken when, on February 22, 1907 at 11:35 A.M., train No. 103 had its passenger combine and a boxcar fall from the highest trestle at Washington Mills. The train had just passed through the rock cut on the far side of the trestle when the last two cars jumped the track.

NARROW GAUGE WRECK. FEB. 22ND. 07

The amazing thing about the accident is the fact that not everyone was killed in the passenger car. Combine 6, had "its sides slammed together, not unlike the covers of a closed book." (*Cascade Pioneer-Advertiser.*)—C. Wyrick

NARROW GAUGE WRECK. FEB.22'ND,.07

It was grim work for the little band of rescuers and to lift heavy fragments and to cut away the parts that pinioned the suffering men was a herculean task but as the news of the wreck spread through the little settlement help arrived to aid the almost exhausted men.

In the rear of the coach was found the body of Mrs. John Rowan of Fillmore, whose death was no doubt, instantaneous and one by one the maimed and wounded were taken from under the wreckage, all suffering from fractured limbs, gaping flesh wounds and sickening abraisions.

Under the northwest corner of the freight car, with only his head visible, and the great bulk of the car resting upon his poor body was Conductor Henry Martin, his tongue protruding and his eyes forced from their sockets, but he was still alive. As rapidly as possible, portions of the car were cut away and his form released. Into the little school house on the north side of the tracks, a few yards from the scene of the tragic catastrophe the dead and wounded were conveyed and where a short time before light hearted children smiled sunnily into each others faces, now bleeding and suffering men and women were laid in a grim row, their features

---

(Upper left) Just as they do today, accidents drew gawkers in 1907. Once the word was passed that the gauge had a fatal wreck, people from the surrounding countryside flocked to the scene. Someone, perhaps the doctor who cared for the injured, arrived in style as evidenced by the horse-drawn buggy in the right foreground.—C. Nemmers

"Under the northwest corner of the freight car, with only his head visible, and the great bulk of the car resting upon his poor body was Conductor Henry Martin, his tongue protruding and his eyes forced from their sockets, but he was still alive." (Cascade Pioneer-Advertiser.) With a flamboyance born of anger and revenge, the editor of the Cascade newspaper held nothing back when he painted as grotesque a picture of the February 2, 1907 wreck on the narrow gauge as good taste would allow. Five days after the accident, Conductor Henry Martin died at Finley Hospital in Dubuque, Iowa.

distorted and unrecognizable through the wounds and cruel mangling received in the fearful plunge....

Of the seven passengers aboard and the four railroad employees and the mail clerk, one woman was killed outright. According to survivors, Mrs. Rowan had been sitting in the last seat next to the toilet. Five days later, Conductor Henry Martin died at Finley Hospital in Dubuque. With the exception of the three train crew members who were in the locomotive, everyone on board was injured to some extent. One other woman passenger remained bedridden the rest of her life because of injuries to her spine.

The cause of the derailment was never discovered. Speed was not to be blamed since everyone agreed the train was moving no faster than eight miles per hour. Another significant aspect was the fact the combine had derailed on the inside of the curve, which allowed the car to tumble off the trestle.

Capitalizing on the situation, the Pioneer-Advertiser quickly went for the jugular vein of the railroad:

Blame cannot be laid to the train men connected with the operation of the train. Responsibility rests directly, clearly and conclusively upon the Chicago, Milwaukee and St. Paul Railroad Company Corporation. The indictment should read plainly no other responsibility will be considered for one moment. The people of this community and along this road, knowing well by observation and experience, the dangerous character of the equipment and methods obliged to be utilized by its employees, have gone to some pains and expense to themselves in the recent past to warn this railroad company of the unsoftness [sic] of travel on this line to say nothing of damage to property. They have officially called detailed attention to the shortcomings of this piece of so called railroad and have predicted the disaster in some form or other that has happened. It was bound to come sooner or later. It was a reference commonly made that only a terrible accident such as has happened would arouse the Company to a realization of the responsibility of maintaining for public use, the inferior equipment in operation upon the narrow gauge. That this accident has not happened before when hundreds of derailments have taken place to the certain knowledge of countless numbers of witnesses of the communities along the line has been due to the kindliest Providence.

Coaches, cars and even engines that should have been condemned, have been continuously sent over the road of the business of hauling freight and passengers, thus jeopardizing the lives without one entangling technicality to bar the way to positive identification of the guilty culprit—the railroad company. The corporation, that has permitted the use of worn out equipment in the operation of its business over this line that has obliged the expediency of using barbed wire torn from the wayside fences to repair worn out, broken rolling stock....the necessity of engineers (being forced to operate) ridiculous devices, leaking unstable and dangerous (and) out of common courtesy are designated as locomotives—they have refused to listen to the voice because that voice few common people who were not supposed to know anything about running railroads but who knew enough to know that sooner or later the penalty would be paid in blood and tears and the cries of mangled men and women, of not only trainmen, but those trusting in them for safe conveyance. The indictment that is found in this sad affair is solely against the corporation—its managers alone are to blame. Upon them rests the blood of the dead, and the blame for the sufferings of the wounded.

Never was a case more clear. Some railroad accidents are traceable to individuals directly concerned in the operation of or direction of moving trains, but in this case no speed limits were violated, no signals were misplaced, no mixed orders were issued, no switches were turned or a dozen other technicalities of railroading that makes possible the daily death list of rail disasters. But on the contrary, the accident at Washington Mills is traceable direct to the fountainhead of responsibility.

As vile as the Cascade newspaper was in its direct attack on the railroad, the company officials were as much in the dark as anyone when trying to find the cause of the accident. Further examination of the approach to the trestle revealed very little damage to the ties or roadbed where the derailed truck had passed.

In fact, no repairs of any type were needed on the track or roadbed. Superintendent W. Stapleton of the Chicago, Milwaukee and St. Paul Railway finished his statement by saying, "The tracks were not torn up, the rails were not broken and the affair promises to remain a mystery." The train crew was absolved of any blame although the engineer, John D. Hanlon, became nervous and ill because of the accident and was granted a short layoff.

The newspaper in Cascade concluded their tirade with, "Derailments have been far too frequent on the narrow gauge to belong to the occult department."

Once any and all claims for personal injuries were settled by the railroad, the accident soon became fodder for conversations that had run out of current topics. To avoid any future duplication of the accident, the trestle was filled in with earth. By the middle of summer the incident had chiefly been relegated to just another episode on the railroad.

Then, on August 15, 1907, another disaster occurred. A tornado swept through Bernard leaving many of the buildings in that town damaged. While the counties of Jackson, Dubuque and Jones were being rain swept, the storm spent its fury on Bernard where "outbuildings, sheds, barns and granaries were leveled." Two and one-half inches of rain fell in two hours and one large store building was completely flattened by the twister. Part of the railroad depot's roof was ripped off.

The passenger station in Bernard was constructed in a manner that enabled baggage trucks to be run into a three-walled room. The fourth wall was missing and opened on that side to the tracks. A walk-up ticket window connected the station agent's office with the public room. A bench, paralleled the nonexistant wall, which provided an open-air quality to the combination waiting and trunk storage room. When the roof was damaged in the August storm, it appeared as though the carpenters had decided to leave town before completing their work.

More disasters were in store for the Slim Princess but after the year 1907 no one could imagine anything worse than the events of that year.

The grade in the right foreground is actually the site of the trestle from which the passenger car plummeted in 1907. Over the years following the accident, the trestle was filled in and today looks like the abandoned fill it is. The school house has long been deserted but a modern trailer home guards the scene of Iowa's Slim Princess's only fatal passenger accident.

Mrs. John (Mary) Rowan of Fillmore, was about fifty years of age when she was killed instantly in the wreck of 1907. According to survivors, Mrs. Rowan had been sitting in the last seat next to the toilet. Just before the car left the tracks, Mrs. Rowan was telling Mary McLaughlin how happy she was to be returning to her home and her ten children. She had been visiting her ailing father who lived in Bellevue. Of the twelve people, including the crew, who were on the train, eight people counting J.M. Fonda, the mailclerk, were in the combine. Mrs. Rowan and the conductor, Henry Martin, who was on the boxcar trying to apply the brakes when the accident happened, were the only fatalities.

When the roof was damaged in the 1907 tornado, the Bernard depot took on the atmosphere of being incomplete. This particular building had no bay at the front to see the track from inside as most depots did.

The Bernard depot (left) had a unique combination waiting room/storage room for the baggage cart. Enclosed on three sides, the fourth wall existed only on the upper two-fifths, allowing easy access to the inside. The broken windows at the depot, the overturned shed, the house twisted off its foundation and downed trees in the background testify to the severity of the tornado that passed through town August 15, 1907. The upper portion of the open wall is gone in the photo above. Perhaps it was removed by the storm.

Despite the economic and physical growth of Cascade as a community, the citizens reminded the Milwaukee Road each year about December 1, of their inabilities to satisfy the needs of the businessmen, farmers, and shippers. Many of the buildings in the early 1900s photo above still stand in 1982.

It's late 1907 and No. 1400 is on the point of westbound No. 103. The switching duties have been completed at Zwingle and the crew stands perfectly still for "just a minute." Left to right the crew members are: Nathan Hunter, fireman (in the cab); Charlie Spielman, engineer (behind Hunter); Ed Gongaware, conductor; Willie Cannon, brakeman (on top of stockcar); Ed Akpock.—*Higbe*

In those days:

D.M. Auten, a portly traveling salesman for Smith Manufacturing Company of Chicago and who lived in Oelwein, Iowa, managed to escape with the least injury of any of the passengers involved in the wreck of 1907. By the following Monday after the Friday accident, he left the hospital in Dubuque and was a passenger again on the narrow gauge by Wednesday. He was quoted in the *Dubuque Telegraph Herald*: "I've been interviewed by the railroad claim agent but don't think the gentleman knows what high prices aerial acts usually bring. And I don't intend to cut prices even if he was young at the business."

Between 1885 and 1904, the Liberty Bell made five trips around the country to be displayed at different expositions, fairs and occasions meriting such attractions. In 1904, the symbol of America's independence and freedom was mounted on a flatcar bound for the St. Louis World's Fair. There were stops scheduled in various centers of population and, since it was being routed west of Chicago on the C.M.&St.P., Dubuque was to be a one-hour stop for the famous bell on June 7. Over 10,000 people climbed the steps leading to the flatcar, passed by the precious cargo, gently caressing it, and descended by means of another staircase. When the "extra" passed through Bellevue, it didn't stop but was required by law to slow to a safe and reasonable speed. Many people lined the tracks that traversed the center of Second Street for most of Bellevue's full length. The gauge had had an extra number of people from the inland towns riding that day to see the Liberty Bell. While Duke Strazinsky, engineer of the "extra," whistled his way through town, one of the Pittsburgh 4-4-0s sat on its narrow gauge track, separated by a short distance from the main line, tooting a steamy salute.

Frustrated because of his train's being stuck in a deep drift, the conductor, Willie Cannon, became concerned about a sizeable amount of perishable express in the baggage car. Without moving an inch all night, the train sat breathing gently, waiting for help. But with the coming of dawn, Cannon set off for the nearest farm. Returning with the farmer, a man named Curoe, the perishable items were loaded on horse-drawn sleds and taken to the farm's storeroom. Once the train was shoveled clear, the items were brought back. Cannon suggested to Curoe that he submit a claim for the service rendered, but the farmer refused, citing "too much red tape" for his reason. Not to be outdone by the farmer, Cannon offered "special service" for him and his family whenever they rode the train. "I'll stop the train close to your farm and let you off instead of at the depot in town." And the train crews did this from time to time. That spring, Mrs. Curoe, along with two of her small children, was heading homeward and stood to get off the train in Bernard. Cannon gently ordered them to be reseated. He would stop the train at the crossing near their farm so they could walk home. As luck would have it, the superintendent of the division was on the train. When the train stopped at the crossing and the woman and children got off, the "super" approached the conductor.

"What kind of railroading is this? Do you stop at every crossing for passengers?"

"You're damn right," Cannon snorted. "We were stuck out here last winter and if it wasn't for those people coming to save *your* express, you'd probably have had a thousand dollar damage claim to pay. As long as I'm running this train, I can stop and pick them up wherever and whenever I want to." The superintendent didn't say another word. [Gerald Feeney interview, 1980.]

A lady from Chicago was traveling to Cascade by way of the narrow gauge. As the train crept along at a slow pace, she began asking questions of Willie Cannon, the conductor. "What's this?" and "What's that?" "Who's that?" and "Who lives there?" were questions she kept asking of almost everything and everyone they passed. Cannon, who had lost the side of one fingertip when a steer in a cattle car had stepped on it, patiently answered each query. When she noticed his notched finger, she asked, "What happened to your finger?" "Oh, I wore that out pointing to the scenery along the narrow gauge!" Apparently, the woman had connections with the *Chicago Tribune* because the anecdote appeared within its pages shortly thereafter. [Gerald Feeney interview, 1980.]

Cascade Line.

		109	105	Mls.	Table 92		110	106			
		PM	AM				AM	PM			
-----	Nos. 105 and 109 Mixed.	†7.15	†9.40	0	Lv....**Bellevue**....Ar		8.25	5.20	Nos. 106 and 110 Mixed.	-----	-----
-----		7.55	10.45	11.4	"......La Motte.....Lv		7.50	4.20		-----	-----
-----		8.10	11.10	15.7	"_____Zwingle_____"		7.38	3.40		-----	-----
-----		8.32	11.35	22.0	"_Washington Mills_"		7.22	2.50		-----	-----
-----		8.45	11.59	25.2	"_____Bernard_____"		7.12	2.30		-----	-----
-----		9.03	12.15	29.7	"_____Fillmore _____"		7.00	2.05		-----	-----
-----		9.25	12.45	35.6	Ar.....**Cascade** Lv		†6.45	†1.40		-----	-----
		PM	PM				AM	PM			

In an attempt to satisfy the shippers, the Milwaukee maintained a schedule requiring four trains daily between Cascade and Bellevue. Trains No. 109 and No. 110 were the fastest ever scheduled on the gauge and the times would never be improved upon. Trains No. 105 and No. 106 handled most of the switching duties enroute and were allowed three hours, five minutes and three hours, forty minutes respectively. At the time of inauguration, Iowa's Slim Princess sported three steam engines. With one locomotive being held in reserve for an extra or sent to Dubuque for backshopping, two engines were always ready. The schedule was designed in such a manner that one locomotive could have handled all four trains should the necessity arise.

No. 1400 has just finished its switching duties at Cascade after bringing a train in from Bellevue. It is being turned with muscle power on the armstrong gallows turntable. When it is pointed east, it will get a drink of water from the tank and be ready for the down trip.

7

1908-1915 The Assault on the Gauge

Turned and watered, No. 1400 is already on the main line. But the brakeman, Art Masters, who is standing on the tender platform and Nathan Hunter, the fireman will have to back up to the train it has put together before leaving.—*C. Wyrick*

By July 4, 1909, the Chicago, Milwaukee and St. Paul Railway completed the extension of their rails, which had begun in 1906, to the Pacific Northwest. One of two railroad companies that could boast of operating between Chicago and the Pacific Ocean on their own rails, the Milwaukee began hauling trains ladened with raw silk from the Orient and other imported freight in direct competition with the Great Northern and Northern Pacific. Shortly thereafter, passenger trains as well, were being hurried to the northwestern corner of the United States by the C.M.&St.P., the acknowledged leader in passenger equipment and expertise in moving people comfortably and safely.

However, the financial burden of building the route to the West did not deter the company from double-tracking its Omaha line across the state of Iowa. Begun in 1912, it was completed in early 1914. With these types of expenditures, operations such as the narrow gauge branch between Bellevue and Cascade were left for the most part to fend for themselves. There was little excess capital available for other than the barest of necessities. The thirty-pound iron rail had been slowly replaced with the fifty-six- and sixty-pound-to-the-yard steel rail. But the distance between the rails remained a constant three feet. Most freight was still being transferred at the Bellevue terminal by hand. A standard hopper carrying thirty tons of coal required two narrow gauge cars to haul the "black diamonds" inland. Four small boxcars were needed to haul grain enough to fill one

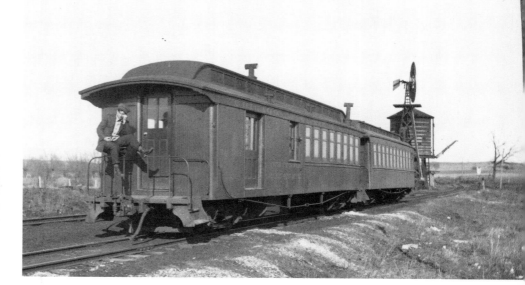

With watertower and windmill in the background, Nathan Hunter poses on the brake wheel of combine No. 8 in the Cascade yards. Looking east in this photo, coach No. 12 is behind the combine.

By 1911 a new depot was built on the site of the one that burned to the ground in 1910. A brick platform replaced the old wooden one. The large elevator as pictured in the previous photo was not rebuilt. However, the stockyards were absolutely vital to the shipment of livestock and they were quickly constructed after the fire. The stub switch in the foreground (center) led to a grain house, coal shed and cement house.—C. Nemmers "wide" gauge boxcar. It took two, twenty-four-foot stockcars to carry enough animals, whether pigs or cattle, to load one regular car. Although the world outside the hills and valleys was picking up speed, in work methods and living in general, the gauge was still operating with the methods in vogue during the 1880s.

Thoughts of consumer discontent were subdued by a July 1910 fire that raged through La Motte. Unusually dry weather had cooked the grass and weeds along the tracks, tinder dry. For whatever reason, since none was ever found, fire broke out and within minutes, the railroad's stockyards and two just-loaded cars of animals were blazing out of control. The La Motte depot, which was nearby, was enveloped in flames and burned to the ground. Before the volunteer fire department could extinquish the holocaust, the flames were destroying one of two grain elevators and a lumber yard. Then, the milk depot that sat next to the tracks went up in sun-bright flames. By 1911, the La Motte railroad structures were rebuilt.

Rumors began circulating in October 1910 concerning the Chicago Great Western and the town of Bellevue. That road, which crossed the Mississippi River at Dubuque over the Illinois Central railroad bridge, was becoming unhappy with the toll it was being charged. Five dollars per locomotive, one dollar per car and fifty cents per passenger totaled more money than they cared to spend. The route of the C.G.W. left Dubuque on that city's north side and circled around to head westerly toward Dyersville and then northwesterly toward Oelwein. Engineers began surveying the territory southeast of Dyersville toward Bellevue. The idea was to skirt Cascade, and to head in an easterly direction toward the Mississippi River, where a bridge owned by that railroad would be built. Serious consideration was being given to buying the right-of-way on which the gauge traversed. Holding their collective breaths, the businessmen, farmers and shippers waited patiently—until January 1911 when the whole project disappeared, not unlike a lot of the railroads Dr. Francis had tried to lure to Cascade. The C.G.W. continued using the I.C. bridge.

Almost a year to the day of the 1910 fire in

La Motte, a similar disaster struck Bernard when a Fourth of July blaze roared through that small town destroying property valued later at $50,000. This community had no volunteer fire department and the only means at hand to fight the fire was a hastily organized bucket brigade made up of several hundred townspeople and farmers. The fire began about 1:30 in the afternoon and wasn't brought under control until 5:00 that evening. The general store, which sold everything, and an attached ice house, two private residences, the town lumber yard, a grain elevator and warehouse along with the gauge's stockyards and six of the small freight cars were nothing but ashes when the last flame was extinguished.

Learning that the Milwaukee was double-tracking the main line across central Iowa, the full wrath of the people of Cascade was aroused. If that main line could be improved, their tracks could be widened. Determined to win their fight for a standard gauge railroad, the customers of the gauge studied their options. First, they would take the C.M.&St.P. to court. If that failed, they would follow through with their overtures to the Chicago and North Western. Several years before, the C.&N.W. had made a survey for a line from Maquoketa on the Midland division, to Cascade. The proposed route followed the Maquoketa River Valley most of the twenty-seven-mile distance. Eager to be of service and open a new territory (and steal some of the Milwaukee's business at the same time), the North Western officials offered their notes on the survey in exchange for the incorporation of a company to build the standard gauge line. This was almost too good to be true. Such a branch line would give them direct access to Chicago, via Maquoketa and Clinton.

In May 1912, a meeting was held at the Columbia theatre in Cascade to formulate their plans for bettering their railroad conditions. Several hundred farmers, merchants and businessmen packed the building to draw up a resolution, which would be their guideline in this fight for standardization of the gauge.

Holding nothing back, the resolution read in part:

Resolved, that it is the sense of this meeting that the narrow gauge railroad between

Cascade and Bellevue, Iowa and maintained by the Chicago, Milwaukee & St. Paul Company, is practically and wholly inadequate in its capacity, character and method of operation to meet the demands and necessities of the traffic of the territory traversed by it, and that by virtue of such inadequacy and lack of fulfillment of the service to which the people are entitled, the community adjacent to its route is made to unjustly suffer in their business welfare. That further...the people of these communities are deprived of the privileges of modern railroading although compelled to pay the same tribute in freight rates, passenger rates and other demands, that are paid for standard gauge service. That a narrow gauge railroad is an obsolete proposition in modern transportation methods....That the resources of the territory...constantly increasing...have overwhelmed its meager capacity in rolling stock equipment and taxed to their utmost its futile motive power in the shape of repatched engines of ancient pattern and lilliputian caricatures of modern railroad machinery. That it is scarcely fit to discharge without mishap the ordinary daily duties imposed...and that any extraordinary demand upon the service burdens it beyond capacity or suspends it altogether....That these conditions impose hardships and losses upon its patrons....That public safety is not reasonably guaranteed....That during the winter months, when most of the shipping is done, a slight snowstorm makes impossible the moving of trains due to poor motive power. And be it further resolved, that we the citizens of the territory...hereby authorize the organization of a movement to carry forward the work of emancipation from present railroad conditions and request the appointment of committees and officers to conduct and direct the desired actions and that funds for the necessary expenses to carry out the aim and purpose of this campaign for betterment be secured by a soliciting committee of reliable men chosen by this assemblage.

Ike Baldwin, who died in 1896, would have been proud.

Throughout the fight for better railroad conditions, the citizens of Dubuque had never offered the shippers along the narrow gauge the slightest bit of encouragement or assistance. The county seat had been interested only once, in 1877, but had been rebuffed. This time, Cascade refused to appeal to the deaf ears to their north. Clinton was not

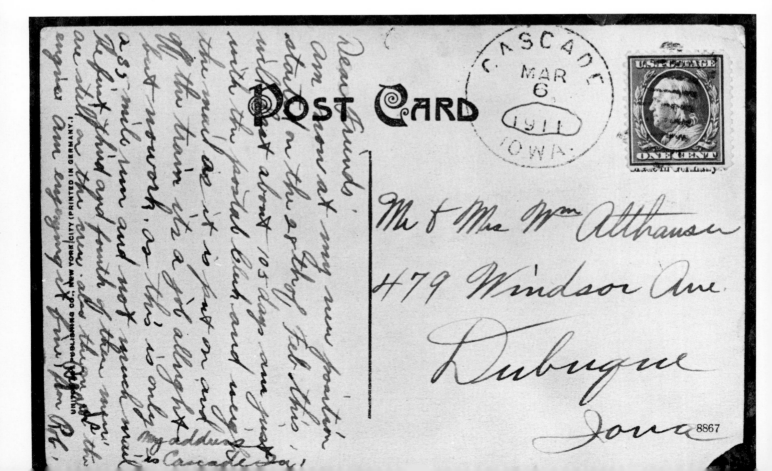

If the history of the gauge is confusing, and at times unclear, it would seem that post marks should help clear up some of the mystery, but not on this railroad. The 1912 cancellation (above) showing it to have been applied on train No. 104 is more than likely correct. However in the cancellation (below) marked June 6, 1913, and as having been applied on train No. 104 seems to suggest a *schedule of convenience* for actual train operations or the mail clerk using whatever cancellation stamp was available and/or within reach. Train No. 104 is listed on a 1903 timetable (see Chapter Six) along with trains No. 109, 103 and 110. No mention of train No. 106. In the timetable included in this chapter, which seems to have followed the 1903 schedule, train No. 106 is included with trains No. 109, 105 and 110. No mention of train No. 104. Another mystery to further confuse the issue. The 1912 cancellation on the above envelope which is from the Jacobson Collection, was probably applied sometime between 1:40 P.M. and 5:20 P.M. by mail clerk James M. Fonda (see train schedule elsewhere in this chapter).—*Above J. Jacobson; below, T. Schnepf from the Earl Moore Collection.*

The card at right was sent from Cascade to Dubuque from a man who had just started a new job as assistant to the postal clerk. It reads, "Dear Friends, Am now at my new position. Started on the 28th of Feb. This will last about 105 days. Am just with the postal clerk and weigh the mail as it is put on and off the train. It's a job allright but no work. As this is only a 35 mile run and not much mail. The first, third and fourth of these men are still on the crew. Also the one in the engine. Am enjoying it fine. Regards from Rob. My address is Cascade, Iowa." The picture on the reverse side was of Pittsburgh No. 1408 and appears in Chapter Six.

In 1912, the Milwaukee renumbered all of its motive power. The gauge's locomotives were all given new identification numbers. Here Pittsburgh 4-4-0 No. 2 sits in the Cascade single stall enginehouse. Note the filled-in slots on the pilot and the extra board above the step. This must have been done for winter running to help push snow aside. Sitting astride the boiler is fireman, Nathan Hunter.—*C. Wyrick*

that much farther away than Dubuque and if Cascade could have standard gauge track running to the former, then who needed the latter?

But Dubuque businessmen *were* concerned. They would stand to lose the business from the southern extremity of the county should this latest plan to connect Cascade to Clinton with standard gauge track materialize. Citing examples where pressure had been brought to bear on the railroad company officials, the Dubuquers showed how they had convinced the Milwaukee to institute regular service between Waukon and Dubuque and the Illinois Central to provide better service to Freeport, Illinois.

There had been much adverse publicity regarding Cascade's fight for a standard gauge. This attention caused Iowa's Thirty-Fifth General Assembly, convening between January 13 and April 19, to consider passing laws in the area of railroad operations. In the past Iowa's general assemblies had not escaped criticism and ridicule from the press for their lack of accomplishments. The usual consensus of opinion when adjournments were reached was, "it might have been worse." The Thirty-Fourth in particular had been dubbed by the press of the state as a "do nothing legislature." Consequently, the Thirty-Fifth General Assembly seemed determined to change its image and, of 1,200 bills that were introduced, 397 were enacted into laws and 13 were adopted as joint resolutions. At least fifteen chapters were passed into law concerning the railroads operating within the state's boundaries. The most curious one was Chapter 170, which read:

> That the Railroad Commissioners of Iowa are charged with the duty, within one year from the passage of this Act, to inspect and examine all railroad lines or branches that are of a gauge less than four (4) feet eight and one half (8½) inches in width of track, and if, considering the interest of the public and the railroad traffic tributary to that line or branch road, and the physical or natural difficulties to be encountered and the expense that would be involved or incurred in changing the track to a gauge of four (4) feet eight and one half (8½) inches in width, and making it practical to operate the said line or branch road on that gauge, it appears to be

"Three Spot" drifts down the main line at Zwingle after spotting cars at the cement depot, grain elevator, and stockyards. Although shippers acknowledged that the little railroad tried valiantly to perform at peak efficiency, they nevertheless wanted standard gauge service.

reasonable and just to require the railway company, which is the owner, to do so, then said Commissioners shall enter an order fixing a reasonable time within which said railroad track is to be changed to a gauge of four (4) feet eight and one half (8½) inches in width.

It shall be the duty of the Railroad Commissioners within one (1) year after the passage of this Act, to examine all the railroads in this state, now in existence, that are less than four (4) feet eight and one half (8½) inches, they shall make their order in writing, fixing such reasonable time within which such a gauge shall be changed to that width. In making such order, said Commissioners shall take into consideration the amount and probably life of the rolling stock of such narrow gauged road, and all other facts bearing on the reasonableness of the time to be allowed to make such change of gauge.

Considering the fact the narrow gauge branch line operating between Bellevue and Cascade was the only such size operation in the state at the time, it would seem rather discriminatory to pass a law aimed at one, and only one, such entity. However, the attention Cascade had drawn to itself in 1912 was apparently going to pay off.

While the Railroad Commissioners were packing their bags and making preparations for a trip on the gauge as prescribed by the new law, and before anything could be done legally about the Slim Princess, the Panama Canal opened in 1914. Within a relatively short period of time, the Pacific Northwest was plunged into a localized financial depression. Ships, which had docked there, were being rerouted through the canal and up along the Eastern Seaboard to ports on the Atlantic and the cargoes' ultimate destination. No longer were shiploads of raw silk being transferred to waiting trains of specially constructed cars that would speed across land to the East Coast, with priority over every other type of train. An era had ended.

The Milwaukee, which had stretched its finances dangerously thin by building its extension to the West Coast, now found itself without the income from transporting exotic Oriental freight. Other staple business from the Northwest began dropping off drastically.

The next ten years would be a trying experience for the C.M.&St.P. and it would not recover until certain legal steps could be taken.

While the full impact of the Canal's opening was being painfully realized, the Iowa railroad commissioners made several trips over the hilly but scenic narrow gauge branch line. Other strangers were also riding the gauge and walking the hills, surveying another route. I.W. Troxel, a civil engineer of national repute, had been contracted by the Farmers and Merchants Tri-County Promotion Corporation, to find a more feasible route to serve them. He reported: "Cost of widening to standard gauge on present alignment, Bellevue to Cascade, $451,115.00. Estimate of cost of widening to standard gauge and reducing the grade to a maximum of 1.5 percent, using the present alignment where practicable, $955,216." Troxel's overall plan called for very little of the present main line to be used and that relocation could have been as far as three miles from the current alignment.

The Milwaukee Road also submitted an estimate made by its engineer, which showed a proposed cost of $555,900 to widen the tracks to standard gauge. The company duplicated Troxel's efforts on reducing the grade to a maximum of 1.5 percent, using the present alignment where possible and showing an estimated cost of $1,941,636.

Moving slowly, the Iowa Railroad Commission conducted its investigation and when all the facts were studied, a decision was handed down December 21, 1915. Referring to the branch line as the "narrow gauge" or "Cascade Branch," the commission gave a brief history of the little railroad. Then it listed the matters to be taken into consideration by them in their investigation:

1. the physical or natural difficulties to be encountered in standardizing the road, and the expense involved
2. the practicality of operating the road as a standard gauge
3. the interest of the public
4. the traffic tributary to the Cascade Branch
5. the rolling stock
6. the feasibility
7. the necessity
8. the order to be rendered by the commission in consideration of their findings

The Iowa Railroad Commission doubted that enough business could be generated to justify broadening the three-foot wide rails of Iowa's Slim Princess. Their report also reflected the impracticability of any attempts to widen the gauge. Although the locomotives had to be transported north to Dubuque on flatcars equipped with rails for backshopping and service, the absence of one locomotive did not make that much difference after the Milwaukee acquired the Brooks Mogul in the photo above. Originally No. 1400, it became No. 1 or "one spot" in 1912.

Even with the modern conveniences such as trains and cars, these Cascade area residents use the more reliable horse and cutter for short distance wintertime transportation.—*W. Talbert*

The commission doubted that enough business would be generated to justify the broadening and decided that the narrow gauge cars could handle the traffic. It also felt that both engineering reports reflected the impracticability of attempting to broaden the gauge. But the hearing was far from being adjourned. Operating expenses were delved into for the three previous years. In 1912, the branch line had suffered an operating deficit of $23,552.00 plus taxes and interest. In 1913, the losses had amounted to $18,770.50 plus taxes and interest on bonds. The figures for 1914, the year the canal opened, showed the narrow gauge losing $17,507.24. The deficits at least, were on a diminishing scale for the time being. Again the taxes and interest due on the funded indebtedness of the branch were not included since neither item was calculated in the financial reports with which the commission was working.

When the matter of the public's interest came to the fore, all hell broke loose. Now the citizens of Cascade would have powerful ears in which to pour their tales of poor service, inadequate equipment and loss of money because of the gauge. Over fifty such formal expressions of discontent were received by the board of commissioners, who quickly categorized the complaints into eighteen groupings. The first half of the list was dispatched with the comment that they were peculiar not only to the narrow gauge operation but to all railroads in general. Slow passenger train service, shrinkage of grain and coal in transit, delays in stock reaching market or produce being shipped in and the like were to be found on the most efficient carriers. The commissioners even went so far as to zealously state that "...a comparison of roads, where the line is under fifty miles in length and terminates at an inland town, shows that the passenger train service on the Cascade Branch compares very favorably with the passenger train service...to and from towns with far larger population than the towns on the Cascade Branch."

The last nine categories of complaints which were individual and isolated cases, were handled singly but did not affect the overall decision of the board.

Each of the eight areas of consideration were

ticked off one by one and the decision was finally rendered when the necessity of widening the tracks was covered. The board stated:

> Our investigation of this matter has convinced us that the Cascade Branch has, for many years, been amply sufficient to carry in and out from Cascade and all the stations along its line, all of the traffic which has been offered to it, and it is our belief that it can, for many years, continue to handle all the traffic which will be originated upon this line....we deem it unnecessary at this time, to pass upon the question as to whether an order requiring the branch line to be standardized would be confiscatory, or in violation of the contract, which the railroad company claims was entered into between it and the state of Iowa.

Interestingly enough, Commissioner Thorne, who chaired the board, dissented. Showing that narrow gauge operations were rapidly becoming obsolete he cited the fact that the C.B.&Q. "has 9,366 miles of track and...only 70 miles of narrow gauge. These are located in South Dakota. The Chicago & North Western has 8,108 miles of track; and there are 16 miles of narrow gauge in Wisconsin; and 21 miles of narrow gauge in South Dakota....There is no narrow gauge in operation on any part of the Atchison, Topeka & Santa Fe, Chicago Great Western, Great Northern, Minneapolis & St. Louis." Thorne continued his recitation of roads, which did not own slim tracks, but to no avail. The majority ruled.

Because of Thorne's dissenting vote, another hearing was scheduled the following year and then cancelled because of Thomas Fitzgerald's death. Fitzgerald had been attorney for the Farmers and Merchants Tri-County Promotion Corporation. This Cascade corporation continued its existence and would from time to time lodge complaints against the gauge. Before another attorney could be hired, the United States became involved in World War I and the matter was never reopened. Iowa's Slim Princess had withstood the toughest test of its existence. It would have more trials and tribulations in the future that would be further complicated by the severe financial troubles in which the Chicago, Milwaukee and St. Paul Railway Company now found itself.

The shippers' anger was growing steadily since most freight still had to be transferred by hand at the Bellevue terminal. The people in Cascade knew the world was picking up in tempo, but their railroad was still operating with 1880s methods. The little boxcars such as those in the photo above were just too inadequate.

Several hundred farmers, merchants and businessmen were packed into the Columbia Opera House to attend a meeting for improving their railroad conditions. The resolution drawn up would have made Ike Baldwin, who died in 1896, proud of his fellow townsmen.

Although the Milwaukee Road had stretched its finances very thin when it extended its rails to the west coast, it did not deter them from double-tracking their main line across Iowa to Omaha, Nebraska. Since money was scarce after these expenditures, just the barest of essentials could be had on branches such as the Bellevue-Cascade line. The rail on the gauge was being slowly replaced with 50- to 60-pound steel but the distance between the rails remained a constant three feet. The steel bridge shown above was located one-half mile east of Zwingle.—*L. Deppe*

The Chicago Great Western was a viable entity in the early twentieth century and offered fast and direct service to Chicago from the north central area of Iowa and from Minnesota. However, the C.G.W. did not like paying exhorbitant fees to the Illinois Central for the use of their bridge between Dubuque, Iowa and East Dubuque, Illinois. Casting about for an alternate solution, consideration was given to buying the gauge's right-of-way and building their own bridge across the Mississippi. The plan never materialized and the gauge continued its own operations. The picture above dates from the Dubuque apparently with doughboys from Europe. Today the station that is in the right background is gone. The Chicago Great Western is gone and the water tank is gone.

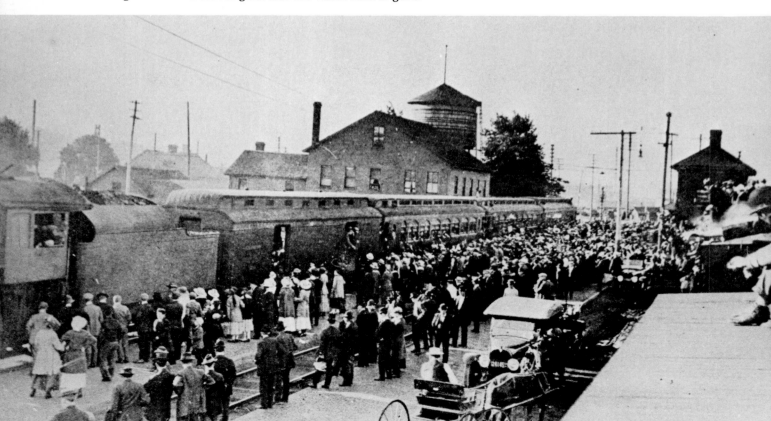

Headed east in the Cascade yards, No. 2 serves as a backdrop for the crew. From left: "Spider" Fagan; Benny Hunter, fireman; Ed Gongaware, conductor; Frank Leffert (whose son Carl took several photos used in this book); Willie Cannon, brakeman; and unknown. Standing on the pilot is Mike Sager.

Charlie Spielman, the engineer immortalized in poetry, looks up from his job of last minute oiling and inspecting, startled to find a photographer aiming at him. Spielman was known for his deft touch on the whistle and could be identified easily by his slouched felt hat.

Taken near Bellevue, this photo shows an early Overland touring car with the driver and passengers dressed in their finest for a picnic outing. The dirt road seen at extreme right, was typical of early roads being usable in fair weather but becoming a nightmare to use after rain or snow.

Although farming with horses remained a common practice until after World War II, this photo from the late teens signals the beginning of the end of that particular era. "One spot," the Brooks Mogul, is shown ready to start the journey to Bernard with six new McCormick 10-20 tractors which were first introduced in 1915.—*Streuser*

In those days:

While heading westbound in number 105 out of Fillmore toward Cascade, engineer Jack Benzer spotted a cottontail rabbit close to the tracks. Slowing the engine, he aimed his ever-present shotgun out the window and brought the animal down. Through experience, "Booby" Dickeman, the brakeman riding in the combine, knew a rabbit had been shot when he heard the gun's report and prepared to drop off the train to retrieve the potential "stew." Before he could complete his half of the job, another blast was heard from the front of the train and 105 ground to a halt enabling Jack Benzer to retrieve a second animal. Then another popped up and the gun sounded a third time. Then a fourth. With each report of the shotgun, Benzer and Dickeman walked a little farther from the train. Carl Leffert, the conductor, walked to the front and ordered young Bill Cook, the fireman, to "take 'er on in to Cascade. We'll do the work and pick 'em up on the way back." A few hours later, the eastbound mixed train hissed to a stop and Benzer climbed aboard the engine and Dickeman threw the day's kill into the baggage compartment of the combine. The crew divided sixteen rabbits that particular day.

Although Bill Cook would one day be employed as an engineer, the other men looked on him as not having "whiskers enough" for the job. He recalled the time the Brooks Mogul blew a cylinder head and "scared the hell out of me." Once he was qualified for the right side of the cab he still preferred firing and did little engineering.

—Bill Cook, April 15, 1981 interview

Conductor Ed Gongaware, left, and brakeman, Phil Webber perch on the pilot, framing "one spot's" face. There's a certain determined look about them that says they are proud to be railroad men.

8

1916-1928 Receivership and The Chicago, Milwaukee, St. Paul & Pacific

When the C.M.&St.P. extended their rails to the west coast and then spent an additional twenty-three million dollars for electrification their purse became pretty thin. Once the Panama Canal opened in 1914, the Milwaukee was hanging on the ropes, gasping for financial air. Box cab electric locomotives, such as the one above, were new and radical and proved their worth by remaining in service until the electrification was taken out over fifty years later. Still, Iowa's Slim Princess could not be improved because the Milwaukee could not entertain thoughts of more expenditures.

In 1916, the Chicago, Milwaukee and St. Paul Railway Company leased for the benefit of its customers along the gauge two, five thousand-gallon tank cars for shipping fuel.[13] Such an action could be interpreted as aiding and abetting the enemy but business was business. There was need for liquid fuel, for automobiles along the branch line and no other way to get it there other than by rail. These cars were leased from the Union Tank Line and would continue in service until the last days of the narrow gauge itself.

The three locomotives, the Brooks Mogul and the two American engines were aging but still performing their duties. The opportunity to purchase another used piece of motive power came from the Colorado and Southern Railroad in 1918.[14] This Cooke built 2-8-0 came just in time since one of the Americans

was on its last legs or wheels, if preferred. Two months after the new locomotive arrived on the property, number "three" gave up. Scalped for parts to keep number "two" running, the hulk was sold for scrap in October 1918. The motive power roster now stood at three engines: one American 4-4-0, Number 2; one Mogul 2-6-0, Number 1; one Consolidation 2-8-0, Number 4.

The next month, World War I ended, and people were ready to begin ordinary living again. When the 1920s began, things were back to normal—weather-wise especially. Old-timers began recalling the blizzards of the 1880s when record-breaking snowfalls whitened the countryside and shut off the gauge. A thirty-four-hour blizzard in April 1921 effectively brought everything to a standstill. The wedge snowplow then being

105

Although some of the stories as related by the old timers who worked for the gauge seem a trifle on the exaggerated side, the above picture proves that Bill Cook's story of the caboose balanced on its right side wheels could and probably did happen just the way he tells it.

Despite bigger locomotives and slightly faster schedules as evidenced by Table No. 316, the railroads were still brought to a complete standstill by the thirty-four hour blizzard in April 1921. If the wide gauge trains were stopped, slim rails, such as Iowa's last narrow gauge operation, were not only stopped but unable to shovel themselves out for several days after the storm passed.

CHICAGO, MILWAUKEE & ST. PAUL RAILWAY 161
Savanna to Waukon and La Crosse — TABLE 316

	GOING NORTH					Miles	STATIONS. Wells-Fargo Exp. Co. June 18, 1916		GOING SOUTH			
No 31 Pass.	No 1 Pass.	No 25 Pass.	No 3 Pass.	No 9 Pass.				No 28 Pass.	No 4 Pass.	No 30 Pass.	No 32 Pass.	No 8 Pass.
Fri. and Sat. only P.M.	Daily P.M.	ExSun A.M.	Daily A.M.	ExSun P.M.			Population	ExSun P.M.	Daily P.M.	ExSun A.M.	Fri. and Sat. only A.M.	Daily A.M.
	a 9 43	b 8 45	a 3 45	b 6 18	0	Savanna 3691		b 2 55	a 5 25	b 9 10		a 3 29
	† 9 51	9 04	3 55	6 30	3	Sabula 944		2 45	5 15	9 00		† 3 20
		9 30	† 4 15	6 55	14	Green Island 128		2 23	4 53	8 40		3 04
		† 9 38			19	Pleasant Creek		† 2 14				
	10 30	9 52	4 38	7 14	23	Bellevue 1708		2 03	4 35	8 23		2 47
		†10 03			29	Smiths		† 1 49				
		10 11	† 4 58	† 7 32	33	Gordon's Ferry 100		1 42	† 4 16	† 8 02		
4 05	11 15	†10 40	† 5 30	8 00	47	Dubuque 41795		1 15	3 52	7 35		2 00
	11 30	11 25	6 00	8 10	47	Dubuque		b 9 50	3 45		10 30	1 51
4 15	11 38	11 32	6 07	8 20	48	Dubuque Shops		9 43	3 38	7 15	10 23	1 44
	11 43	11 35	6 11	b 6 45	48	Dubuque Shops		9 41	3 35	b 3 15	10 20	1 40
				† 7 00	53	Edmore				3 50		
4 35		11 55		† 7 20	59	Specht's Ferry		9 20	† 3 17	2 45	9 56	
				† 7 38	66	Cameron				† 2 25		
4 49		12 08		7 43	67	Waupeton		9 05		2 23	9 41	
4 58		12 17	6 52	8 00	70	Buena Vista 162		8 55	2 57	2 10	9 31	
5 08	†12 42	12 27	7 02	8 30	75	Turkey River 53		8 45	2 48	1 35	9 21	
				8 35	75	Turkey Rv. Junction				1 04		
5 23	1 05	12 43	7 16	9 45	81	Guttenberg 1886		8 28	2 33	12 43	9 04	12 38
				10 00	86	Eckards				11 52		
5 42		1 04	7 35	10 30	91	Clayton 141		8 05	2 14	11 40	8 40	
				10 40	95	Sny Magill				11 20		
6 03	1 47	1 24	7 55	11 05	100	McGregor 1283		7 50	1 57	11 05	8 20	11 59
6 07	1 55	1 30	8 00		101	North McGregor 675		7 40	1 50	10 16	8 12	11 50
6 19 see Table 324		1 55	b§8 10	12 10	101	North McGregor		7 25	b 1 35	9 20	7 55	see Table 324
6 26		2 05		12 25	105	Yellow River		† 7 15		9 05	† 7 45	
6 36		2 18	8 30	12 40	109	Waukon Junction .58		7 05	1 17	8 55	7 35	
b 7 05		b 2 45	b 8 35		0	Waukon Junction		b 6 30	b 1 00	b 7 25		
7 35		3 30	9 05		9	Waterville 192		6 00	12 30	6 57		
		† 3 50	9 25		15	Rossville 189		5 30	12 01	† 6 42		
8 25 see Table		4 30	10 00		22	Waukon 2168		5 15	11 30	6 20		
321	2 18	8 30	1 17		109	Waukon Junction 58		b 7 05	1 17	8 30	see Table 321	
No 33 Pass.	2 28	8 38	1 40		118	Harper's Ferry ..315		6 55	1 05	8 15	No 34	
P.M.	† 2 43		2 00		121	Heytman's		† 6 40	†12 49	7 35	A.M.	
	3 00	9 05	2 45		128	Lansing 1655		6 25	12 34	7 15		
ExSun	3 25	9 28	3 13		139	New Albin 613		6 00	12 10	6 15	ExSun	
5 10	3 41	9 50			147	Reno 113		5 45	11 53		9 37	
5 25	3 56	10 04			154	Browns 361		5 30	11 30		9 02	
5 45	4 15	10 23			164	La Crescent 872		5 06	11 16			
					166	North La Crosse		4 55	11 00			
	6 10	4 30	10 35		167	La Crosse 30417		4 45	10 56		8 45	

No. 10 connects at Savanna for Davenport see table 1123.

Marie Weber waited with several girlfriends in Sullivan's pasture to get this picture of a Sunday extra headed toward Bellevue. As the Brooks Mogul roared past with Engineer Jack Benzer at the throttle, Marie snapped this picture with her husband-to-be Bill Cook, the fireman, perched on top of the cab.—*M. Weber Cook*

operated on the narrow gauge was simply not efficient enough in such conditions. By 1928, the accumulated snowfall would total over twenty-one feet.

Then in the spring of 1925, the record snowfall melted in record time and Cascade was inundated by what has become known simply as *The Flood*. Although only two lives were lost, over one hundred buildings were damaged by the rampaging waters of the Little Maquoketa and property loss was fixed at one-half million dollars.

The fledgling automobile, which had fuel delivered by the gauge, gained a significant advantage in 1927. That year, the Old Military Road, was paved. Now, those who owned a car, could whisk into Dubuque within an hour or two and the passenger business on the Slim Princess began falling off. Hamstrung because of the terrain over which it ran, the narrow gauge branch line was still operating under the rules established in 1880. Trains were not to exceed twenty miles per hour and were to reduce speed to ten miles per hour when descending the grades at Washington Mills, La Motte Hill (eastbound) and Sylva Hill (westbound).

The competition from the automobile and the direct frontal attacks in the wintertime by snow could have been coped with if the Milwaukee itself was not suffering from lack of money and business. The once financially strong granger road had become the victim of circumstances where its West Coast extension was concerned. The project had cost $234 million when it was completed. That total was increased by another $23 million when electrification was added across two mountain ranges. To better understand the cost involved, consider the Northern Pacific. When that road's rails had been extended to the West Coast in 1880, the total cost amounted to $70 million. However, the Northern Pacific had also received grants of land equivalent in area to the state of Missouri. The C.M.&St.P. had been forced to negotiate purchases of all the land on which its rails were to be laid.

When the Panama Canal opened, the three transcontinental railroads serving the Pacific Northwest were at each others' throats for the existing business. To make matters worse, the Union Pacific was thrusting its rails in the direction of the Great Northern, the Northern Pacific and the Milwaukee.

In 1917, the Federal Aid Road Act was passed and trucks and busses began helping automobiles eat away at the railroads once impregnable position. Soaring taxes, higher maintenance costs, improvements costs and federally-ordered increased wages had set the

This is the depot around which the inhabitants of Cascade lingered to keep abreast of the World Series game in 1917. Urban "Red" Faber, a Cascade native son would win three of the four games that year to crown the Chicago White Sox as World Champions. Since there was no radio, the quickest means of finding out about world events was over the telegraph at the railroad station. The man on the right, Harry Care, was station agent in Cascade for many years.

stage for the U.S. Railway Administration to make its appearance during World War I. The government operated all of the privately owned railroads and managed to do this at a substantial loss. When the individual roads regained control of their property in 1920 they were expected to pick up where the government had left off and recoup the privations that had been incurred during the prior three years.

Then the Milwaukee acquired the Chicago, Terra Haute & South Eastern Railway Company in 1921 and the Chicago, Milwaukee and Gary Railroad in 1922. Now there was a direct route to the coal fields in Indiana.[15] No sooner had they acquired these two lines, than a coal strike was called in 1922. This was followed by a governmental order to reduce freight rates.

In 1905, the Chicago, Milwaukee and St. Paul Railway's stock had sold for 199⅝ on the market. Twenty years later, it was selling for $5.00 a share. In 1920, the Milwaukee line hauled sixteen million passengers. By 1930, that figure would be more than halved.

While the customers along the branch line

were not delirious with joy over the performance of their railroad, they gritted their teeth hoping for better service. One bit of legislation, which had been passed into law almost unnoticed, required inspectors representing the railroad commissioners to travel each line at least once a year. During these trips they were to watch for safety measures that were employed, regard for freight and the customers' satisfaction. By late 1924, the inspectors had not yet ridden the gauge and it seemed as though things began going wrong in anticipation of their arrival.

First, number "four," "the big one," as it was referred to by many, went to the Dubuque shops for regular servicing. It was no sooner on its way, than number "two," the remaining American Standard 4-4-0, tipped off the tracks and "one spot," the Brooks Mogul was left to do all the railroading. The screams of shippers in Cascade and Bernard could almost be heard in Bellevue. Twenty carloads of cattle were waiting at the western terminal while twenty-five similar carloads were waiting at Bernard. The backlog of freight building up in Bellevue

Leasing the two 5,000 gallon tank cars for the benefit of its customers, the gauge could have been accused of "aiding and abetting" the enemy. The narrow gauge tank cars were brought to Bellevue on standard flatcars equipped with rails and are sitting on the siding that led to the ramp for unloading.

The tank cars, which were acquired on a lease basis from the Union Tank Line in 1916, were destined to spend the next twenty years on Iowa's Slim Princess.

When No. 3 wore out, parts were cannibalized to keep No. 2, above, running. From left to right, are: Art Masters, brakeman; John Graham, roundhouse hostler; Art Lynch, fireman; Charlie Spielman, engineer. With its stack bobbed, No. 2 took on a long, sleek appearance.

prompted the railroad officials to issue an order refusing any new freight until matters were cleared up in the river town.

Then the inspectors arrived. They made their trip and left to write their report. However, by the time the report was made out after consulting with the Milwaukee people, all three locomotives were in service and matters quieted down for the Christmas holidays.

Although the C.M.&St.P. Railway's directors voted for receivership in 1925, they were not deterred from purchasing still another used locomotive for the gauge in 1926. This was probably out of concern over the 1924 incident when the road was underpowered. An outside frame 2-6-0 Baldwin steam engine was brought on the property and given the number "three." Five months later, in August, the remaining American was sold for scrap and the branch line continued operations with three locomotives.

A singular distinction was bestowed on the gauge that same year when the Chicago and North Western narrow gauge line between Fennimore and Woodman, both towns in Wisconsin, was abandoned. This left the narrow gauge branch line to Cascade the only such operation in the Middle West. Several years earlier, the last remnants of the three-foot line between Galena, Illinois, and Benton, Wisconsin, had been torn up.

The following year, in 1927, the Chicago, Milwaukee & St. Paul Railway became, through reorganization, the Chicago, Milwaukee, St. Paul and Pacific Railroad, a 10,891-mile network of rails. Included, were the thirty-six miles of narrow gauge tracks running between Bellevue and Cascade. A new president was brought in from the Union Pacific where he had served as one of that road's vice presidents. H.A. Scandrett would prove to be one of the most dynamic presidents the Milwaukee would ever have.

The new corporation's papers were filed March 13, 1928, and three months later Iowa's Slim Princess was treated to its last steam driven engine. Another outside frame 2-6-0, a twin to the other Baldwin, was purchased and the gauge now boasted four steam engines. Since the scheduled runs had been reduced to one each way in 1927, the new power was going to be uitilized for double heading longer trains.

Under Scandrett's guidance, the Milwaukee began cutting back its passenger service, substituting mixed regular passenger trains in at least twenty-five instances. Sixty-six passenger trains, which operated over twenty-six hundred miles daily were eliminated. However, the mixed trains inaugurated on the gauge in 1880, continued to ply the hills and valleys in Jackson and Dubuque counties.

Taken about 1900 near Golden, Colorado, this photo shows No. 55 of the Colorada and Southern double-heading with another locomotive. As the B.&C. branch was short of motive power, the C.&S. was ordered by the U.S.R.A. in 1917 or 1918, to ship the Cooke built 2-8-0 to the Milwaukee. Requiring numerous repairs before it was put into service on the B&C as No. 4, the above transfer caused a dispute between the two roads as the U.S.R.A. went out of existence before a price was agreed upon.

The "big one," as the Cooke 2-8-0 soon became nicknamed by many, lost its fancy stack when it came to Iowa, but remained for the most part readily identifiable as an iron horse from out west. No. 4 is taking on water at Cascade preparatory to coupling to the down train and will be Bellevue-bound shortly. The man on the tender is unidentified. John Fuerst, the fireman, is on the tender platform and Jack Benzer will be on the throttle and working the whistle.

No. 2, the last Pittsburgh 4-4-0 to operate on the gauge is just leaving Zwingle. The competition is becoming more obvious as the years roll by. There are three cars and four horse-drawn wagons at the depot area. The crossing just ahead of the locomotive would be the scene of an accident in time to come.

Six stock cars are waiting to be loaded and taken to Bellevue. First point of business will be to rehang the door on car No. 113. Note the swaybacked baggage truck in the foreground on the Cascade station platform. Sometime around 1920.— *Neiers*

Backshopped, and ready for service "four spot" is just off the turntable at the Dubuque shops. The sand drying building just behind the sand tower still stands today but the water tower is long gone. On one particular occasion, while the Cooke built off the tracks and Iowa's Slim Princess was operating with one locomotive, the Brooks Mogul.

"Two spot" tipped off the rails in December 1924 while the Cooke consolidation was in the shops for service. The overload of work on "one spot" caused the Milwaukee to stop accepting any new business for the gauge until such time the bottleneck in Bellevue could be cleared up. Charlie Spielman stands on the tender platform while he considers the job of turning the 4-4-0 by hand on the turntable in Cascade. The gallows type table had been replaced around the turn of the century.

A latter day photo of dam and mill at Cascade during high water conditions gives a graphic illustration of the origin of the town's name.

Although the Milwaukee inaugurated four scheduled runs daily except Sunday and that pattern remained in effect until the late 1920s, the fact remained that the gauge was operating by the same rules as the ones established in 1880. Trains could not exceed a maximum speed of twenty miles per hour. The branch line ran nothing but mixed trains. With Highway 151 paved, the passenger business began falling off during the warm months when it "made more sense" to go by auto.

6 WESTWARD · BETWEEN BELLEVUE AND CASCADE SUBDSIVION · EASTWARD

SECOND CLASS 121 Mixed Daily Except Sun.	SECOND CLASS 105 Mixed Daily Except Sun.	Capacity of Siding in Cars Passing Tracks	Capacity of Siding in Cars Other Sidings	Distance from Bellevue	Time Table No. 16 In Effect 6:01 a.m., March 8, 1925 STATIONS	Office Closed Week Days	Distance from Cascade	Telegraph Calls	SYMBOLS See Special Rule, Page 8	SECOND CLASS 102 Mixed Daily Except Sun.	SECOND CLASS 106 Mixed Daily Except Sun.
L 5.10PM	L 8.10AM			116	BELLEVUE		35.7	BU	RBWCTJ	A 2.25PM	A 3.15PM
6.05	9.05	27		11.4	11.4 LA MOTTE	5:00PM to 8:00AM	24.3	AM	WD	1.25	2.15
6.30	9.30	17		15.7	4.3 ZWINGLE	5:00PM to 8:00AM	20.0	WI		1.01	1.50
7.05	10.05	14		22.0	6.3 WASHINGTON MILLS	No Office	13.7		CWD	12.25	1.15
7.25	10.25	25		25.2	3.2 BERNARD	5:00PM to 8:00AM	10.5	BR		12.11PM	1.00
7.45	10.45	30		29.8	4.6 FILLMORE	No Office	5.9			11.50	12.40
8.10PM	102 11.10AM	54		35.7	5.9 CASCADE	5:00PM to 8:00AM		CD	RBWCTD	L 11.25AM	105 L 12.15PM
3.00	3.00				Schedule Time					3.00	3.00
12.0	12.0				Average Speed per Hour					12.0	12.0

SPECIAL RULES

EASTWARD TRAINS ARE SUPERIOR TO WESTWARD TRAINS OF THE SAME CLASS

Trains must not exceed maximum speed of 20 miles per hour.

All eastward trains reduce speed to 10 miles per hour descending Washington Mills and LaMotte hill, and westward trains descending Sylvia Hill.

All regular branch freight trains will carry passengers.

In the spring of 1925, the winter's record snowfall melted in record time and Cascade was inundated by what has become known simply as "the flood." The Maquoketa River swept out of its banks, destroying over one hundred buildings and causing a half-million dollars worth of damage. During the crisis, the falls, that gave Cascade its name, was dynamited to lower the water level.—C. Wyrick

Only one of the American 4-4-0s was operating well. The other was beginning to spend more and more down time as it aged. "One spot," the Brooks Mogul, was performing admirably but that fact did not preclude the idea that more and better motive power was needed. No. 1 is just about ready to whistle out of the Cascade yards as the engineer checks for the conductor's signal.

The ivy covered bank in Zwingle must have shuddered in 1925 when its neighbor, the Chicago, Milwaukee and Saint Paul Railway, voted for receivership, only to turn around and purchase another steam locomotive in 1926. The following year, the Chicago, Milwaukee, Saint Paul and Pacific Railroad emerged.—*Neiers (8-15-25)*

It is difficult at best to understand today, how a railroad could make money shipping 125 pounds of anything for 50¢. Granted the dollar value was considerably higher—but 50¢? Regardless of the monetary element, the school children at Zwingle would not have any reason for being short on vocabulary once the carton of dictionaries arrived.

"Three spot," the new Baldwin outside framed Mogul, is eastbound as its whistle barks a warning for the grade crossing in Zwingle. The squared off headlight, which was a Milwaukee peculiarity, enabled people to distinguish between "three spot" and its twin, "two spot" when it showed up on the property since the latter carried a round headlight.

The Baldwin 2-6-0 above was acquired in 1926, possibly to avoid a similar lack of power as the one that occurred in 1924. The outside framed Mogul was considerably bigger than the other locomotives and was more powerful. The snowplow on the front of "three spot" would prove to be inadequate once the heavy snow storms hit the Hawkeye state.—*J. Adney*

No. 3, the latest engine acquired for the gauge breathes gently as it sits on the Cascade turntable after being turned. The engineer and fireman are probably breathing harder than the locomotive.

"One spot" eases forward with the brakeman sitting on the pilot. The train will head east until the last car clears the switch by the water tank. Then it will back up and couple to the stockcars sitting on the next track. It's shortly after 1927 and the Milwaukee's official name is now the Chicago, Milwaukee, St. Paul and Pacific Railroad. Note the logo on the tender.

The fireman's side of the new "two spot" as it posed on the turntable at Cascade. At first, there were few cosmetic differences between the two Baldwin locomotives other than the headlights. "Two spot" had a conical shaped spark arrestor as opposed to a cylindrical one on "three spot." There were a few variations in the piping. Carrying one of its classification lights in a horizontal position above the handrail would not count as a difference.

119

Nightmare of potholes and ruts near Cascade in the 1920s graphically illustrates the hazards facing motorists in the pre-paving era.

Going to Dubuque by automobile was a sheer joy once the Military Road (Highway 151) was paved. Hardly a thought was given the gauge when zooming across the tracks between Fillmore and Cascade above. The track is receiving some attention from a section gang—probably replacing some spikes.—*L. Deppe*

Milwaukee Road section crew in Cascade yards on July 2, 1928. Note the smoke flap on the chimney of the one stall roundhouse at left. The gondola at right had a 60,000-pound capacity. The only identified crew member is Bob Holmer, at far right.

When 1927 arrived, the people of Cascade were overjoyed when Highway 151, Lyman Dillon's old furrow, was paved. When Main Street would be covered with concrete, the elements would no longer turn the thoroughfares into a muddy quagmire.

"We shoveled by the hour for pay and anything over eight hours, we got time-and-a-half. I think it was around forty cents an hour. That was 1926 when I was about fifteen years old." From a taped interview with Gerald Feeney of Bernard, Iowa in 1980.—*L. Deppe*

Some of the drifts could be as high as the train itself. It's not surprising then to hear of an instance where all four of the steam engines would be employed to push the wedge type snowplow in an attempt to open the main line. This picture was copied from a local newspaper but clearly shows the weather element in full display.—*J. Thomas*

122

With a blanket of snow on its roof and more tucked around the bottoms of the windows, the gauge's only caboose waits on a siding, ready to be of service. Note the interesting walkway around the cupola, which was added to both sides at the Dubuque Shops when the crummy was backshopped.—*R. Bogue*

Because the last American, "two spot" had given up the struggle in August 1926 and because the then newly acquired Baldwin 2-6-0 had performed so well, the Milwaukee jumped at the chance to buy another used piece of Baldwin equipment. "Two spot" would prove to be the last steam power purchased and would operate the longest of the locomotives on the roster. It must be shortly after its arrival on the property since it carries a number on the cab but no logo on the tender. The conductor, Walter Graham is on the left; Richard Sullivan is the brakeman; Charlie Spielman, engineer and Michael Galvin, brakeman. It's a cold morning in Cascade as No. 2 marks the gray sky with its smoke.

The turntable and roundhouse at Bellevue in later days. When the possibility of more than three locomotives became apparent, additional space would be needed to house the extra motive power. The building into which the tracks of the turntable are leading was built with additional sheathing on the inside and was much warmer in the winter than the two-stall roundhouse. During the gauge's existence, the turntables at Bellevue and Cascade remained man-powered as evidenced by the armstrong handles at either end.—*L. Deppe*

Irony dictates that a new storage tank delivered to the Standard Oil house at the Cascade yards be delivered by truck. With the oil facility at far right, a lumber shed can be seen at far left, and the grain elevator partially obscured by the new tank.

"Two spot," the latest steam power acquisition blasts over Whitewater Creek, framed by the bridge spanning the water. Headed east it will arrive in Bellevue with its trainload of freight in several hours. Its first stop will be Fillmore, which is less than a mile away.—*C. Leffert*

Taken looking east from the depot in Cascade, this photo shows the Standard Oil facility in the Cascade yards. Included are, from right, Standard Oil house, pump house, and three oil tanks. Note the horse-drawn tank wagon in front of the far left tank. One of the passenger cars is seen behind a switch stand at extreme left.

Horses remained the mainstay of farm work for years until after World War II. The automobile gained popularity rapidly—especially for a means of conveying the family. There the horse lost out quickly. In the scene of Bernard, there are three teams of horses visible, three narrow gauge freight cars and only one automobile. At best, the tin Lizzie looks benign and poses hardly a threat to either the horse or the railroad.

In those days:

In the fall of 1916 I was firing for [Frank] "Sonny" Widman. We were in "three spot," heading east down the La Motte hill with two stockcars and the caboose. The freight cars were loaded to the roof with shingles. Apparently, the air brakes didn't engage completely and when I looked out my side, back at the train, I could see the two stockcars, which were top heavy, rocking back and forth. I knew they were bound to go over any minute and yelled to "Sonny." Before either one of us could do anything, both cars, first one and then the other, went off the track and down an embankment. The caboose, went up on its right wheels and stayed there, balanced so a person could have tipped it over with one finger, if he'd had a mind to do something like that.

—Bill Cook, April 15, 1891 interview

One of the few times the gauge made the big city newspapers was in the October 15, 1917, issue of the *Chicago Tribune*. James A. Cruisenberry, a native of Cascade, and a reporter for the "Trib," wrote:

No doubt most of the inhabitants of Cascade were hanging around the narrow gauge railroad station getting the clicks off the wire, because Cascade knew it was up to Red Faber, prominent citizen of the town, to come forth and save the game.

The game, Cruisenberry was referring to was the sixth game of the World Series. The White Sox and the Giants were battling and Urban "Red" Faber of Cascade, Iowa, and a future member of baseball's Hall of Fame, would win three of the four games needed to decide the championship for the Chicago team.

The following is an excerpt from the *Prairie Farmer's Home and Country Directory of Dubuque County* for 1924. It was written by a "folksy" columnist who used the name John Turnipseed, and is about his visit to Dubuque County.

Well, I guess you all feel that you are nigh on to bein' acquainted with me through my writin's in *Prairie Farmer* and if you ain't been readin' my "sputin' off" you better look for it in the next copy of your *Prairie Farmer*. I've been doin' a little travelin' around in your county and I'm goin' to try and tell you about seein' some of the things in the county and meetin' with you folks.

I got started out on that little railroad of yours in the south part of the county and I certainly enjoyed my ride on it. I was talkin' with Melloy that lives near Bernard and he says, "It's small, it's slow—but it gets there," and I guess that's about right but he didn't say when it gets there. It travels pretty fast, 'cause the day I was on it the thing stopped just after it left Zwingle and I asked the motorman what was the matter and he said there was a critter on the track and so we soon got goin' agin and then when we was agoin' down hill on the way to Cascade we stopped agin and I asked him agin what was the matter and he said, "There's a critter on the track again" and I says, what another critter, and he says, "Nope, it's the same one again, we just catched up with it." Well, I guess this contraption gets anyone back and forth between Zwingle and Cascade and thats what it was made for.

The day I was on it there was several politicians on it and they had us fellers all a smokin' some of them cigars that the cigar manufacturers get rid of every election time. We had them cars so full of smoke that you couldn't tell where the engine was at. It poured out of the windows as fast as it came out of the smoke stack of that 'er engine.

There was one woman on the train that weighed about 250 pounds and this little train was rather crowded and she wanted me to get up and give her my place and I asked her where she was goin' and she said she was goin' to Fillmore to a Suffragette meetin'. So I ask her if she believed in women votin' and she said she most certainly did and I said do you believe in women takin' the place in life a man takes and she said she did and that I should hurry and get up and give her my place. Well, I said, do you believe in takin' responsibility a man takes in life and a man's place and she said she did so I told her to stand up like a man then. We went around one of them curves and the car made a side-swish and she fell right down on me and smashed all the political cigars and also my last year's hat that I was still wearin' in hopes corn would go up so's I could buy a new one. Well, folks I certainly was glad to give her my place in that car after she tumbled.

Sincerely yours,
John Turnipseed

During one of the "usual" Iowa winters in the late twenties, all four of the locomotives were being used to push the wedge snowplow in an attempt to open the line. Jack Benzer was engineer of "four spot" and suddenly along with the other three men, felt a sudden lurch. As one, they applied the brakes and brought their strange train to a halt. Roadmaster Norman Kelsey, who was riding with Benzer, led his four train crews to the point of the train to see what had happened. The snowplow had jumped the track on a tight curve and careened several car lengths down a slight embankment into a farmer's pig pasture. After several moments discussion, Jack Benzer convinced Kelsey and the others that the four engines could pull the plow back to the track. His reasoning was simple. If the "damned thing plowed its own track of snow, we'll pull it back on the same track." Cables were attached to the errant plow and to the lead engine. All four engines backed up slowly, pulling the connection tight. Then with smoke belching from their stacks, the engines barked a staccato accompaniment to the humming cables. Slowly, the snowplow edged toward the track and eased back on to the rails. It was the only time the snow had ever worked to help the little railroad out of a tight spot.

—Jack Benzer, 1959 interview

Following the end of World War I, more and more cars were showing up in the towns along the gauge. Because the roads weren't graveled yet, train travel was still the most reliable, especially in the winter and spring when the roads were impassable. The biggest hazard in automobile travel then, was the number of horseshoe nails littering the roads. If a trip to Dubuque was successful, as far as flat tires were concerned, the expression was, "I went clear to Dubuque and back and never had to change a tire."

I shoveled snow on the line between here [Bernard] and Cascade. The cuts would get plugged up [with snow]. They had a snowplow ahead of the engine and they'd buck into the snow drift and it would get stuck and you'd have to go in and shovel it loose. They'd get jammed and couldn't go ahead or backward and you'd have to shovel out along side of the engine and snowplow both. When they got the rotor out [after 1929] of course they blew the snow. That was a special made rotor. What I shoveled out was a V-shaped plow [the wedge plow], mounted on a flatcar and loaded with rock. It would hit a hard spot in the snow and go right up on top of the drift. There were places where the snow got eight—ten feet deep. We'd have to dig along side, then back it out and clean out between the rails and flanges. The snow would get packed against the rail and the engine couldn't get a grip.

We went on the payroll. We shoveled by the hour for pay and anything over eight hours, we got time-and-a-half. I think it was around forty cents an hour. That was 1926 when I was about fifteen years old. The shoveling crews were young fellas up to about twenty-two years old. Another fella and I were youngest.

—Gerald Feeney, July 18, 1980 interview

With large facilities to service locomotives at Marquette, Dubuque and Savanna, farther south, it became necessary for the Milwaukee Road to abandon one. Because Dubuque was located fifty miles south of Marquette and forty-five miles north of Savanna, it was the logical choice for abandonment but that made it necessary for the little locomotives of the gauge to travel 140 miles round trip for backshopping.—*J. Adney*

9

1929-1933 The Spiral Downward

Another view of No. 1 that has been backshopped at Marquette and is ready for its trip back to Bellevue, seventy miles to the south.—*J. Adney*

With the paving of roads and the cost of new 1929 automobiles as low as $495, the railroads were not adjusting quickly enough to compensate for the immediate losses in business to trucks, busses and automobiles. The gauge, like other railroad companies, was in disordered step with the times. To streamline their overall operations in the Mississippi Valley, the Milwaukee Road closed the shops in Dubuque. The narrow gauge equipment was then transported for servicing to the Marquette facilities, seventy plus miles north of Bellevue. The Dubuque offices were moved to Savanna when the divisions were shuffled in a consolidation effort toward more and better service to the customer.

Although none of the ills, which had plagued the gauge since its inception, could be defined as peculiar where other roads were concerned, it seemed as though the thirty-six miles of railroad had had more than its fair share. The amount of snow that fell in 1929 amounted to 55.2 inches—not much spread over an entire year. However, 34.3 inches of it fell in the month of January during fourteen snow days. As a result, the constant problem facing Roadmaster Norman Kelsey, involving the gauge, was the matter of keeping the line open during the winter months.

Finally, a decision was reached and the Klauer Manufacturing Company in Dubuque was approached. Six years earlier, in 1923, this concern had introduced a revolutionary plow, which utilized a combination of augers that pulled snow to the center of a scoop. The screws in turn, forced the snow into a powerful blower that spewed it many feet away from the road. Could something such as their "Sno-Go" plow be adapted for use on a railroad?

The main endeavor of the Klauer Manufacturing Company, from its early beginnings in 1870, had been the fabrication of sheet metal products. The firm's policy and philosophy from the first year of business, was based on giving the customer the highest quality

131

"Four spot" has been turned, watered, and fed after reaching Cascade. Engineer Charlie Spielman, checks the 2-8-0 before departing Cascade for Bellevue.

product possible but never losing sight of the fact that economy was equally important. Their policy and philosophy were clearly demonstrated in their Sno-Go plow. The first model was hand built in 1923 and was capable of clearing not only snow but ice as well. (At this writing, there have only been thirty-five hundred of these units sold and each one was and still is hand built.)

Impressed by the operation of the street model, the Milwaukee Road ordered a three-auger plow during the heavy snows of 1929. The unit would be mounted on a flatcar with an enclosed cab housing not only the controls but the two powerful Climax engines that drove the augers and blower. Because of the meticulous approach taken by the manufacturer, delivery could not be made before the end of the year. What difference would a year or so make? The gauge had operated without

this blessing in the disguise of a snowplow for fifty years. Once this marvel was on the property, it could snow all it wanted. Snow would no longer be a problem.

Then, before 1929 was over and "Black Friday" could throw everyone into a financial tailspin, another tragedy took place. The diminutive work train, which kept the tracks in order and maintained the bridges, was parked on the siding at La Motte. The bridge crew foreman, who was confined to bed because of an illness, burned to death when a fire broke out in the bunk car.

Although, the Depression began in October 1929, monies allocated and commitments made for the paving of roads were still channeled to the Iowa State Highway Department. The road from Dubuque to Davenport, which passed through Zwingle, was paved in 1930 and many of the county roads plying the

Grading the west approach to new highway bridge over Whitewater Creek near Fillmore is shown in July 1929. The paving of this road added another nail to the coffin of the gauge. The grove of trees at the right obscures the railroad bridge and right-of-way.

The above picture taken July 2, 1928 looks northeast to the yard in Cascade at the time of the paving of the highway from Cascade to Dubuque. At the center a crane and dry mixer of paving materials can be seen in front to the water tank. At this time of financial struggle for the branch, it is ironic that not only was the yard used for mixing the pavement, but most of the equipment and materials for the project were hauled to Cascade on the narrow gauge. The large shed at left was a temporary structure used to protect cement from the weather.

Looking west toward water tank at Washington Mills with a gondola on the siding, at left.—*C. Leffert*

Bellevue-Cascade
Narrow Gauge

READ DOWN   READ UP

		81 Mix. Ex. Sun.	Miles	Table **70**	82 Mix. Ex. Sun.		
		AM			PM		
....	....	7.20	0	Lv.....**Bellevue,** 66.....Ar	**2.40**	.....	
....	....	8.20	11.4	.......La Motte........	**1.40**		
....	....	8.45	15.7	.........Zwingle.........	**1.10**		
....	....	9.15	22.0	..Washington Mills..	**12.30**		
....	....	9.40	25.2	.........Bernard.........	**12.15**		
....	....	10.00	29.7	.........Fillmore.........	11.50		
....	....	10.35	35.6	Ar.........**Cascade**.........Lv	11.25		
		AM			AM		

Reference Notes for Tables 66 to 70, Inclusive

† Except Sunday. * Daily. § Sunday only. § Except Saturday.
f Stops on signal. kSaturday only. xConnects with LaX River Div.
train 55 at La Crosse. yConnects with Ia. & So. Minn. Div.train 158.
① Stops to leave from east of St.Paul. ② Stops Sundays on signal.
④ Stops Fridays only.
Time shown in light figures indicates a.m. **Time shown in dark figures indicates p.m.**

The Milwaukee Road continued operating only one train each way daily but the competition from trucks and busses continued eating away at the very existence of the gauge. If an extra was needed on Sunday, a train was put together and the run was made. Otherwise, the rails would be silent from Saturday until Monday.

No. 3, Class Nm2, Baldwin 2-6-0 plying the hills of eastern Iowa with a string of cattle cars. This locomotive came originally from the Cattskill and Tannersville Ry.

They were a different breed of men altogether, those hoggers of a bygone era. Standing with Charlie Spielman, (extreme right) who could make a whistle talk, and Dick Bogue (second from right in white cap) who was a railroad man's railroad man, is Dick Sullivan (second from left). Sullivan began his railroading career in 1905 as a call boy and eventually became a brakeman and then a conductor. In the above photo, Sullivan was working as a brakeman. The man on the left is not identified. When jobs were scarce and the calls for work scarcer during the depression, employees of the Milwaukee Road would jump at the chance to work on the gauge.

hills between Bellevue and Cascade were upgraded with gravel. Now trucks, busses and privately owned cars began eating away at the gauge's profits more than ever. Hardly accustomed to its new corporate name, the Milwaukee Road reeled under the impact caused by the collapse of Wall Street.

As winter approached, the snowplow was slowly taking shape in the Klauer shops. On December 2, 1929, the C.M.St.P.&P. took delivery of the snowplow. It was transported on the wide gauge flatcar with rails to McGregor where it was painted boxcar red and stenciled with, among other data, the date of 12-15-29.

To inaugurate the new plow's presence on the railroad property, the railroad crew dumped almost two feet of snow on the slim rails in January 1930. The amount of snow was hardly a challenge for the Sno-Go since it could handle drifts as deep as twelve feet. But the end results were mixed. It was not a question of the Klauer plow handling the job of opening the line when it was blocked with snow. The fault, if it could be termed a fault, was in the manner of moving the piece of equipment. Klauer's street models had their own source of movement and a slow speed, which was the secret of the plow's success, could be maintained. The steam locomotive, which was to be the means of moving the plow on the gauge, was a tempermental beast and could not move slowly enough to make the plow 100 percent efficient. The Sno-Go was used again in March to remove another foot of snow and then set off on a siding to wait for the next winter's onslaught. The total cost for the new piece of equipment was $17,000 from designing board to delivery. A lot of money for the time but not when the longevity of the Klauer product is taken into consideration.

Where the railroad officials and workmen had in the past, dreaded the thought of winter coming, they almost anticipated the coming in the fall of 1930. They were ready. The gauge *would* get through. By the end of December, barely six inches of snow had fallen. But wasn't January the notorious month? Not in 1931. During four snow days 7.9 inches fell. February—1.4 inches. March, which could produce some horrendous spring blizzards, failed when four snow days averaged only 4.5

inches each time. Hardly a decent test for the plow. As a result, the $17,000 snowplow sat in the Bellevue yards, waiting for a true moment of glory. It was not to come in the fall of 1931 for October, November and December produced only a total 5.7 inches of snow.

Even though the lack of heavy snow falling kept the Slim Princess operating, the Depression and the competition from trucks and busses caused business on the gauge to decline. Trucks and busses were offering faster and more dependable service, and people in business had to get their money's worth out of transportation because of the Depression. When service on the gauge had been cut back to one scheduled run per day in 1927, trains became longer and were often double headed. Still, the efficiency seemed to be lacking.

Something had to be done to overcome the snow. The Milwaukee Road officials were impressed by the Klauer Manufacturing Company's street model snowplow. In the photo above is one of the very early models that helped sway the owners of the gauge to order a specially built Sno-Go for the narrow rails of Iowa's Slim Princess.

The Milwaukee Road felt it was a red letter day when they took delivery of Klauer's Sno-Go plow. After it was readied in Marquette, the plow was taken to Bellevue. Above, it is pictured on the turntable, ready and waiting for the heavy snows of a typical Iowa winter.—*Streuser*

Less than a month passed before the Sno-Go plow was given its initial test when two feet of snow were dumped on the gauge. The above view shows clearly how the Klauer product worked. Snow was pulled into the blower by the three augers in front. A four-cylinder Climax engine turned the blower at approximately 1,000 rpms.—*Streuser*

The above rare photo shows the Sno-Go in operation under the Milwaukee. Although the steam engine used to propel the snow remover is obscured by snow, it's smoke plume can be seen rising above the cloud of snow from the Sno-Go at the extreme upper right. Photo was taken about one mile west of Bernard with the Sno-Go and engine headed west.—*Jack Otting*

Sno-Go in action near Zwingle. Men at left are members of section crew and extra snow shoveling gang.—*Ray Kemerer*

No. 3 is ready to be backshopped in Marquette sometime in 1930. Note the plow mounted on the pilot.—*J. Adney*

Typical of early road conditions encountered in Iowa, the above photo shows a Wills-Knight auto battling the mud and snow about three miles north of Bernard in the early 1930s.—*Jack Otting*

In this view looking southwesterly in the Bellevue yards, the Cooke consolidation is moving toward the company coal house. The buildings on the engine's right are the repair shop, the sixty-foot long enginehouse (later referred to as the Sno-Go shed) and the two-stall roundhouse. The bluffs in the background are typical of the terrain with which the gauge had to contend until it reached Bernard some twenty-five miles to the west.

During the 1915 hearings, the bookkeeping system then in use had made it difficult to determine exactly how much money was being made or lost on the branch line between Bellevue and Cascade. Accounting methods and practices were then changed and the Milwaukee Road officials had their eyes opened when business of 1931 was reviewed. The Depression, the competition from trucks and busses and the cost of ordinary maintenance earned the gauge an operating deficit of $66,000 for the year. Although the little trains continued chugging up the grades and whistling through the hills, business continued to dwindle. The picturesque and bucolic anachronism was living on borrowed time.

In compliance with the law governing abandonment procedures, the Milwaukee Road set up a series of meetings at the towns along the branch line in the spring of 1932. Since the Chicago, Bellevue, Cascade & Western Railway had been granted a lease from the railroad commission which lasted until 1979, it was necessary for the Milwaukee Road to secure a release before stopping all service on the line. The railroad's alternate plan was to substitute truck service and maintain a station and stationmaster at

Cascade, Bernard, Zwingle, La Motte and Bellevue. This idea was met with total opposition from the shippers. Antagonism rose as the efforts to widen the gauge of the track were recalled and the period of days the communities had gone without rail service because of snow, recounted. Nothing was agreed upon at the April 29 meeting and more were scheduled. Disregarding the future meetings, the Milwaukee executives applied to the Interstate Commerce Commission for permission to abandon the gauge knowing it would take time to gain the authority.

A meeting at Bernard without the railroad officials produced a petition that was to be signed by residents and then presented to the railroad company. Bernard, located off the highway leading to Cascade and Dubuque, had remained one of the best shipping points on the line. Customers who needed building materials and bulky, heavy assignments were vigorous in their protests. Another meeting was scheduled, once the petition was completed. A committee of three, Louis F. Meloy, Joe Noonan and Dr. D.C. Shields, was appointed to represent Bernard at another hearing with the Milwaukee officials at Cascade.

Two days after the Bernard meeting an

Built in seven days to welcome the new iron horse just before the line was completed, the depot in Cascade measured 24' x 50'. In this photo the daughter of station agent Harry Care, Ruth Care Ganfield, stands in the doorway.

Merchants and businessmen in Cascade depended heavily upon the narrow gauge, despite service problems associated with equipment and weather. In this view looking west in the Cascade yards, a freight house can been seen at left center with lumber and coal sheds partially obscured by gondolas at the right.—*R. Bogue Collection*

Westbound, the Baldwin-built No. 2 approaches the crossing at Highway 151 with two gondolas, one boxcar and a combine in tow. The photo would have been taken after 1929 when paving of that portion of the highway was completed. Engineer Charlie Spielman is at the controls.

Looking east in Zwingle with the depot to the left of the boxcars on the siding. Old Highway 61 bisects the photo just beyond the switch.

interesting editorial note appeared in the Dubuque *Telegraph Herald.* The apparent answer to the bus question had been found in France with the development of a rubber-tired rail car. No one could imagine at the time that such an innvoation might affect the gauge— however, in time it would.

The financial problems besieging the nation and the world were taking up much of the space in the newspapers and the people along the branch line were finding it difficult to have their case presented fully. Wall Street experts were predicting a market resurgence that would return prosperity. Then, as if to crowd the plight of the customers along the narrow gauge track even farther back in the news, the body of Charles Lindberg's kidnapped baby was found. For weeks, that story held the front page.

The meetings continued but the railroad people knew they would have their way in the end. The deficits were too overwhelming. The business involved did not justify the continuation of service. They were merely going through the motions of attending the different hearings, listening to the disgruntled shippers plea for their railroad's continuing operation.

That summer, R.E. Molster, an examiner for the commission, heard the case, including all

testimony, at Dubuque. The petitioners and the Milwaukee Road filed briefs of their position, after the testimony, with their representative. Molster then read the arguments and took the case under advisement.

While Molster was mulling the pros and cons of abandonment, winter gradually approached. As if mocking the snowplow, which sat forlornly in the Bellevue yards waiting for a sizeable snowfall, winter arrived almost unnoticed. In October, November and December 3.4 inches fell. January, the notorious month, enjoyed unseasonable weather with only 1.1 inches of snow. It would only snow eight more times, averaging less than two inches in each instance, before spring.

Molster reached his decision and granted the C.M.St.P.&P. the right to abandon the line. But those opposed were not finished with their fight. They were given an oral hearing before Division Four of the Interstate Commerce Commission in Washington, D.C. Nothing was gained at the hearing and the decision remained intact.

Although it might have seemed as though the commissioner was siding with the railroad, it became apparent that he had given every consideration to the people involved along the branch line. In his report, prefatory to the order permitting abandonment of the branch, Molster stated that

> ...doubtless the effect of abandonment on the towns of the branch would be disastrous. Cascade, much isolated, would be a heavy sufferer. Dealers at these towns would be placed at a rate disadvantage in comparison with those at nearby railroad points. Various business enterprises in the different towns would doubtless be abandoned. The evidence shows that the feed mill at Cascade would be worthless, lumber and coal yards could not operate and shipping associations could not function.

Nevertheless, he found that "the branch had been operated at a substantial loss for the past four years, and the record affords little hope if continued in operation, it would ever pay operating expenses. Under these conditions the continued operation of the branch would be a constant drain upon the resources of the parent company and a burden on interstate commerce. The record clearly shows an urgent necessity for conserving the applicant's system income."

On March 20, 1933, authority to abandon the Bellevue-Cascade narrow gauge branch line was handed down to the C.M.St.P.&P. The commission's decision provided that the certificate of public convenience and necessity permitting abandonment shall be effective after ninety days. This was to "afford opportunity to develop plans of substitute," which the Milwaukee was willing to do. There was, however, no stipulation made that such plans be developed to make the authority legal. If the C.M.St.P.&P. would renege, there could be no recourse on the part of the people or the Interstate Commerce Commission.

Despite the apparent hard-heartedness of the officials, they showed a spirit of romanticism when they approached Allen Woodward about a special job. Woodward, who was seventy-eight years of age at the time, was still an active engineer on the Milwaukee. Since he had piloted the first train into Cascade, the road's superintendent, L.F. Donald, assigned the aged engineer to the task of taking the last train out of Cascade.

June 20, 1933 would see the end of Iowa's Slim Princess.

Although the above view of the depot at Bellevue (far left) with a variety of rolling stock seems to indicate that business was good, accountants had to inform the Milwaukee Road that the branch line had lost $66,000 at the end of 1931.

Standing in front of the first driver of the "four spot" in Zwingle is Carl Leffert. Leffert, whose father was employed by the railroad, used a box camera to record some of the photos in this book. Standing on the pilot is Donald Datisman.

The Milwaukee wanted to abandon the narrow gauge branch line but was met with stiff opposition from the shippers along the gauge. They felt trucks could not get their livestock and other produce to market as well as Iowa's Slim Princess. Above, No. 2, one of the Baldwins breathes gently, waiting for the engineer's command to move.

More and more cars were beginning to show up on the highways in the early 1930s, testing not only narrow gauge railroads such as the Cascade branch line, but standard gauge lines as well. From the looks of the traffic jam on the south side of the bridge, there might be an auction sale going on some place in Zwingle.—*R. Kemerer*

The daily mixed train ambles toward Zwingle behind one of the Baldwin outside framed 2-6-0s. Even though the hearings concerning the future of the little railroad continued, the Milwaukee Road was merely going through the motions of cooperating.

Bellevue-Cascade

READ DOWN   *Narrow Gauge*   **READ UP**

	81 Mix. Ex. Sun.	Miles	Table **47**		82 Mix. Ex. Sun.			
	AM				PM			
....	....	7 00	0	Lv ....**Bellevue**......... Ar	2.30	See table 27,		
....	....	8.00	11	.........La Motte.........	1.30	page 28, for		
....	....	8.25	16	.........Zwingle.........	1.00	connections		
....	....	8.55	22	......Washington Mills▲.....	12.20	at Bellevue.		
....	....	9.20	25	.........Bernard.........	12.05			
....	....	9.40	30	.........Fillmore▲.........	11.40	....	....	....
....	....	10.15	36	Ar ....**Cascade**......... Lv	11.15	....	....	....
	AM				AM			

Early 1933 saw a slight change in the scheduling on Iowa's Slim Princess. No matter how the time table above is interpreted, it still took three hours and fifteen minutes to travel the length of the gauge—the same time established in 1880 when the C.B.C.&W. began operations.

Early 1930s photo showing boxcars in front of Geo. Wassenaar's feed mill in the Cascade yards. This view showing the east side of the mill, is looking northwest from the south side of the right-of-way. The men are, from left: Earl "Lad" Loes, Ralph Ganfield, and standing in front of the International truck is Francis "Butch" Loes.—*Neiers*

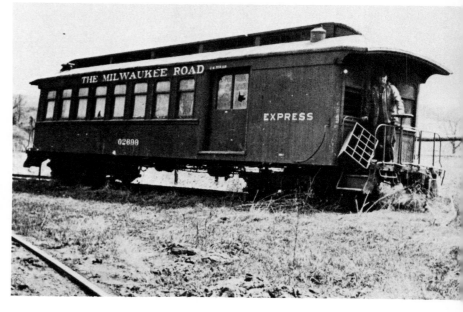

Carrying late Milwaukee No. 02699, this combine rests on a siding at Bellevue after abandonment, with Lester Deppe standing on the platform. According to an equipment list at the time of abandonment, compiled by Ted Schnepf, combine No. 02699 had formerly been No. 8.

Brakeman Dick Sullivan stands by the tender of No. 2 at Zwingle in the summer of 1933.—*Ray Kemerer*

Reflecting the spiral downward which the Milwaukee Road was experiencing at the time, a westbound mixed train with only one boxcar and a combine on the rear, prepares to leave La Motte for Zwingle.

The gauge was always good copy for the Bellevue and Cascade newspapers. The photo above was taken shortly before the Milwaukee Road transferred ownership. The caption read: "This group of young ladies took a day off to take a ride on the Narrow Gauge, travelling from Cascade to Bellevue and back to Cascade. The gentleman with them was a taxi driver in Bellevue. He took the group sight-seeing in the great metropolis of Bellevue. Reportedly, most of the day was spent travelling between the two cities because trains on the Narrow Gauge did not move at excessive speeds. The group managed to get back to Cascade at 9 p.m. after having left early that morning. From left are Rose Moorman, Clara Moorman, Helen Kurt (McNally), Laura Moorman (Rollinger), Frances Moorman (Koppes), Frances Kurt (Burlage), Margaret Kurt and Ann Kurt (Luber). *(Photo courtesy Rose Moorman)* [sic]"

It's a lazy summer day in the early 1930s and westbound train No. 81 drifts into Zwingle with a couple of stockcars, three boxcars and combine No. 02699.

In those days:

Railroad trains had always seemed fair game for bandits and highwaymen over the years. Coping ingeniously with the possibility of being robbed, railroad officials and employees tried many devious methods designed to foil would be Jess Jameses and in later days, John Dillengers. During the 1890s for example, the Burlington ran a dummy train that was held up by a gang in Missouri. The would-be desperadoes, got away as clean as the train had been of money. A year later, the same gang held up the same train and got away with a considerable amount of cash the second time. The gauge and its employees were no different when it came to feeling fits of apprehension whenever money was to be carried to the banks along the line. Although there was a stout safe in one of the combines, Dick Bogue, a veteran engineer, thought up the scheme of hiding the heavy canvas bag containing money under the coal in the combine's bunker next to the potbellied stove. Any would be train robbers would have been in for a disappointing surprise had they held up Iowa's Slim Princess.

> During January of 1929, the westbound got caught in a heavy snowfall and it wasn't long before we couldn't move an inch. We were stranded for four days and had to rely on farmers for our food when we were isolated in the caboose. So we had plenty to eat. I never worry when I have something to eat.
>
> —Dick Sullivan, 1980 interview

THE WEATHER
Somewhat unsettled tonight and Saturday. Not much change in temperature.

The Telegraph-Herald
and Times-Journal

EVENING EDITION

DUBUQUE, IOWA, FRIDAY, JUNE 9, 1933 · PRICE 3 CENTS; VOLUME 91, NUMBER 115—14 PAGES

WON'T ABANDON NARROW GAUGE

SEEK 90-CENT WHEAT TO HELP GRAIN GROWERS

Advancing Season Is Spurring Action By Administration

Editor's note: Administration policies toward American agriculture are rapidly taking shape although few of the immense executive powers in the farm relief act have been exercised. This dispatch describes the trend in the government attitude toward the farm problem.

By WILLIAM A. BELL, JR.
United Press Staff Correspondent
(Copyright, 1933, by United Press)
Washington, June 9 —(UP)—The farm relief administration is preparing for easy action on a program involving several hundred million dollars of cash awards to farmers substantially reducing or promising to reduce their production of major crops.

Officials emphasized today that no specific course of action yet has been adopted but that definite trends in their price-raising plans are apparent. Pressure of advancing seasons and relief petitioners is accelerating their conclusions and midsummer may see...

Fire Destroys Grill Home on Asbury Road

Fire, which followed the upsetting of a gasoline stove in the kitchen, Friday noon completely destroyed the home of Reuben H. Grill located on the Asbury road near the Home of the Good Shepherd with a loss estimated at between $8,000 and $9,000. Part of the loss was covered by insurance.

The home, a two story brick structure, was completely burned to the ground. Only a few pieces of furniture were saved.

The fire occurred at 12:01 o'clock. Miss Emma Strobel, 75, aunt of Mr. Grill, was burned about the face following the explosion. She was taken to a physician's office where her burns were treated. Her condition is not considered serious.

Mrs. Theresa Grill, wife of the owner, and his mother, Mrs. Carrie Grill, and the family's only son, Jack, 9, were in the kitchen awaiting the arrival of the father when the explosion occurred. The youngster, according to reports, hurried into the kitchen and his clothing brushed against the gasoline tank on the outside of the stove, causing the explosion. The gasoline splattered over Miss Strobel's face and clothing.

An alarm was sent to fire headquarters and engine company No. 4, in conjunction with several firemen from fire headquarters, responded.

Continued on Page 10, Column 2.

MORGAN GROUP BOWS TO POWER OF U. S. SENATE

Lamont Describes Deals That Reduced His Income Taxes

Washington, June 9. —(INS)—Secretary of Treasury William H. Woodin, and the late Senator Dwight W. Morrow and Owen D. Young, head a list of J. P. Morgan and Co. "favored clients" sold Johns-Manville stock at sub-market prices, it was revealed this afternoon at the senate banking inquiry.

There were two groups of clients—one left in on the "ground floor" the other in the "basement" in June, 1927.

The "ground ground" clients paid $57½ a share while the "basement" group paid $47½. The stock later went as high as $234 a share.

Washington, June 9.—(INS)—The great banking firm of J. P. Morgan and Co., bowed to the power of the U. S. senate today when one of its younger partners, Thomas S. Lamont, fully described at the senate banking inquiry a series of personal stock transactions that reduced his income taxes in 1931.

He followed the instructions of J. P. Morgan in testifying about the...

Compromise on Veterans' Cuts Is Acceptable

Washington, June 9—(AP)—The house democratic steering committee today unanimously accepted a modification of President Roosevelt's compromise proposal on veterans cuts and made plans to bring it up for house action tomorrow.

The decision was reached at a joint meeting of the special veterans committee and the steering committee.

Representative Pou (democrat, North Carolina), who acted as spokesman for the steering committee, said:

"We had a harmonious meeting. We substantially agreed to the form of a rule which will probably be presented to the house this afternoon and considered tomorrow."

Pou declined to make public details of the compromise.

SPEED ACTION ON INDUSTRIAL RECOVERY BILL

Washington, June 9—(UP)—Leaders drove with speed on the industrial recovery bill today, hoping congress might adjourn tomorrow night...

MATTERN STILL HOPES TO SET FLYING RECORD

Roaring Over Siberian Wastes; Chita Is Next Goal

BULLETIN.

Moscow, June 9—(AP)—Jimmy Mattern, round-the-world flier, landed at Beloye, Siberia, about fifty miles from Irkutsk, at 3:45 p. m. today, Moscow time, (7:45 a. m. Eat).

He intends to remain there until tomorrow. No details were available here but the aviator presumably was in good health and his plane functioning well.

Moscow, June 9—(AP)—Jimmy Mattern, American round-the-world flier, passed over Nizhni Udinsk, in eastern Siberia, at 2:05 p. m. Moscow time (6:05 a. m., E. S. T.) today.

Nizhni Udinsk is about one-third of the distance between Krasnoyarsk, Siberia, Mattern's last taking off place, and Chita, apparently his next objective. It is about 1,300 miles from Krasnoyarsk to Chita.

Moscow, June 9—(AP)—Jimmie Mattern continued his 'round-the-world flight today by hopping off from Krasnoyarsk, Siberia, a little more than four hours after he had arrived there...

Roosevelt Will Give Out Plums Of Patronage

Washington, June 9—(UP)—The patronage mill was grinding at top speed today as the administration moved feverishly to obtain senate approval of dozens of important appointments before adjournment.

Postmaster General James A. Farley, who has been consulting daily with the president on patronage, expected Mr. Roosevelt would be able to clear the slate of nearly all diplomatic appointments and scores of offices upon which action has been deferred.

Friends of the president expected him to name an ambassador to Germany within 24 hours.

Mr. Roosevelt was prepared to announce selections of John Cudahy, Milwaukee, Wis., real estate operator, as minister to Poland, a position declined by Mayor James M. Curley of Boston.

It was felt he would attempt also to dispose of some of the diplomatic plums in the Latin American countries, few of which have been dealt out to date.

New Romance?
***
Elliott Roosevelt May Have Found New Love Down in Texas

Dallas, Tex., June 9—(AP)—Miss Ruth Googins, 25-year-old attractive Fort Worth brunette, declares there is no romance between her and Elliott Roosevelt, second son of the president.

Her statement came after Mrs. Franklin D. Roosevelt, flying to Washington, D. C., after a short visit with Elliott on the Pacific coast, declined to comment on the reported romance, saying:

"Really couldn't say anything about that. You see Elliott still is married."

Young Roosevelt, general manager of a west coast airline, has established residence in Nevada so that his present wife, the former Elizabeth Donner, of Philadelphia, may sue for divorce on grounds of incompatibility. He could not be located immediately for comment, but previously had declared there was no "triangle element" involved.

Mrs. Roosevelt stopped briefly in Fort Worth last night. Early in the day, at Los Angeles, she had disclosed that her son and his wife planned a divorce. Her disclosure, made as she left a hotel to take a plane for the national capital, was immediately confirmed by Elliott.

"Too Bad," Says Girl

Miss Googins, a Wellesley college graduate, said her introduction to the president's son was in Dallas and that they had been invited to several gatherings in Forth Worth. Then she added...

CASCADE LINE WILL HAVE NEW MANAGEMENT

Milwaukee Is Selling Road to Firm in Minneapolis

The narrow gauge railroad serving the district between Cascade and Bellevue, abandonment of which was decided upon several months ago after long litigation, will not be junked after all and the facilities of the railroad will be at the disposal of that particular district soon under the management of private investors.

This information was contained in a letter received today by Mayor H. E. Scandarett, president of the Milwaukee railroad company, present owners and operators of the line.

Make Contract

The railroad president's letter stated that the railroad company had entered into contracts with E. C. Bradley of Minneapolis, president of the Twin City Coach company, for the sale of the line and...

U. S. DELEGATES STILL SILENT ON

The only other time the gauge made the headlines on page one of the Dubuque paper had been in 1907 following the accident at Washington Mills. In a day when businesses were going broke every day, it was big news when one that was slated for extinction, suddenly received new life.

10

1933-1936
The Bellevue and Cascade Railroad

The Canary drew crowds at every station along the gauge when Earl Bradley took it to Cascade the first time. Completely new, totally different and innovative, No. 5 could have been the salvation of the Cascade branch line. Design problems showed up early when the *slow* speed of the reverse gear was discovered. Speeds of over thirty miles an hour were gained by the Canary over the slim rails, according to Ralph Otting who road with John Bradley during one such achievement. However, a ground hog could and did on more than one occasion, derail the unit if the animal was unlucky enough to be on the tracks at the wrong time. One or two cars proved to be the limit for the Canary and when the engine block froze one cold November night before proper maintenance could be had for the cooling system, Earl Bradley's "brain child" finished its days on a siding.—*A. Hachmann*

An eleventh hour stay of execution magically materialized when the Milwaukee Road entered into negotiations with Earl W. Bradley, district sales manager of the Twin Coach Company. Residents along the branch line had already accepted the inevitable abandonment of the gauge and were delighted with the sudden turn of events. The idea of purchasing one of the diminutive steam locomotives for display in the lofty park overlooking Bellevue was dropped. Apparent-

ly, the narrow gauge was going to overcome adversity once more.

There was a front-page headline announcing that the gauge would not be abandoned, which appeared in the June 9, 1933, issue of the Dubuque *Telegraph Herald*. Then, on June 15, articles of incorporation for the Bellevue and Cascade Railroad Company were filed. The amount of authorized capital for the new corporation, which reflected the value of the dollar during the Depression, was set at

The Depression produced few heroes but to the people along the gauge, Earl W. Bradley was exactly that. When Bradley, who was district sales manager of the Twin Coach Company, entered into negotiations with the Milwaukee Road to purchase the narrow gauge branch line, the shippers hopes soared. They would not lose their railroad after all.

Sam Goldish, a Duluth, Minnesota businessman, was the real "brain trust" who operated the narrow gauge railroad for Earl Bradley.

Experiments in France led to the development of the Micheline rubber-tired railroad truck. One of the first models in the United States was a single car unit built for the Reading Railroad (below). It, like its successor (above), which was built for the Texas and Pacific, were both retired soon after completion because of power plant failures. The units were built by Budd. Note that only the trailer car on the T.&P. train has rubber-tired wheels.

$30,000. The shares of stock were divided as follows: twenty-five hundred shares of preferred stock at a par value of ten dollars per each share and five thousand dollar shares of common stock at the par value of one dollar each.

The purchase price agreed upon between the two companies included everything connected with the three-foot system: one disabled and three working steam locomotives, three passenger cars, one hundred and ten freight cars, one caboose, ten maintenance-of-way cars including the $17,000 snowplow; all buildings and 35.72 miles of narrow gauge track. The price—$18,000—was to be paid in monthly installments of $150 plus 5 percent interest.

The transfer of ownership was to be made July 22, one month and two days after the Milwaukee Road had planned the abandonment. At 11:50 A.M. that day, the last train operated by the Milwaukee was scheduled to leave Cascade. A small gathering of Cascaders were at the depot to usher an era out of their community. When Conductor Walter Graham shouted, "All aboard," the brakeman, Dick Sullivan, led the group of people in singing "The Little Pink Box on the 7:29." For some unknown reason, Allen Woodward, who had been asked to take the last train out of Cascade earlier in the year, was not at the throttle. Instead James Crawford of Dubuque was on the right hand side of the cab and Joe Reding was firing. The passengers making the last Milwaukee Road narrow gauge run of all time, were: Norman Kelsey, the roadmaster, and his two sons Milton and Robert; P.L. Mullen, the Milwaukee Road chief mechanic at Savanna, Illinois, and his son, Frank; Royal Holbrook of the Iowa Historical Society. Holbrook had come to Cascade on the gauge that morning and claimed the distinction of purchasing the last ticket sold by the Milwaukee in Bellevue and in Cascade. They would prove to be the last tickets ever sold. The little train puffed sadly out of Cascade toward Bellevue to welcome the new owners.

At 6:45 that evening, Earl Bradley, president of the B.&C., rolled into Cascade at the controls of the unit he hoped would revolutionize the gauges business. The rubber-tired unit would haul light freight and express over the line and carry whatever passengers there might be. With Bradley were S.L. Goldish, the road's secretary and acting general manager, William F. King, superintendent of the rolling stock, and other members of the crew.

While John Bradley, Earl's nephew, would eventually be the general manager of the B.&C. on paper and sign the annual reports for the Iowa state railroad commissioners, it was Sam Goldish who would run the show.

The main attraction that day was the new, bright yellow motorized unit that had brought the officials to Cascade. It was much smaller than the steam locomotives and was shaped something like a milk truck. People swarmed around it while Bradley proudly answered questions put to him. It was expected to move fifty tons of rolling stock over the line with ease and would be able to make the trip between the terminals much more quickly than the old, outdated steam engines. Bradley demonstrated the unit's unusual adaptability to conditions and took many of the onlookers for short rides up the track from the station and back, just like Allen Woodward had done fifty-three years before. Despite stops at every station where people flocked around the "Canary," as it was quickly dubbed, the new unit had made the trip from Bellevue to Cascade in two and one-half hours.

Because of his association with the Twin Coach Company, Bradley obviously had some clear-cut ideas about the future of railroading and interurban transportation. Experiments had been held in France using pneumatic-tired Micheline trucks, which were the newest innovation in railroading at that time. Many railroad executives must have felt that this was the logical next step in improving their mode of transportation. The industry as a whole, had watched closely, the experimental models produced by Philadelphia's Budd Company. In 1932, that company's rubber-tired, stainless steel gasoline cars were a novelty and had been built for the Pennsylvania and Reading railroads. However, engine failures soon retired the models. Then, in 1933, Budd produced its most ambitious pre-Zephyr model when it designed a two-car motor train for the Texas and Pacific Railroad. This time only the trailer car or passenger car

Fourteen-year-old John D. Smith used his family's railroad pass to take the train from his home in Marion, Iowa to Green Island, Iowa where he caught a northbound train to Bellevue. He made the up trip to Cascade behind Baldwin No. 2. While waiting for the return trip, he made several pictures of the locomotive including the one above taken by a boyhood friend who caught John. Smith's trip was taken eight days before the Milwaukee turned over the operation of the gauge to the newly formed Bellevue and Cascade Rail Road Company. Smith's father, a Milwaukee engineer, urged his son to make the trip because he didn't think the gauge would last much longer.—*John D. Smith*

utilized the Micheline trucks. The 1932 models had used six rubber-tired wheels per truck while the Texas and Pacific model was built with eight per truck. Again, the model was retired because of engine complications.

The thing Bradley needed was a railroad on which he could experiment with ideas of his own concerning rubber-tired vehicles. For all practical purposes, his Canary was a truck on rails. With four 35 x 5 tires and sliding doors on each side, it could be easily mistaken for a milk truck or bread van.

Another practical innovation Bradley quickly implemented was the cessation of passenger traffic. The previous fiscal year had tallied $70 in tickets and $75 spent for insurance to cover the passengers while riding. Anyone needing transportation was welcome to ride the Canary free of charge. All the B.&C. required was a signature on a waiver form, which freed the railroad of responsibility should an injury occur. The forms were seldom, if ever used.

Bradley insisted the success or failure of the railroad was almost entirely dependent on the communities served. He promised prompt, adequate and courteous service and that he would make a valiant effort to enlist the support and cooperation of the public.

While the Canary was expected to do the fast work required, the steam engines would be used for heavier traffic until such time as a motor unit capable of hauling two hundred tons could be purchased. The taxes had been greatly reduced along with the general overhead, and if the company payroll could be held down along with the operating expenses, a new locomotive could be a reality in a short time.

To further streamline his operation, Bradley appointed the managers of various shipping associations along the route as local station agents. The B.&C. elected to retain the one round-trip, which the Milwaukee had instituted in 1927, and extras would be run when needed.

Almost immediately, business began picking up and another motorized unit, this time a more conventional twenty-ton Plymouth Locomotive Works switch engine, was acquired from the S.J. Groves and Son contracting firm in Minneapolis. Because of its deep throated horn and ability to move more weight than the Canary, it was nicknamed the "Ox," and was first used to push one and sometimes two steam engines hauling up to forty-eight cars. When more than one train was to be operated, one of the passenger cars would be pressed into service as a caboose.

In addition to transporting livestock, coal, feed, lumber, grain and petroleum products,

Despite stops at every station where people flocked around the new Canary, as it was quickly dubbed because of its bright yellow paint, the new unit had made the trip from Bellevue to Cascade in two and one-half hours. The unique gas powered, rubber-tired unit had been built according to Bradley's specifications, and if the experimental innovation worked, the gauge could look forward to years of prosperity. In this photo, Arne Hachmann is standing at the door.—J. Bradley

Number 2, Class Nm2, Baldwin 2-6-0 has been turned and serviced for the down trip to Bellevue. In the photo above it is sitting just west of the grain elevator in Cascade. Photo was taken about 1929.—*John D. Smith*

When Bradley took over, the motive power roster included "four spot" that was sitting on a siding in Bellevue. One of the cylinders had cracked, and because the cylinder block was incorporated into the frame casting, it was impossible to repair.—*J. Adney*

Earl Bradley needed a railroad on which to test his rubber tired Canary. When he bought the gauge he had just what he needed. Above, Bill King (left), the master mechanic for the road and Sam Goldish, examine the Cascade terminal facilities.

John Bradley, above, Earl's nephew, was a college student who worked on the gauge and served as general manager of the little railroad for his uncle.

In a 1972 interview, former railroad employee Richard Bogue said "she was 36 inches wide, 36 miles long, and took 36 hours to run" in recalling the fitfull operations during the line's last years of existence. Considering the general state of the equipment and the track, one can only speculate about the length of time required to make the above run. Pictured eastbound in La Motte, two steam engines (at far right) are seen pulling at least twenty-four stockcars with the Ox pushing.—*J. Bradley*

157

When the Ox burned out a rod and was disabled until new parts could be acquired, the two steam locomotives still running, "one spot" (above) and "two spot" were quickly readied and put into service several weeks before the B.&C. had planned. Even though the Milwaukee Road only held the mortgage due on the branch line, the B.&C. never removed the C.M.St.P.&P. logos from the tenders or freight cars. Note that the old C.M.&St.P. lettering is beginning to show through below the cab window. Soon after the above photo was taken, "one spot" suffered a broken driving axle, and was moved eventually from La Motte to Bellevue where it was parked next to No. and No. 3. "Three spot" had failed to operate properly after an I.C.C. required overhaul. None of the people in the above photo are identified.

the little railroad began hauling logs, which were to be used as piles in constructing the new government locks and dam at Bellevue.

As winter approached in 1933, the residents along the main line and the employees of the Bellevue and Cascade Railroad held their breaths once more. Would the winter be as mild as the previous one? The middle section of the United States was experiencing the worst drought of the twentieth century and moisture was needed to insure a good crop the next year.

When the last snow had fallen, the total inches only amounted to 19.8 and the railroad had relatively smooth running until the Ox burned out a rod halfway between Zwingle and Sylva Switch,[16] a siding which was seldom used. The train was left standing on the main line and the Plymouth switcher limped into Cascade. Although the steam power was being used, age was telling on the venerable locomotives. "Four spot," the 2-8-0, had been inoperable since 1932, and "three spot" had

been decommissioned following a three thousand dollar overhaul. The B.&C. had elected to not use steam power until spring. "One spot" and "two spot" were quickly readied and began running before schedule. Once the new parts arrived for the disabled Ox, it was given a general overhaul and the railroad continued operating it as a pusher since the two steam locomotives were running well. To prepare for an onslaught of livestock business, two trains consisting of over forty cars were to take the bulk of the stockcars to Cascade and other points. The first train was pulled by "two spot" and had the Ox pushing. "One spot" headed the second train. When the first train reached Bernard, the agent advised John Bradley, the conductor, that the second train was in trouble at La Motte. The driving axle had broken and the train was blocking the main line. The Ox was dispatched back to pull the disabled locomotive off the main line and bring the second train into Cascade. That particular round-trip took sixteen hours. Shortly

Even though passenger service had been eliminated, one of the functions of the Canary was to carry people who were willing to sign a waiver form, freeing the Company of any liability in the event of an accident. The steamers were still to be used for the heavy hauling of freight. The combines, although serving as cabooses, did not carry passengers. In the photo above, from left to right: unknown; Ed Green, fireman; Charlie Spielman, engineer; unknown.—*Streuser*

The seldom pictured No. 3 Baldwin pictured eastbound in Cascade with two boxcars and a combine.

Because business began picking up immediately after the takeover by the B.&C. another motorized unit, this time a more conventional 20 ton Plymouth Locomotive works switch engine was soon acquired from the S.J. Groves and Son Contracting firm in Minneapolis.—*C. Leffert*

Probably because of its deep throated horn and ability to move more weight than the Canary, the Plymouth engine was quickly nicknamed the Ox. Above, it is westbound at Washington Mills. At the extreme left of the photo part of the coaling tower and storage shed are visible.—*L. Deppe*

An inexperienced engineer on his first run, was initiated into the gauge's way of handling trains when he approached the trestle bridge at Lytle's Creek at Washington Mills. His two-car train left the tracks, but the Ox managed to stay on the rails. The empty cement sacks that filled both cars were salvaged but the overturned boxcars were left along the embankment since the B.&C. had no crane with which to right them.—*R. Bogue*

In addition to transporting the usual livestock, coal, feed, lumber, grain, and petroleum products, the B.&C.'s revenue was increased when the little railroad began hauling logs, that were to be used as piles in constructing the new government locks and dam at Bellevue. The Ox is heading east across Lytle's Creek at Washington Mills with four gondolas and the caboose.—*R. Bogue*

thereafter, the Brooks Mogul was coupled to an eastbound train and parked near "three spot" and "four spot" in Bellevue.

The one accomplishment of the B.&C., which stood above anything the Milwaukee had ever done, was to successfully use the Sno-Go. Because the Ox could move forward at a slow, steady pace, the augers had a chance to work in the manner for which they were designed. Where steam had moved the machine forward in spurts, the Ox proved that the internal combustion engine was the type motive power needed. A bell system was rigged between the plow and the cab of the Ox. A code of rings enabled communications between the two vehicles.

The rest of the summer passed uneventfully for the little railroad and when winter approached the question again was, Would their luck hold out? It didn't. Shortly after the "two spot" was sidetracked because of a lack of funds for its five-year overhaul and before any snow fell, the Canary cracked its block when the water hadn't been drained properly before the cold weather set in. It would remain in Bellevue, inoperable along with the four steam engines. Then, early in 1935, an inexperienced engineer, who had had a dragline operating background, failed to properly lubricate the Ox's governor, which in turn burned out. Without the governor working, the engine would run too fast going upgrade in low gear. As a result, another rod was thrown, which in turn went through the side of the block, ruining the engine. Funds were short and a new engine block was out of the question.

Casting about for a solution, the Sno-Go, which had spent the summer in the single-stall engine house next to the roundhouse at Bellevue, came under consideration. Equipped with two engines for the augers and blower, the plow, which had been used the two previous winters, was moved out of its building. Removing the Leroi six cylinder from the Plymouth locomotive, the Ox was repowered with the six-cylinder Climax from the Sno-Go. This engine did not work all that satisfactorily since the 91-horsepower Climax was designed to turn at 1,000 rpms (for operating the blower) and the 150-horsepower Leroi was geared much slower. Other problems presented themselves as soon as the engine was ready to roll. Now the shift lever was too far removed from the engineer's area, making it difficult to operate. In almost all cases, someone had to shift gears while the engineer operated the clutch.

The Sno-Go was relegated to the roundhouse and the Ox began spending the cold winter nights in the shed recently vacated by the snowplow. The Plymouth switch engine was difficult to start on cold mornings and the building had sheathing on the inside of the walls as well as a large coal stove. At least, the Ox could be started easier under these circumstances than when it sat in the roundhouse, which only had two small stoves. The heat from the steam locomotives had done the bulk of the heating when they were in use.

Being familiar with the tales of blocked cuts and draws during the winter months by word of mouth only, John Bradley and Sam Goldish began worrying about keeping the track open without the Sno-Go. Fortunately for the company, 32.4 inches fell all winter in twenty-seven snow days. Whenever snow presented a problem, crews were hired to help shovel the gauge clear and operations continued.

By spring the finances were slipping out of control because of the lack of dependable motive power. Earl Bradley applied to the Reconstruction Finance Corporation (R.F.C.) for a loan of $25,000 with which he hoped to purchase a new diesel-electric locomotive. Throughout these negotiations, the railroad haphazardly continued to operate. Meanwhile, the only way possible to arrange the financing of a new piece of motive power was to secure a guarantee of minimum tonnage from Cascade and the other shipping points along the gauge. This plan was met with some opposition in Cascade. However, to satisfy the R.F.C., the Interstate Commerce Commission was contacted to inspect the property and make an evaluation. Their study showed that a minimum of $300,000 was required to refurbish the line and make it profitable. Disheartened, Bradley applied for abandonment. His railroad scheme had not worked out. According to the terms of the purchase, it was provided that should the Bellevue and Cascade Company fail to make the required payments, or abandon operations within eighteen months from the effective date of the agreement, the Milwaukee, at its option, could cancel the agreement and the branch line

One thing the B.&C. could do that the Milwaukee Road had not had too much success with, was the operation of the Sno-Go plow. Since the Klauer unit had no motive power of its own, unlike the street models, the steam engines had not been able to move it slowly enough. That problem was solved when the Ox was utilized to push the plow. *From left to right:* Ben Roehl; unknown; Richard Bogue.—*J. Bradley*

Propelled by the Ox the Klauer Sno-Go spits snow for yards to clear the main line between Fillmore and Cascade. A simple battery powered bell system was devised by Sylvester Otting, who operated the Sno-Go, to signal his brother Joe who was usually at the throttle of the Ox. A third brother, Ralph, also worked for the gauge while only a teenager.—*J. Bradley*

When the Ox threw another rod, this time through the block wall, the Sno-Go was robbed of its six cylinder Climax engine to power the ailing Plymouth locomotive. Recalling the tales of blocked cuts and draws during the winter months they had been told, John Bradley and Sam Goldish held their breath. Without the Sno-Go, they wondered how they would keep the tracks clear. A wedge plow was mounted on the front of the Ox and they began praying for as little snow as possible. The Ox and caboose, sans Sno-Go, attempts to open the gauge's tracks between Fillmore and Bernard.—*R. Bogue*

The above photo speaks eloquently for the design of the Klauer plow. Snow could be hurled to either side and drifts as high as ten or twelve feet could be handled quite easily.—*J. Bradley*

Bell knew what it took to run a small railroad. The thing he didn't know was the fickleness of the Iowa winters. The cold seasons had not produced anywhere near the normal snowfall since the Sno-Go had been acquired. With the plow disabled because of the Ox's engine troubles, when the snow began falling in January 1936, the game was over. True to his word, William Bell, began abandonment proceedings immediately when the line could not be opened by shoveling. Above, the Ox walled in by snow early in the winter of 1935-36.—*L. Deppe*

Once the main line was opened after a winter storm, the clearing distance on either side of the train was minimal at best because of the banks of snow, as evidenced in the photo. —*L. Deppe*

Giving a graphic demonstration of deep snows that occurred during the winter of 1935-36 when the B.&C. gave up operations, the photo at bottom shows area residents hand shoveling a county road about one mile north of Bernard.—*Jack Otting*

would revert to it. Apparently, the idea of controlling the gauge did not appeal to the former owner since no move of any type had been made when Bradley was slow in making his payments. Money was also owed for material, coal and transfer expenses at Bellevue. If for no other reason, the gauge would give up the ghost because of a lack of "horses." Had there been the motive power, enough business could have been generated to succeed, even with the financial arrangement with the Milwaukee. Outbound freight originating along the branch line would pay the Bradley people 60 percent with the remainder going to the Milwaukee, who in turn hauled it out of Bellevue. Incoming freight paid just the opposite: 60 percent for the Milwaukee and 40 percent for the gauge. But now, it was apparently over and the papers were once more filed for abandonment.

As had happened in 1933, however, the gauge was miraculously saved and this time by William G. Bell and Joseph Shoenthal. Bell, who was considered an expert in the management of short rail lines, was president of the Cincinnati and Georgetown Railroad Company; first vice president and treasurer of the Ohio and Morenci Railroad Company; general manager of the Springfield Suburban Railroad Company and manager of the Toledo and Western Railroad Company. Shoenthal operated a scrap iron and steel company in Columbus, Ohio. The manner in which these two men operated was simple. Find a small railroad that was for sale or in trouble financially and buy it. Operate for a while and if it could be made to pay a profit—fine. If it could not, then tear it out for the scrap metal. Either way, they could succeed.

A purchase price of $37,500 was agreed upon between Bell, Bradley *and* the Milwaukee Road. Out of this amount the Milwaukee Road was paid, as per the 1933 sales agreement, the amount due for principle and interest, plus the amount due in the open account. The Milwaukee Road also received one-half, about $3,800, of the monies remaining after all obligations of the Bellevue and Cascade Company had been satisfied.

By November 14, 1935, the newspapers were heralding the fact that new owners were operating the gauge. When Bell and Shoenthal took over, the Ox represented the only motive power.

With one locomotive, the Ox, which was not powered correctly, the B.&C. continued operations. Bell did not pull any punches. He alerted the shippers along the branch line to the fact that if they stood by him and the railroad, using it to the fullest, he would put it into shape. Better equipment would be forthcoming and schedules and service improved. If the support was not apparent from the outset, the line would simply be abandoned. Torn out. Erased from the face of the earth.

Frank McDermott, who managed the shipping operations in Cascade, quickly circulated a petition for signatures supporting the rail line. McDermott, as well as others, instinctively knew that this was the little railroad's last chance.

When "two spot" was sidetracked in the summer of 1934 because of a lack of funds for its five year overhaul, and the Canary cracked its block when the water hadn't been drained properly that fall, the Ox was the only motive power still operating. Soon it, too, would become affected by the jinx seemingly plaguing the gauge.—*R. Bogue*

At 9 A.M., July 3, 1934, less than a year after the Bellevue and Cascade Railroad Company had taken over, a semi-truck came careening downhill into Zwingle, its brakes gone. The early morning westbound freight with "one spot" on the point had just begun crossing the highway when the runaway truck struck the second car in the consist. The boxcar was turned over and salvaged but the truck's tractor was crushed. The driver of the truck suffered a broken hip and burns but recovered. The Dubuque fire department was summoned to help extinguish the gasoline fire that followed the collision. A passenger in the truck suffered severe burns over his entire body when his clothes were soaked in flaming gasoline, and died the next day at a Dubuque hospital. In a curious sidelight to the accident, Iowa's Governor Clyde Herring, visiting Cascade as part of that town's centennial celebration, had toured the line with other dignitaries in the Canary the previous day.—*All, C. Leffert*

With the Cascade depot to hide behind, the Ox seems to be trying to avoid the stock truck parked on the other side. Trucks, busses, and automobiles were the cancer eating at Iowa's Slim Princess. Since Earl Bradley could not negotiate a loan for a new diesel powered locomotive, he was about ready to throw in the sponge and call it quits.

While Earl Bradley applied for a loan from the Reconstruction Finance Corporation, the Ox continued pulling its short trains through and over the hills. The caboose looks every bit the part of an anacronism waiting for the proverbial sword to fall as it heads east in Mill Creek flats after descending the "summit."—L. Deppe

With the wrong type of power plant in the only operating engine, westbound trains were considerably shorter than before. The Ox heads west with two of the bigger 1930 built gondolas and one of the smaller, earlier vintage cars. Photo was taken from the caboose.

168

Most of the steel shipped out of Bellevue, the steel that had once been the track for the gauge, was sold as scrap. Some of it, along with what had been the locomotive's, according to several rumors then circulating, was sent as far away as Japan. According to John Bradley, the Canary was outfitted with a new engine and rigging and was used on the streets as a milk truck. When the branch line no longer existed, and the rolling stock and locomotives were gone, the Ox was loaded onto a flatcar and shipped to the Ohio and Morenci Railroad. Only the Sno-Go remained and then, it too, was shipped back to the Klauer Manufacturing plant. The builders had agreed to buy it back at a reduced price since one of the Climax engines was no longer inside.

With the removal of the Sno-Go, the gauge was no more. Other than the grade, and depots at La Motte, Zwingle, Bernard and Cascade, every vestige had been removed. The farmers took over the land on which the little trains had operated and began sewing crops wherever it was feasible.

Today, many people recall the gauge with affection. They get a far away look in their eyes when they speak of it, seeing sights that no longer exist. Gone forever are the bad feelings because of poor service and being snowed in without the trains moving. Only the good memories are retained and that's the way a friend who has gone away, should be remembered—forget the bad and recall only the good. That's the way it should be. That's the way it is today along the route of the Chicago, Bellevue, Cascade and Western Railway.

Petitions aside, there was no controlling the weather. The intentions of the shippers could have been of the highest quality and more than likely were. Still, the winters for the past three years had been uncommonly mild for the area. By the end of December 1935, 9.9 inches of snow had fallen. Then, January and February struck with all their might. Snow amounting to 33.4 inches fell and with ice forming on the top, the shovelers found it next to impossible to open the tracks.

Bell considered John Bradley's suggestion of purchasing a new Leroi engine for the Ox and reinstalling the Climax in the Sno-Go. But after spending almost $700 for shovelers without opening the line, he decided against the plan. The track was eventually cleared by April 1 but Bell knew when he was licked. It was foolish to consider the continuation of operations. He repetitioned the Interstate Commerce Commission immediately for permission to abandon the branch line. The official order read in part:

> Pursuant to authority granted by the Interstate Commerce Commission in Finance Docket Number 10815,...the Bellevue and Cascade Railroad Company will abandon all of its railroad in Jackson and Dubuque Counties in Iowa, extending from Bellevue to Cascade.
>
> W.G. Bell, President
> Bellevue, Iowa

Service was formally stopped on Saturday, March 14, 1936, when Lester Deppe, a young engineer, braked his eight-car train to a stop in Bellevue.

The next month, Laverne Ferneau of Dubuque, Iowa, purchased forty-six boxcars and thirty-six stockcars. These were sold at auction and were to be used for sheds, corn cribs and whatever other purpose could be thought of by the ingenious farmers of the area. The gondolas, flatcars and maintenance-of-way cars were to be utilized in tearing up the track before their disposal.

Sam Goldish, who had operated the branch line for Earl Bradley, apparently was enticed to stay on to work for William Bell since he was in charge of tearing out the track. On Monday, April 20, the crew of men directed by Goldish, began taking the track up in Cascade. The rails were taken to Bellevue and in turn shipped out on the Milwaukee.

With the incorrectly powered Ox as its sole piece of motive power, the Bellevue and Cascade Railroad continued operating under the new management of William G. Bell, who was considered an expert in the management of short rail lines. The Ox pauses with a work train on the bridge one-half mile east of Zwingle.—*C. Leffert*

Service was formally stopped on Saturday, March 14, 1936 when Lester Deppe, a young engineer, braked his eight car train to a stop in Bellevue. Deppe stopped his train at the foot of the summit in Paradise Valley, crawled over the barbed wire fence bordering the tracks and took this photo.—*L. Deppe*

170

In April 1936, Laverne Ferneau of Dubuque, purchased all of the boxcars and stockcars, which were in turn sold at public auction. A stockcar is unceremoniously, but carefully, taken from the tracks to be hauled by truck to a farmer's property. The stockcars and boxcars were put to many uses by the purchasers.—*C. Leffert*

Sam Goldish who had worked for Earl Bradley, was apparently enticed to stay on and work for Bell since he managed the entire salvaging operation. Looking west from Fillmore, the distant crew is already beginning to pull spikes while the salvage train itself will soon back into position. By the next day, Iowa's Slim Princess will only be a memory. The small white building in line with the pulley in the gondola was the station for Fillmore.—*L. Deppe*

The salvage crew tore the rails from the earth rendering a structure such as the La Motte depot, useless. Eventually, it was restored for the town's centennial celebration. See Appendix on Memorabilia.—*L. Deppe*

The citizens at Zwingle would not be affected by the gauge's demise because of the highway passing through town. The station was purchased for use as a home and still stands today. See the Appendix on Memorabilia.

Rumors began circulating along the once popular branch line that the steel rails, locomotives and hardware from freight cars were being shipped as far away as Japan. It won't be long now since the salvage train has reached Paradise Valley, that elysian picnicking spot frequented by young Bellevue lovers in the past.—*L. Deppe*

When steel bridges were encountered by the wrecking crew, they, like the rail, were removed. The timbers, those that still remained, which had been cut by George Runkle, were tossed aside to rot.—*L. Deppe*

At least the death of the gauge meant that some family men were able to work, thus feeding their families during the darkest of economic times in the United States' history. The crossing near the lumber company office was the scene of the semi-truck/train accident in 1934. Once the rails are gone, the highway will be free of hazards caused by the once-needed line.—*L. Deppe*

On Monday, April 20, 1936, the job of taking up the rails was begun in Cascade. Men who had found it difficult to work at a job steadily because of the Depression, were thankful for the temporary employment—even if it was to rip out *their* railroad. After pulling the spikes, the 60-pound rail was winched into gondolas.—*R. Bogue*

Once its task of tearing the rails up was completed, the Ox was lettered for the Ohio and Morenci Railroad Company, one of William G. Bell's more successful enterprises. Loaded on a flatcar, the Plymouth locomotive was shipped east while the Canary was equipped to run on regular streets and roads. Bradley's experiment served out its days delivering milk.

By the late 1930s and early 1940s, the gauge was a mere memory. However, Bellevue still had rail service as evidenced by the splendid photo of a Milwaukee Road F3 Pacific passing down Railroad Street. For years, Milwaukee employees who had worked the gauge, and still headed south out of Dubuque on the River Road, would look westerly, past the Bellevue depot, and wish for the good old days. The train above is southbound, headed for Green Island, where the passengers in the streamlined combine will meet the westbound Midwest Hiawatha.—*R. Courtney*

In those days:

Of the twenty-seven employees, both full- and part-time, who worked for the Bellevue and Cascade Railroad, there was one young, energetic fellow who was always looking for the easy way of doing his job. Assigned to cut weeds along the main line, he took one of the motorized handcars and began his seemingly endless task. Then, inspiration struck. Remounting the car, he started out of Bellevue at a speed of about ten miles an hour and held the long handled scythe firmly along the edge of the track. Wonder of wonders! It worked—until he hit a sumac sapling growing among the weeds and found himself unceremoniously yanked off the handcar, which continued along the track until it ran out of gas several miles west of Zwingle.

On April 19, 1936, Bellevue attorney Frank Schwirtz was talked into a last ride on the gauge by Sam Goldish. They took the only locomotive. "It was really a foolish trip," Schwirtz said years later in an interview, "...with Sam at the controls, we tooted at every house and crossing between Bellevue and Cascade." The next day the crew of men, under Goldish, began taking the tracks out.

The photo above was reproduced from the original glass negative as were several other original Wyrick pictures contained in this book. Most notably the pictures of the passenger cars, No. 8 and No. 12; No. 1401/2; No. 1400 at the water tank in Cascade all of which appear in Chapter Seven. The interior of No. 2s cab in this chapter is also a Wyrick original. Railroad modelers wishing to duplicate in miniature any of the motive power or rolling stock that was used by the gauge, will appreciate the crystal clear detail of the Wyrick photos.—C. Wyrick

11

Motive Power

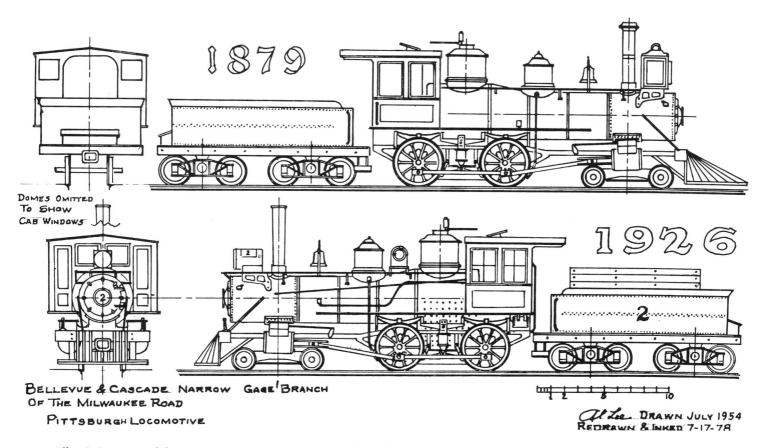

1879

DOMES OMITTED
TO SHOW
CAB WINDOWS

1926

2

BELLEVUE & CASCADE NARROW GAGE BRANCH
OF THE MILWAUKEE ROAD

PITTSBURGH LOCOMOTIVE

Al Lee DRAWN JULY 1954
REDRAWN & INKED 7-17-78

Albin L. Lee, one of the progenitors stirring interest in the Bellevue-Cascade narrow gauge branch line, has done much research concerning the history, motive power and rolling stock used between 1879 and 1936. The schematic drawing of the Pittsburgh locomotive is very accurate and representative of the machine. The two Pittsburgh locomotives were classified as NG.

If the narrow gauge railroad running between Bellevue and Cascade and its history have been maligned over the years, then certainly the background, history and knowledge of the first locomotives have been jumbled into an almost unsolvable puzzle. It has been said that the C.B.C.&W. had *one* locomotive to start business; that the C.B.C.&W. had *two* locomotives at the beginning; and that the C.B.C.&W. had *three* locomotives in 1879. Which is correct? Actually, it is the belief of the authors that all three theories are accurate—to a point. In truth, probably five locomotives ran on the rails the first year or so.

The first argument is substantiated by the *railroad commissioner's report* for the year 1880, when the C.B.C.&W. had been in business for only six months. One locomotive is listed along with its cost. (See Appendix V for this report.)

Still, an almost unimpeachable source would have to be the engineer of the first train into Cascade. Many reports state, "engine number two, with Allen Woodward at the controls," referring to the first train that ran to Cascade. That was mystifying until a newspaper interview conducted in 1933 with the engineer in question was uncovered. In the interview,

Probably the most unique photo in this entire book is this one of No. 2's cab interior. Even though the little Pittsburgh 4-4-0 would have been considered simple and extremely basic if compared to a Union Pacific "Big Boy," the basic components to operate a steam locomotive are all there.—C. Wyrick

Woodward stated, "In November, 1879, they loaded my engine on a flatcar and sent me down to the Bellevue-Cascade narrow gauge under construction at the time. They put me out on the uncompleted part of the line towards Cascade. Another engine pulled cars out of Bellevue carrying materials as far as Washington Mills. This train would unload there and the materials loaded onto my string of cars."

Apparently, there were two locomotives, which were referred to as "one" and "two," reflecting their position in construction work. But only one was owned at the time by the gauge itself. The other belonged in Minnesota where it had run on the Reno-Preston narrow gauge branch of the Chicago, Clinton, Dubuque and Minnesota. In February 1880, Woodward and his locomotive were transferred to the narrow gauge Waukon & Mississippi, north of Dubuque. When Woodward was assigned to the wide gauge locomotives, the engine he had piloted into Cascade, was sent somewhere else on the Milwaukee system or was sold, since it wasn't

around in 1882. That year the W.&M. branch of the C.M.&St. P. acquired a nifty little Grant 2-6-0 when the Iowa Eastern from which the new locomotive came, was widened. (See picture of the 2-6-0 in Chapter One.)

Now the gauge is back to one locomotive. But what about the idea that there were three? How could that possibly be correct in light of Woodward and his engine?

To understand this theory, it is necessary to study the locomotives acquired by the Milwaukee when it purchased the C.C.D.&M. in 1880. There were twenty locomotives involved in the sale. Of these, there were no less than seven narrow gauge locomotives. Fortunately, there are people like John Adney of Miles, Iowa, who worked for the Milwaukee for many years and who has taken an interest in maintaining the historical records of locomotives of various lines. With the full list of locomotives owned by the Milwaukee in 1882, the reason why the first two engines were numbered 416 and 419 becomes a little clearer. Table 1 shows the numbering as done by the C.M.&St.P. in 1880 when it acquired

The right-hand view of No. 2 showing the pump for the air brakes and other details. Photo was made at Cascade after 1912.

the River Road, as well as subsequent renumberings. The numbers assigned to the C.C.D.&M. locomotives, 400-419, were in sequence with other C.M.&St.P. steam power.

Then, just about the time the numbering was making sense, along comes Albin L. Lee, who has done more for perpetuating the accurate history of the gauge than anyone, with a letter from the Milwaukee Road, dated 1952. The letter states in part, "the third locomotive, numbered 1401, was used to haul the Car Department transfer table at Milwaukee Shops....This engine was scrapped in 11-'05." Backtracking that particular number, 1401, in the *Railroad History Bulletin* #136, which deals with the Milwaukee Road, it is discovered that the pre-1880 number was 413. Prior to that it was Chicago, Bellevue, Cascade & Western Number One. Without a doubt, that particular locomotive, with its 11" x 16" cylinders, proved to be too light for the grades on the gauge and was replaced by two locomotives from the Caledonia, Mississippi & Western, which the Milwaukee also acquired in 1880. Engine 417, a sister or cousin to 416 and 419, and originally from the C.M.&W., was brought in to run on the gauge at least once, as attested to by the picture of it on the long Washington Mills trestle, in Chapter Two and Chapter Four.

Locomotives Purchased from C.C.D.&M. By C.M.&ST.P. In 1880

Year Built	Builder	Type	Dia. × Stroke	CLS	Gauge	Origin. Road	Pre 1880 Number*	CM&St.P. No. '80	Re '99	Re '10	Re '12	Disposition
1872	Manchester	4-4-0	16 × 24	H3	4' 8½"	C.C.&D.	1	400	1272	1438		Scrapped 1912
1872	Manchester	4-4-0	16 × 24	H3	4' 8½"	C.C.&D.	2	401	1273	1439		Scrapped 1913
1872	Manchester	4-4-0	16 × 24	H3	4' 8½"	C.C.&D.	3	402	1274	1440	144	Scrapped 1917
1872	Manchester	4-4-0	16 × 24	H3	4' 8½"	C.C.&D.	4	403	1275	1441		Scrapped 1910
1871	Manchester	4-4-0	14 × 24	H1	4' 8½"	C.D.&M.	1	404				Scrapped 1899
1871	Manchester	4-4-0	14 × 24	H1	4' 8½"	C.D.&M.	2	405				Scrapped 1899
1871	Manchester	4-4-0	14 × 24	H1	4' 8½"	C.D.&M.	6	406				Scrapped 1899
1871	Manchester	4-4-0	14 × 24	H1	4' 8½"	C.D.&M.	9	407	1412			Scrapped 1906
1871	Manchester	4-4-0	14 × 24	H1	4' 8½"	C.D.&M.	10	408				Scrapped 1899
1871	Manchester	4-4-0	14 × 24	H1	4' 8½"	C.D.&M.	11	409				Scrapped 1899
1871	Manchester	4-4-0	14 × 24	H1	4' 8½"	C.D.&M.	7	410	1413			Scrapped 1910
1871	Manchester	4-4-0	14 × 24	H1	4' 8½"	C.D.&M.	8	411	1414			Scrapped 1910
1871	Pittsburgh	4-4-0	15 × 22	?	4' 8½"	C.D.&M.	?	412	1419			Sold 1901
1871	Hinckley	4-4-0	?	?	4' 8½"	C.D.&M.	22					Sold 1879
1879	Pittsburgh	4-4-0	11 × 16	?	3'	C.B.C.&W.	1	413	1401			Scrapped 1905
1875	Pittsburgh	4-4-0	10 × 16	?	3'	W.&M.	**	414				Scrpd. or Sold
1877	Pittsburgh	4-4-0	11 × 16	?	3'	Reno/Preston	2(?)	415	1402***			Sold 1903 (?)
1879	Pittsburgh	4-4-0	12 × 18	NG	3'	C.M.&W.	1	416	1405	1402	3	Scrapped 10/18
1879	Pittsburgh	4-4-0	12 × 18	?	3'	C.M.&W.	2	417	1406			?
1880	Pittsburgh	4-4-0	12 × 18	?	3'	C.M.&W.	3	418	1407			Scrapped 1901
1880	Pittsburgh	4-4-0	12 × 18	NG	3'	C.M.&W.	4	419	1408	1401	2	Scrapped 8/26

*C.C.&D. locomotives 1 & 2 were named Peter Kiene and J.K. Graves; 3 & 4 originated on Central Railroad of Iowa. C.D.&M. locomotives were named: 1 - J. Merrill, 2 - J. K. Graves (Graves was an official on both roads); 6 - Joseph Rhomberg; 9 - Platt Smith; 10 - Guttenberg; 11 - Lansing; 7 - General Booth; 8 - General Clark; 22 - Dubuque. The C.M.&St.P. abandoned naming locomotives in 1876.

**The Waukon & Mississippi apparently only named this locomotive (Union Prairie) and did not number it.

***Numbers 1403 & 1404 were narrow gauge locomotives elsewhere on the C.M.&St.P. when they were renumbered in 1899.

180

Table 2: River Road's Seven Narrow Gauge Locomotives

1880 C.M.&St.P. Number	Cylinder Size × Stroke	Delivered	Pittsburgh Builder's Number	Original Road and Number	Operated on the Bellevue Cascade Branch
413	11 × 16	7/79	392	C.B.C.&W. #1	Yes, 1879-1880. Used as transfer table power; renumbered #1401 in 1899.
414	10 × 16	10/75	350	Waukon & Mississippi first locomotive, Union Prairie	No
415	11 × 16	1877*	?*	Caledonia-Preston branch on C.C.D.&M.	Yes. 11/79 to 2/80; went to W.&M. as #2
416	12 × 18	8/79	394	Caledonia, Mississippi & Western #1	Yes. Renumbered 1405 in '99; 1402 in '10; 3 in '12
417	12 × 18	8/79	395	C.M.&W. #2	Yes (as per picture)
418	12 × 18	10/80	401	C.M.&W. #3**	No
419	12 × 18	10/80	402	C.M.&W. #4**	Yes. Renumbered 1408 in '99; 1401 in '10; 2 in '12

Railroad Bulletin #136 shows a building date of 8/79 and a Pittsburgh builder's number of 393. It could be. However, Allen Woodward's engine went to the C.B.C.&W. in 11/79 and he was engineer on that particular locomotive from September 1877. He and the locomotive went to the W.&M. for a brief time where the number 2 was given it and a subsequent renumbering in 1880 of 415.

**418 & 419 (C.M.&W. #3 & #4) were undoubtedly ordered before the C.M.&St.P. purchased the River Road since they were delivered the same month the new owners took possession. When the Milwaukee took over, 419 was sent to the gauge in Iowa.

The men above are partially obscuring the face of No. 1, the Brooks Mogul. Note the difference between it and the face the 2-6-0 received in a backshopping by the Milwaukee Road in the late 1920s. (The *John Adney* photo elsewhere in this section.)

When the Milwaukee renumbered all of their locomotives in 1880 following the acquisition of the River Road, the seven narrow gauge locomotives were numbered in sequence with the standard gauge motive power. Still, it is interesting to note that the sequential numbers as applied to the three-foot gauge steam power were begun at the southern most point, which happened to be the Bellevue-Cascade branch line. Their number "one" locomotive was renumbered 413. Moving north, the next narrow gauge branch was the Waukon & Mississippi, which had at the time two locomotives, the Union Prairie and Allen Woodward's engine. They were numbered 414 and 415, respectively. The remaining four numbers, 416 through 419, were applied to the existing and forthcoming motive power in Minnesota on the Caledonia, Mississippi and Western Railroad. (See Table 2 for capsulized data of these seven locomotives.)

So, how many locomotives did the Chicago,

Bellevue, Cascade & Western begin operating with? Take your pick. Anywhere from one to five locomotives. Eventually, two were used and they were 416 and 419. That fact is in the records of the Chicago, Milwaukee, St. Paul and Pacific Railroad.

These two locomotives served a combined eight-five years on the gauge. Number 416 worked for thirty-nine years and 419 lasted for forty-six years. Both were products of the Pittsburgh Locomotive and Car Works, which was established in 1865 under the guidance of Andrew Carnegie. The first locomotive rolled out of the shops in Pittsburgh in 1867, and the company continued erecting standard and narrow gauge steam engines under the P.L.&C.W. name until 1901, when it merged with the American Locomotive Company.

The locomotives were built in 1879 and 1880. They were numbered 416 (Pittsburgh #394) and 419 (Pittsburgh #402) by the C.M.&St.P. in 1880. See previous tables for subsequent renumberings.

The fireman's side of the American 4-4-0 No. 2 shows the different appliances and necessary wiring to maintain the electric headlight. More piping has been added over the years to increase the efficiency of the little Pittsburgh locomotive.

Locomotive builder	Pittsburgh
Builder numbers	394 - 402
Years built	1879 - 1880
Class	NG
Wheel arrangement	4-4-0
Cylinders	12" x 18"
Valve gear	Stephenson
Valves	Slide
Valve travel	
Diameter of drive wheels	42"*
Drive wheel journal	
Engine truck wheel	20"**
Truck wheel journal	
Rigid wheelbase of engine	7' 3"
Total wheelbase of engine	18' 4"
Total wheelbase engine and tender	35' 6"
Boiler type	
Boiler pressure	125 p.s.i.
Boiler diameter (inside first course)	
Number of tubes and diameter	102 - 2"
Length of tubes	8' 9"
Firebox dimensions	60" x 19"
Grate area	7.92 sq. ft.
Heating surface of tubes	465 sq. ft.
Heating surface of firebox	57 sq. ft. (approx.)
Tender journals	
Tender water capacity	
Tender coal capacity	
Weight on drivers	27,300 lbs.
Weight on engine truck	
Weight of engine and tender	41,350 lbs.
Weight of engine and tender in working order	61,000 lbs.
Tractive effort	6,557 lbs.
Factor of adhesion	4.16
Spread of frame centers	?

* Some references show 38", 38¼" and 42". John Adney's records, which were meticulously copied by hand from the C.M.&St.P. records, dated 1882, show 38". However, 42" was used in determining the tractive effort in the table above.

** Some references show 24" wheels.

Source:
   All information concerning the above locomotives compiled from Milwaukee Road records dated 1882; Albin L. Lee and *Railroad History Bulletin #136.*

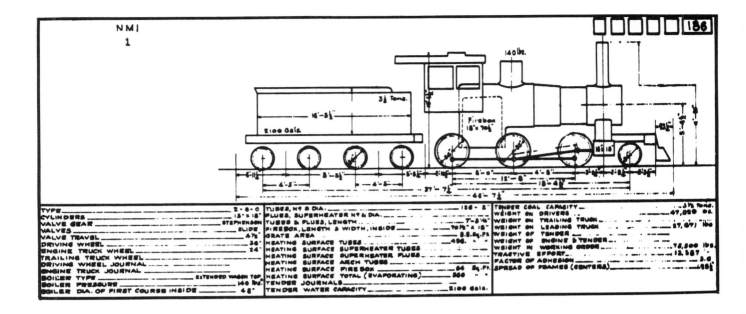

Originally classified NM (Narrow Mogul) the Brooks locomotive became Class NM1 when the Baldwin Moguls came on the property. There are some interesting discrepencies between the blueprint (reproduced above as a black line drawing) as used by the Milwaukee shop crews and Albin Lee's schematic (below). Actually, Lee's is by far and away the more accurate since the drivers' spacing is accurate on his and the blueprint merely gives the proper measurements but are drawn equidistant from each other. Still, Lee shows the old boiler face on his lower drawing instead of the virtually flat one used after 1930.

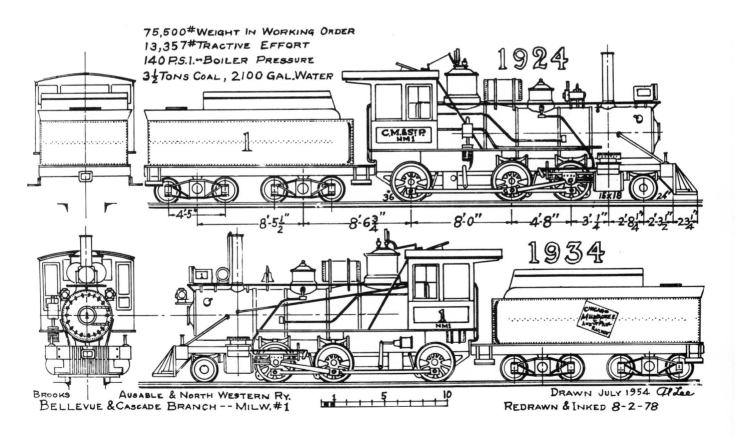

Class NM1—The Brooks Mogul

In 1889, twenty years after the Brooks Locomotive Works began business, it built a 2-6-0 Mogul-type locomotive for the J.E. Potts Salt & Lumber Company. It was numbered "three" while there and became number "eight" when it was sold to the Ausable & North Western Railroad. According to Railroad *History Bulletin #136*, the C.M.&St.P. acquired it from the Banner Lumber Company in 1905 but no number was indicated. This locomotive was numbered 1400 when it came to the narrow gauge property in Bellevue. At

that time, numbers 1401 through 1408 were in use on narrow gauge motive power. However, there was a #1409 (ex-NYO&W 4-4-0) wide gauge locomotive then in use. Consequently, the lower number, 1400, was assigned to the Brooks Mogul, which operated for a total of forty-six years. Thirty years were spent on the gauge. In 1934, it suffered a broken axle and was not repaired. Parts became difficult to acquire when repairs were needed and many replacement parts were built in the Dubuque Shops. In 1912 it was renumbered "one."

Locomotive builder	Brooks
Builder number	1555
Year built	1889
Class	NM1
Wheel arrangement	2-6-0
Cylinders	15" x 18"
Valve gear	Stephenson
Valves	Slide
Valve travel	4½"
Diameter of drive wheels	36"
Drive wheel journal	
Engine truck wheel	24"
Truck wheel journal	
Rigid Wheelbase of engine	12' 8"
Total wheelbase of engine	18' 4½"
Total wheelbase of engine & tender	35' 9¾"
Boiler type	Extended wagon top
Boiler pressure	140 p.s.i
Boiler diameter (inside first course)	48"
Number of tubes and diameter	126-2"
Length of tubes	7' 5¼"
Firebox dimensions	70½" x 18"
Grate area	8.8 sq. ft.
Heating surface of tubes	496 sq. ft.
Heating surface of firebox	64 sq. ft.
Tender journals	
Tender water capacity	2100 gal.
Tender coal capacity	3½ ton
Weight on drivers	47,829 lb.
Engine weight in working order	75,500 lb.
Weight of engine & tender (working order)*	123,915 lb. (approx.)
Tractive effort	13,387 lb.
Factor of adhesion	3.6
Spread of frame centers	28½"

*The total weight of engine and tender combined in working order has tender weight (empty) estimated at 23,922 lb. plus weight of water and coal.

With its new face lift, No. 1 drifts to a halt in Bellevue in June 1933, shortly before the Bellevue and Cascade Company took over. The assortment of locomotives on the gauge was an interesting one, especially when the roster included "one spot" (above); "two spot," the Pittsburgh 4-4-0; "three spot," the first of the two Baldwin outside frame 2-6-0s and "four spot," the Cooke 2-8-0.—*J. Adney*

The Brooks Mogul was a classy little engine and performed heroically until it broke its main drive axel after the Bellevue and Cascade Railroad took over. Its husky lines indicated it would not fool around by slipping too much if put on the point of a heavy train. The spacing of the main drive wheel and the last drive wheel is reminiscent of the *Petticoat Junction* locomotive. It would be a challenge to model this particular engine but it could probably be accomplished.—*Streuser*

Class NC1-The Cook Consolidation

What was to become the Cooke Locomotive and Machine Company first produced textile machinery and was managed by Charles Danforth. In 1852, he combined his facilities with a patternmaker, John Cooke, to produce locomotives under the name Danforth, Cooke and Company. The Cooke family remained in control of the company until they merged with the American Locomotive Company. In 1882, Cooke built engine number 1502, a 2-8-0 Consolidation-type, for the Denver, South Park and Pacific who numbered it 67. It was renumbered 216 for the Denver, Leadville and Gunnison road in 1885. Then, in 1889, it came under the ownership of the Union Pacific where it retained the number 216. Ten years later it was renumbered again—this time for the Colorado and Southern, where it bore number 55. In August 1918, the Milwaukee

bought it and numbered it "four," since the Mogul and two Americans had been renumbered in 1912 as "one," "two" and "three," respectively. When number "three" was scrapped in October 1918, the locomotives were numbered in the spasmodic sequence of "one," "two" and "four." "Four spot" had a major change made in its running gear when the main rod was altered to drive the third set of wheels as opposed to the second as the manufacturer had produced it. (See Albin Lee's schematic drawing.) The Cooke locomotive lasted fifty years, fourteen of which were spent on the gauge. In 1932, one of the cylinders, both of which were built as part of the frame, cracked, and it was the first of the last four locomotives to be retired. It sat on a siding in Bellevue, quietly rusting and waiting for the end of the gauge.

Classified NC1, the Cooke 2-8-0 performed well. Used on many different roads as outlined in the text, the "big one" as it was called by many of the people living along the gauge, underwent several interesting backshopping changes during its service. Most notable was the relocation of the main rod from the second driver to the third. The Milwaukee blue print (right) shows it connected to the second set of wheels as it was when it came on the property in 1918. Albin Lee shows it connected to the second in his 1921 version (lower drawing) and to the third in his 1933 version.

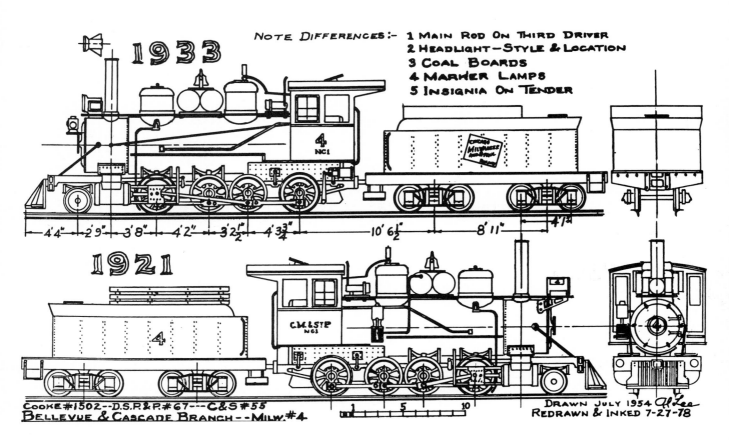

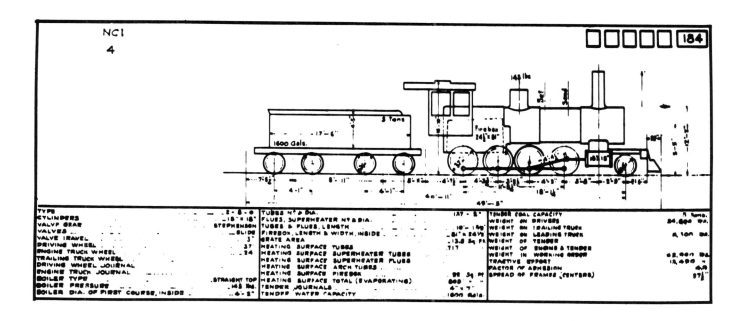

Locomotive builder	Cooke
Builder number	1502
Year built	1882
Class	NC1
Wheel arrangement	2-8-0
Cylinders	15″ x 18″
Valve gear	Stephenson
Valves	Slide
Valve travel	3″
Diameter of drive wheels	37″
Drive wheel journal	
Engine truck wheel diameter	24″
Truck wheel journal	
Rigid wheelbase of engine	11′ 8½″
Total wheelbase of engine	18′ 1¼″
Total wheelbase of engine & tender	41′ 7¾″
Boiler type	Straight top
Boiler pressure	140 p.s.i.
Boiler diameter (inside first course)	50″
Number of tubes and diameter	137 - 2″
Length of tubes	10′ 1⅝″
Firebox dimensions	81″ x 24½″
Grate area	13.8 sq. ft.
Heating surface of tubes	717 sq. ft.
Heating surface of firebox	92 sq. ft.
Tender journals	4″ x 7″
Tender water capacity	1600 gal.
Tender coal capacity	5 tons
Weight on drivers	54,600 lb.
Saturated light weight of engine	62,900 lb.
Weight of engine & tender (working order)*	110,150 lb. (approx.)
Tractive effort	13,490 lb.
Factor of adhesion	4.0
Spread of frame centers	27½″

* The total weight of engine and tender combined in working order has tender weight (empty) estimated at 23,922 lb. plus weight of water and coal.

With lots of "spaghetti" and "cans 'n things" hung on its boiler, the Cooke 2-8-0 was an interesting little locomotive with lots of personality. In this photo, taken shortly before 1928, "four spot" is sitting on the turntable at Cascade. Note the squared-off headlight, a Milwaukee Road trademark.

Because the cylinders and frame were one casting, "four spot" was relegated to a siding in Bellevue when one of the cylinders cracked. Unrepairable, the little consolidation was the first of the four remaining locomotives to be set aside to rust. When the B.&C.s Ox arrived, its braking ability was improved when the brake valve and pump was taken from No. 4 and installed in the Plymouth switcher.—*Streuser*

The clean, simple, front end belies the jumbled side elevation of No. 4 seen here at Cascade, Iowa.

Class NM2—The Baldwin Moguls

The Baldwin Locomotive Works turned out more steam powered locomotives than any other builder. In 1901, it erected locomotive number 18884, an outside frame, 2-6-0 for the Catskill and Tannersville Railroad, where it was numbered "two." In June 1928, through the Birmingham Rail and Loco Company's efforts, the Milwaukee Road purchased this outside frame engine and as the second "two spot" it was the last to operate on the gauge. Then, in 1908, locomotive number 32715 was built and sent to the Catskill and Tannersville Railroad. This locomotive, numbered "one" on the C.&T.R.R. preceded its twin to the Milwaukee, via the same dealer, the Birmingham Rail and Loco Company, by two years. When it was acquired in 1926, it was numbered "three." Then for a period of four months or so, the gauge was at full strength with four locomotives numbered in sequence. However in August of that year, number "two," the remaining Pittsburgh 4-4-0 gave up the ghost and the roster number sequence was

"one," "three" and "four." When the second outside frame Baldwin arrived, the number sequence was complete again. The two Baldwin locomotives were the most powerful of the steam roster employed by the gauge. "Two spot" proved to be the workhorse—especially once the Bellevue and Cascade took over. The only major problem with these two engines was the design of the firebox. Both engines were designed for and used in the southern part of the United States before coming to Iowa. As a result, when cold winter air hit the hot flue sheet the flues would start leaking. "Three spot" was decomissioned first when a three thousand dollar overhaul, (as required by the I.C.C.) proved unsatisfactory. On its first trip following the overhaul, the water foamed in the boiler. One of the ten employees felt the water was too low in the boiler as it topped the summit. More than likely the life was gone out of the metal lining the fireboxes. Both locomotives were plagued with leaky flues and staybolts.

If "one spot" looked husky and "four spot" was called the "big one" then the ungainly-appearing Baldwin outside frame 2-6-0s proved themselves to be the *big husky ones* almost immediately. With a bigger boiler because of the wider, outside frames, the locomotives weighed more and had twice the tractive effort of the original Pittsburgh 4-4-0s. Classified NM2, the Baldwins performed well and "two spot" was the last to operate on the gauge. The Milwaukee Road roundhouse blueprint gives all the pertinent information concerning the engines while Albin Lee's drawings give all the pertinent detail needed to model one of these interesting engines.

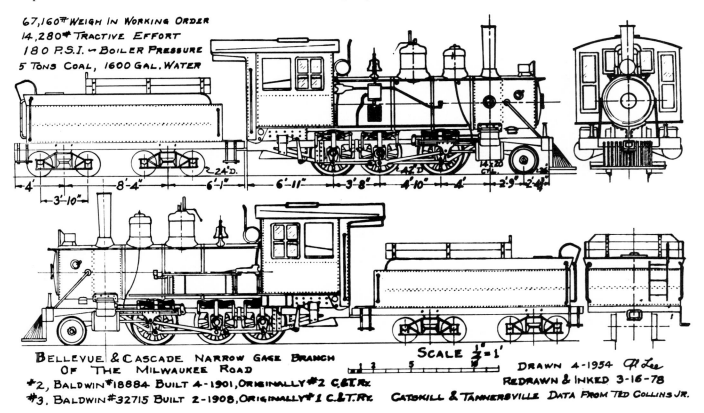

67,160# WEIGH IN WORKING ORDER
14,280# TRACTIVE EFFORT
180 P.S.I. — BOILER PRESSURE
5 TONS COAL, 1600 GAL. WATER

BELLEVUE & CASCADE NARROW GAGE BRANCH
OF THE MILWAUKEE ROAD

SCALE ⅛"=1'

DRAWN 4-1954 Al Lee
REDRAWN & INKED 3-16-78

#2, BALDWIN #18884 BUILT 4-1901, ORIGINALLY #2 C.&T.Rx.
#3, BALDWIN #32715 BUILT 2-1908, ORIGINALLY #1 C.&T.Rx.   CATSKILL & TANNERSVILLE DATA FROM TED COLLINS JR.

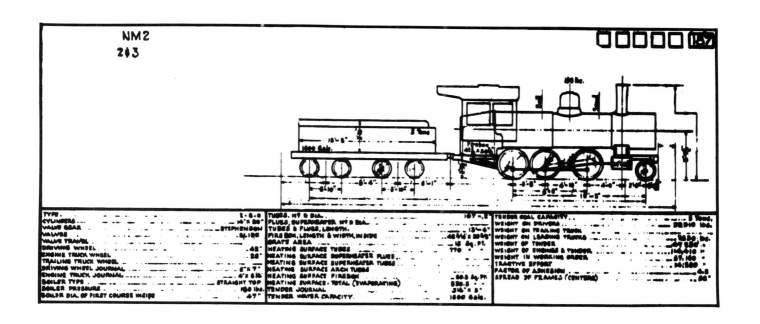

Locomotive builder	Baldwin
Builder numbers	18884-32715
Years built	1901-1908
Class	NM2
Wheel arrangement	2-6-0
Cylinders	14″ x 20″
Valve gear	Stephenson
Valves	Slide
Valve travel	
Diameter of drive wheels	42″
Drive wheel journal	6″ x 7″
Engine truck wheel	26″
Truck wheel journal	4″ x 6¼″
Rigid wheelbase of engine	8′ 6″
Total wheelbase of engine	15′ 3″
Total wheelbase of engine & tender	38′ 6″
Boiler type	Straight top
Boiler pressure	180 p.s.i.
Boiler diameter (inside first course)	47″
Number of tubes and diameter	107-2″
Length of tubes	13′ 4″
Firebox dimensions	42 3/16″ x 50 5/8″
Grate area	15 sq. ft.
Heating surface of tubes	770 sq. ft.
Heating surface of firebox	60.5 sq. ft.
Tender journals	3¼″ x 5″
Tender water capacity	1,600 gal.
Tender coal capacity	5 tons
Weight on drivers	59,910 lb.
Saturated light weight of engine	67,160 lb.
Weight of tender	47,250 lb.
Weight of engine & tender (working order)*	114,410 lb.
Tractive effort	14,280 lb.
Factor of adhesion	4.2
Spread of frame centers	52″

* The total weight of engine and tender combined in working order had tender weight (empty) estimated at 23,922 lb. plus weight of water and coal.

A remarkable close up of "two spot's" face as it is pushed on its flatcar into the roundhouse at Marquette. About the only difference between No. 2 and No. 3 was the style headlight. No. 3 had the more traditional, squared-off Milwaukee type headlight while No. 2 had the round style.

The chunky proportions of the Baldwins denied them any aesthetic lines, but they could perform and that was what the Milwaukee Road wanted when they bought the two Moguls.

When the Bellevue and Cascade Railroad Company purchased the gauge from the Milwakee, the four steam engines went along as part of the deal. "Four spot," the 2-8-0 Cooke Consolidation, had cracked a cylinder in 1932 and was impossible to repair. As a result, it never operated for the new owners. However, the other three did until one by one, they were retired because of mechanical problems that could not be remedied. "Two spot" ran the longest until its staybolts in the firebox began leaking badly. About the middle of winter in 1934, it too was parked in Bellevue to rust. When the road was finally torn up for

salvage by Shoenthal, the locomotives were cut up and shipped out as scrap. One of the whistles was purchased for $1.50 by a Zwingle farmer, Ray Kemmerer, who wanted it for his steam traction engine. Today, when that whistle eerily wails, memories of a bygone era are recalled. Kemmerer's steam tractor is fired up each year for a threshing meet at Mt. Pleasant, Iowa. All four locomotive bells were saved and are proudly displayed at three private homes and at New Mellery Monastery. The fifty-pound bells were bought for seven and one half-cents per pound.

The only major problem with the two Baldwin 2-6-0s was the design of the firebox. Both locomotives had been designed for the use in the southern part of the United States. Iowa's cold winters greatly affected the hot flue sheets, causing leaks. A required I.C.C. overhaul of No. 3, proved unsatisfactory, when the boiler water began foaming on its first trip following the extensive repair job.

The Baldwins were relatively clean as far as accessories are concerned. Certainly they did not have the garbage hanging from their boilers like the other locomotives on the gauge.

A schematic profile drawing of the Canary as rendered by Albin Lee for this book. The side elevation should be about two feet longer as per the side views in the various photos in *Iowa's Slim Princess*. Other than that, one minor flaw, the dimensions seem to be relatively close.

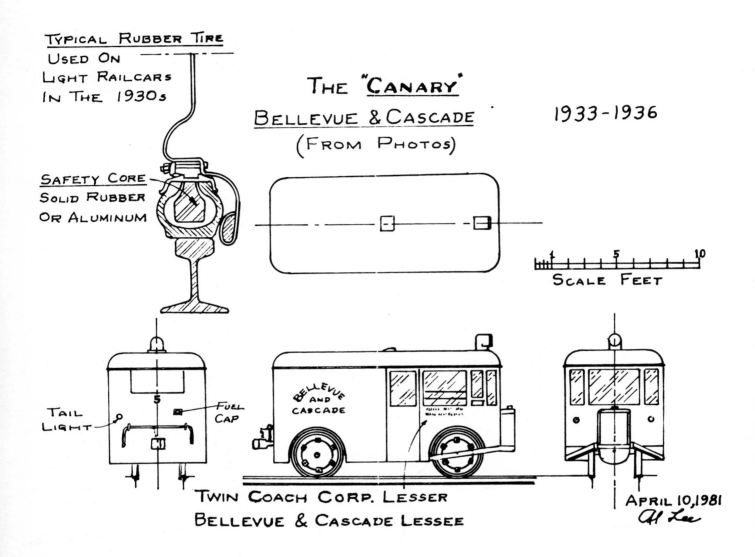

TYPICAL RUBBER TIRE
USED ON
LIGHT RAILCARS
IN THE 1930s

SAFETY CORE
SOLID RUBBER
OR ALUMINUM

THE "CANARY"
BELLEVUE & CASCADE
(FROM PHOTOS)

1933-1936

SCALE FEET

TAIL
LIGHT

FUEL
CAP

BELLEVUE AND CASCADE

TWIN COACH CORP. LESSER
BELLEVUE & CASCADE LESSEE

APRIL 10, 1981
Al Lee

The Canary. Earl Bradley pinned his hopes for success on this little machine. Although it looked like a bread van or milk truck, it covered the distance between Bellevue, where this photo was taken, and Cascade thirty-six miles distant, in better time than the steam locomotives. Its biggest single drawback was its inability to pull more than one or two narrow gauge cars. When an employee neglected to protect the cooling system with anti-freeze, the motor block cracked and the Canary was finished on the gauge. Notice that the lessor was the Twin Coach Corporation and the Lessee, the Bellevue and Cascade Rail Road Company.—*Ted Schnepf*

The Canary

The Canary was the most unusual piece of motive power on the gauge, and, as it turned out, not a very successful one. Because the Canary only ran for about fourteen or fifteen months, there are very few pictures of it. It was built by the Twin Coach Company of Kent, Ohio, which exists today as part of the Grumman Flxible Company of Loudonville, Ohio. Erected per Earl Bradley's instructions, the Canary was owned by the Twin Coach Company and leased by the Bellevue and Cascade Railroad. At another time in history, a vehicle such as the Canary might ultimately have been proven a success, but the age of streamlining was just dawning. Radical innovations such as the Micheline rubber-tired truck and the B.&C.'s yellow railway van with rubber tires were tested in passing but never given too much consideration.

Earl Bradley designed the unit, combining essentials of both railroading and the automotive industries. The inspiration for the Canary had been a bus, developed by the Twin Coach Corporation, which was built to run on rails as well as on roadways. This particular vehicle had a small set of steel, flanged wheels, which could be lowered in front and in back of the normal, rubber tires, for operating on rails. However, the Canary was radically different. Its wheels had a steel rim and the rubber tires, which were demountable, were held to the rim by lugs in a manner similar to the automobiles of the 1920s and early 1930s. Inside each of the 35 x 5 tires was a special wide tube as well as an aluminum rail. This rail was in three sections and was bolted to the wheel rim. In the event of a blowout or slow leak, the rubber tire retained its shape because of the aluminum

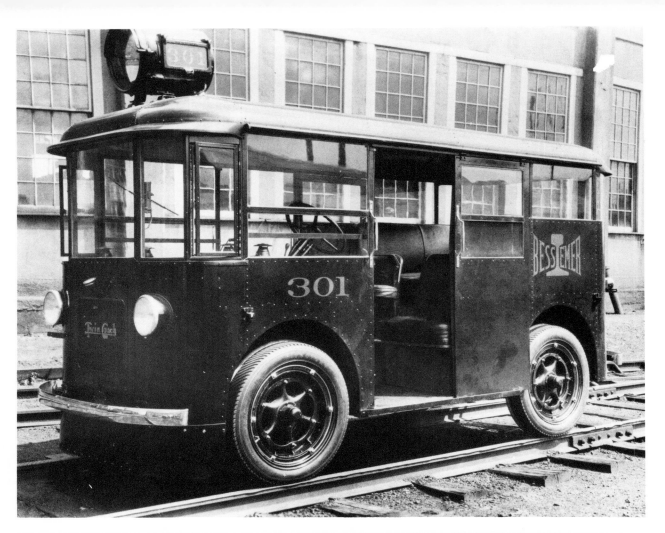

rail, and the motor unit would remain on the track. Its frame was not unlike a ton-and-a-half Diamond T truck frame, complete with suspension system and all. The body, with its sliding doors, big windshield and small rear window, resembled a milk truck or bread van.

Whatever it lacked in design aesthetics and power, it made up in comfort. The ride was exceedingly smooth and quiet, according to those who rode it. "Like riding on air," one described the experience many years later. And sometimes the Canary *was* doing just that. For example, a ground hog who was unfortunate enough to be on the three-foot track at the wrong time, was capable of derailing the unit. The Canary proved difficult to start on wet and even damp rails. Nor did the eighty horsepower Hercules straight six-cylinder engine pack enough wallop in its gearing to move more than one or two loaded freight cars at a time.

Ralph Otting, who braked as a teenager on the gauge, recalled one ride with Johnny Bradley: "Johnny showed me what it would do and we must have been clipping along at about thirty miles per hour. The Canary was swaying back and forth and I was glad when he slowed it down. I never went over the line that fast before."

The Canary was brand-new in 1933 when the Bellevue and Cascade bought the branch line from the Milwaukee. The unit was used primarily to haul express but people were welcome to ride inside. Although there were no regular seats as such, straight-backed chairs were used and the ride was "surprisingly comfortable." With three speeds forward and only one (very slow) in reverse, the Canary was not thought too highly of for switching purposes. With a coupler at the rear, a plank was attached across the front for pusing cars. Ralph Otting recalls: "I can remember one time, when Johnny Bradley took the Canary to La Motte to delivery some express. Since there was no way of turning an engine around at that town, he had to back all the way into Bellevue. It took him a lot longer coni..ng back than it did going there."

The vacuum clutch caused the air pressure for the brakes on the unit to decrease when going downhill or decelerating. To remedy this, the transmission was put in neutral and the throttle was opened almost wide to keep the engine running fast. The racing engine would keep the air pressure up and the brakes could then be applied.

Because there were no connections for air pressure between the engine and its cars, it was necessary to have a brakeman along to control the car or cars being hauled. Ralph Otting describes his job: "When we would start downgrade, I'd crawl through the back window and onto the top of the car. Then, through a series of signals on the horn, the engineer could let me know when to apply the brakes or release them. During the nice weather, I would just ride up on top of the car."

There was no snow in November 1934, but the weather was cold. The Canary met its match in freezing temperatures when its radiator was not drained and the water froze, cracking the block. Because it was nothing more than a glorified truck on rails, the engineers and crews did not really mourn its passing. The gauges experiment in streamling was finished.

Bessemer and Lake Erie's No. 301 (above left) is another good example of a Twin Coach product. It appears as though it might have been a bit smaller than the narrow gauge Canary that ran between Bellevue and Cascade. Used on the Bessemer & Lake Erie from 1933 to 1939, this "cousin" had a 40-horsepower engine and used rubber tires with steel flanges.—*Professor D.F. Wood Collection*

Imagine crawling out of the rear window and onto a freight car to apply the brake in freezing weather. That is what Ralph Otting had to do as a teenager when he worked as brakeman on the gauge. Except for the knuckle coupler and gear at the back of the Canary, it looks for all the world like a bread van or milk truck. When the motor was replaced, a front-end suspension and steering linkage were installed and the Canary spent its last days as a milk truck. It is sitting in the weeds at Bellevue after its block cracked one cold November night.

When Bell's threats of abandoning the gauge had no effect on the weather, the petition for abandonment was submitted and granted. Because the underpowered Ox was the only piece of motive power operating, the task fell to the Plymouth switch engine and its engineer, Lester Deppe, to pull the salvage train. Note the higher exhaust pipe above the hood of the Ox. The Climax operated at a much higher rpm than the Leroi and, even without the side panels in place, the extra heat had to be carried off and away from the engine.

BELLEVUE & CASCADE RAILROAD
MARCH 1933 TO JAN. 1936

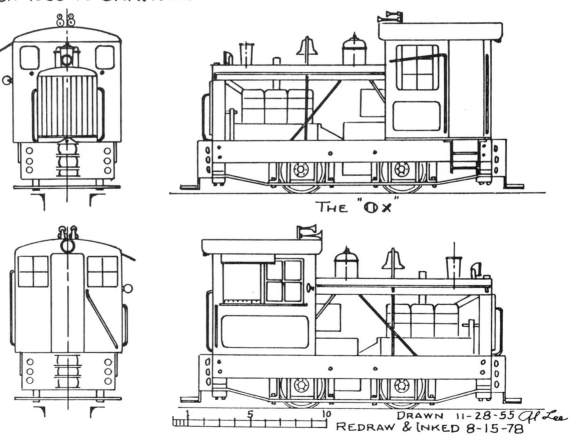

THE "OX"

DRAWN 11-28-55 *Al Lee*
REDRAW & INKED 8-15-78

This schematic of the Ox, as drawn by Albin Lee, is a faithful reproduction and is extremely close to scale. According to Ralph Otting who rode the Ox with his engineer brother, Joe, the standard-gauge Plymouth switch engine on display at the Mid-Continent Railway Museum at North Freedom, Wisconsin, is exactly what the Ox looked like when it operated on the B.&C. except for the difference in gauge.

The Ox

Of the two motorized units, the Ox was by far the superior piece of motive power. Built by the Plymouth Locomotive Works, it came to the Bellevue & Cascade from the S.J. Groves and Son Construction Company of Minneapolis, Minnesota. Rated at twenty tons, it was powered by a 150-horsepower Leroi model RXS six-cylinder engine. According to Ralph Otting, the Ox was exactly like a standard gauge Plymouth switcher now on display at the Mid-Continent Railway Museum in North Freedom, Wisconsin.

At first, the Ox was assigned to pushing service to help the aging steam engines up the summit and any other grade that might prove difficult. Its only drawback as a locomotive was its lack of producing air for braking an entire train. Designed primarily for switching duties, the brakes were never intended to stop more than three or four cars on level or close to level track. With more than that, the locomotive was in trouble and unable to stop—especially on a grade. When the steam power began to fail, the B.&C. got a retired railroad man who lived in Bellevue to take the brake valve out of one of the old steamers and install it in the Ox. Because "four spot" was the first deactivated steam engine, it is likely that the valve came from it.

Once the Leroi engine had thrown a rod through the block, the Ox lost much of its effectiveness with the Climax engine from the Sno-Go. The latter was designed to turn at 1,000 rpms and produced only 91 horsepower. The rpms were too fast for the transmission of the Ox.

When the job of taking up the track was completed, the Ox was loaded on the flatcar with rails and shipped to the Ohio and Morenci Railroad.

When the Ox first arrived on the B.&C. property, it had two horns and was ready for action. When an inexperienced engineer failed to lubricate the 150 horsepower Leroi engine's governor, a piston rod was thrown through the wall of the cylinder block. In the photo above, with its side panels in place for the cold months, the Ox is prepared to go to work. Broken rods, wrong engines are still in the future.

In time, more horns were added until they numbered four. The only solution available to solve the power plant trouble with the Ox was to take the six-cylinder Climax from the Sno-Go plow. The Plymouth originally was rated at 150 horsepower when the Leroi was in place. When the Climax was installed, its 91 horsepower was geared to turn the plow's blower at 1,000 rpms. As a result, the Ox still had its throaty horn but its power had been greatly diminished.

CHICAGO, MILWAUKEE & ST. PAUL RY.
DUBUQUE DIVISION, CASCADE LINE.
THE LAST NARROW GAGE IN IOWA.

NARROW GAGE COMBINATION CAR

0 1 2   5   10

INKED 7-5-78

A.L. LEE

Albin Lee's scale drawing of combine No. 7 as used on the
C.B.C.&W. is an excellent representation when compared
to the picture of the same piece of rolling stock.

12

The Rolling Stock

Combine No. 7 has a definite resemblance to Chicago, Burlington and Quincy passenger cars of the late nineteenth century. Because of James F. Joy's close association with that railroad, it is believed that the C.B.&Q. shops were probably instructed to build the above car for the new narrow-gauge line plying the Iowa hills.

Why should the records of the rolling stock of the gauge be any different then its history or locomotive data? All that can be presented is what has been found, along with a little speculation. The reader can decide what is fact.

The railroad commissioner's report of 1880, which covered half of the previous year, represents the only time the C.B.C.&W. actually reported while operating under that name. It shows the gauge purchasing one combination passenger, mail and baggage car. "Twenty five freight and other cars" were also listed as having cost $9,024.49. Included with that second listing was, in parentheses, one combination. If that "one combination" is taken to be a freight car, the C.B.C.&W. paid an average of $360.98 per car. According to the same report, the Waukon & Mississippi paid

$9,081.45 for thirty "freight and other cars," for an average price of $302.72. Did the C.B.C.&W. get taken or was the "one combination" another passenger car? The one passenger car listed cost $1,600.00. If the total spent on freight cars by the C.B.C.&W. is reduced by $1,600.00 or the cost of one passenger car, the total for twenty-four freight cars becomes $7,424.49 or an average cost of $309.35—much closer to the neighboring road's cost. It has always been stated in newspaper reports, and the timetables of the era seem to bear out the fact, that two passenger cars were in service on the gauge from day one. The "hidden" passenger car could have been an attempt by the C.B.C.&W. to prevent possible reprimands from the commissioners for overextending on

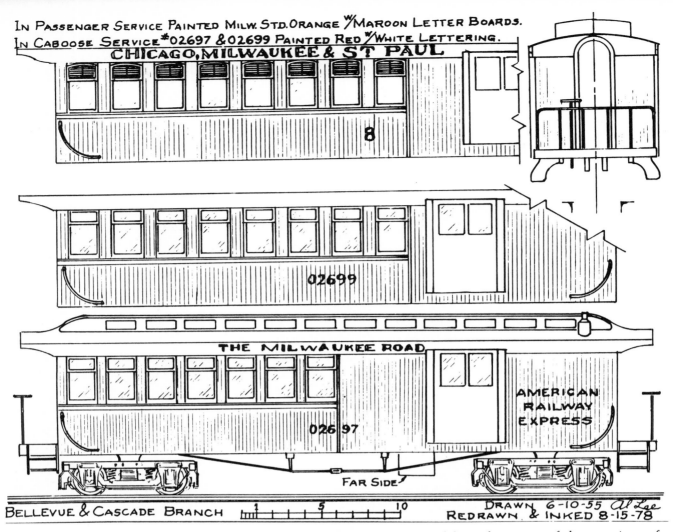

In Passenger Service Painted Milw. Std. Orange w/Maroon Letter Boards.
In Caboose Service #02697 & 02699 Painted Red w/White Lettering.
CHICAGO, MILWAUKEE & ST PAUL
8
02699
THE MILWAUKEE ROAD
026 97
AMERICAN RAILWAY EXPRESS
FAR SIDE
BELLEVUE & CASCADE BRANCH
DRAWN 6-10-55 Al Lee
REDRAWN & INKED 8-15-78

Lee's drawings of the two Milwaukee Road built cars, above were rendered from the picture of the two pieces of passenger equipment in this chapter. The distance between the windows of the coach are a little too widely spaced and should resemble the combine windows' placement more.

passenger cars.

Because of Joy's past affiliation with the Burlington lines, those early passenger combines could easily have been built by that company at Joy's behest. The configuration around the windows of the passenger compartment and throughout the rest of the car matches almost exactly pictures of Burlington passenger cars in service at that time. Also, bear in mind that Joy was ousted from power on the Burlington when he attempted to have the larger company serve the interests of the smaller. It is logical, but there is no proof.

The passenger car, number twelve, resembles in many ways, if not precisely, the design of cars in service and built by the Milwaukee. During the latter part of the nineteenth and early twentieth century, the Milwaukee Road was renowned for "the best passenger service west of Chicago." The much larger windows on the coach and later combines, as evidenced by the pictures as well as the number of vents in the clerestory, could be the results of backshopping by the Milwaukee. When all are totaled, the passenger car roster reads:

Number six, began service in 1880 and was destroyed in the 1907 wreck at Washington Mills. Built about 1879.

Number seven, could have been built by the Burlington shops, was inherited by the Milwaukee and could have undergone several window/door changes when being backshopped in Dubuque. Built around 1879.

Number two, could conceivably have been number seven as a result of backshopping. Built——?

Number eight, is probably a Milwaukee Road product. Built 1883.

Number twelve, a coach, could be a Milwaukee product. Built 1883.

An alternate choice to accepting the backshopping theory is replacement of the combines from other narrow gauge railroads, which the C.M.&St.P. company acquired and subsequently widened. The Milwaukee took over the Waukon & Mississippi in the purchase of 1880 and was widened about 1885-86; the Iowa Eastern was widened in 1882 and one of its locomotives sent to the W.&M. (#64, the Grant 2-6-0); the Minnesota Midland was widened in 1903. There were other roads also widening narrow gauge tracks about the same time. The Chicago and North Western converted the Des Moines & Minneapolis in 1880; the Chicago, Burlington and Quincy widened the Burlington & Northwestern Railway at about the same time. As a result, there should have been a glut of narrow gauge passenger and freight cars on the used market. Some of the rolling stock used on Iowa's Slim Princess could have come from these other roads.

One hundred years after the fact, it is more than difficult to determine exactly what did happen. Not all of the information dealing with passenger cars could be double checked and at best the above information is a calculated guess.

The balance of the rolling stock as listed in the 1880 report reads: "15 eight-wheel box-cars; 10 eight-wheel stockcars; 5 eight-wheel platform cars." Obviously, that totals thirty cars which conflicts with the twenty-five (or twenty-four) cars inventoried as being purchased in the same report for expenditure purposes. Still, it is logical to assume that the platform cars and several boxcars were used to built the line and were brought in, again at Joy's orders, from another narrow gauge line.

Combine No. 8 and coach No. 12 were excellent renditions of the passenger car construction art as executed in the late nineteenth century. The Milwaukee Road had the reputation of being the best passenger mover west of Chicago. Even a narrow gauge branch line such as Iowa's Slim Princess were treated to fine rolling stock. Cars were painted orange, maroon, and brown.—C. Wyrick

No. 02697, according to the Milwaukee Road inventory, which is dated 1933, had previously been No. 2. The origin of this car is a bit of a mystery. It could have been purchased from a foreign road or sent to the gauge from another Milwaukee branch line. It does appear to have C.M.St.P.&P. characteristics. When the cars were renumbered with five digits, they lost their standard Milwaukee orange sides, maroon letterboard, and brown roof color schemes. They were repainted boxcar red and served as cabooses when necessary. The lettering was white.

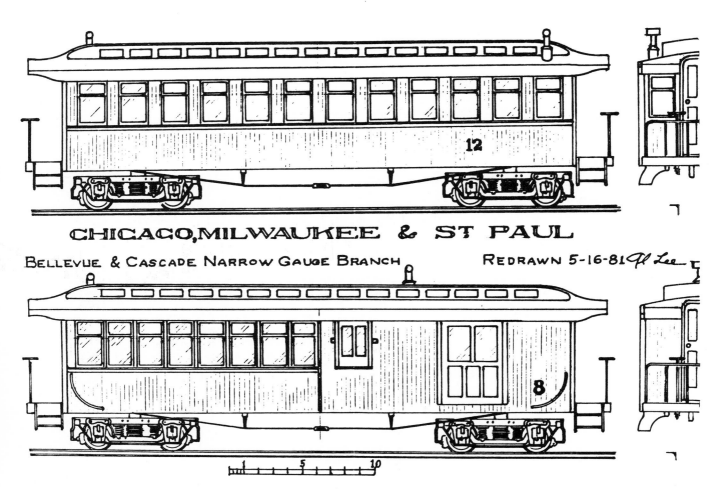

The differences in window configuration and door placement among the existing photos of the gauge's passenger equipment can be readily seen in Lee's drawings and in the accompanying photos. It is not known whether the changes took place as a result of backshopping over the years or were different pieces of rolling stock obtained from different narrow gauge roads when their rails were widened.

Such shuffling of equipment was common, especially when one man had control over more than one line.

To further confuse the issue, the "combination car," as listed in the purchased cars listing, could have been the caboose. Early photos of it show the car with a small, almost all-windows cupola. Later pictures show a more Milwaukee-type cupola again probably the result of backshopping in Dubuque. More than likely this caboose was built by the Ohio Cab Company of Jeffersonville, Indiana, in 1879 or 1880. Its original number was 55, not 055 as the distorted history has claimed. This was pointed out most emphatically to the authors by Dick Sullivan, a retired Milwaukee Road conductor who rode many miles in the caboose. "It was 55, not 055," he said. "The zero in front would have designated a main line caboose and the gauge was not a mainline. In the late twenties, it was given the number, 055. Why? I don't know. But it only carried that number for about seven or eight years." Early pictures bear Mr. Sullivan's account out

completely and the number was indeed 55. Today the caboose's remains are owned by Jim Schroeder, a Bellevue contractor, who has constructed a full-size duplicate as complete in detail as the original.

The commissioner's report dealing with the 1915 hearing that concerned the widening of the gauge, listed a 1914 inventory of rolling stock for the purpose of helping to decide the issue. That inventory showed: forty-eight stockcars, forty-two boxcars, nine freight cars (gondolas and flatcars), one caboose and three passenger cars.

The final rolling stock inventory was made for the purpose of abandonment by the Milwaukee Road in 1933.[17] Indexed under file number 360.017-30 which is dated September 13, 1933, Account #53 listed the freight cars along with their numbers, type of construction and capacity. Many of these cars had been built in the late nineteenth and early twentieth centuries, and the year of construction is given where available.

The blurred number stenciled beneath the windows in this photo apparently is 02698. According to the Milwaukee Road inventory of rolling stock, which was prepared for the sale of the gauge to the B.&C., No. 02698 had been previously No. 12. No. 12, though, was the Milwaukee Road built coach. According to Ralph Otting, that particular car sat in Bellevue until the tracks were pulled up. At this late date it is difficult at best to sort out the facts.

Excellent side view of the caboose with an obviously repaired section beneath the windows. A duplicate of the caboose has been constructed by Jim Schroeder, a Bellevue contractor, who bought the decaying remains of the original from which all the measurements were made. (See Appendix on Memorabilia)—*L. Deppe*

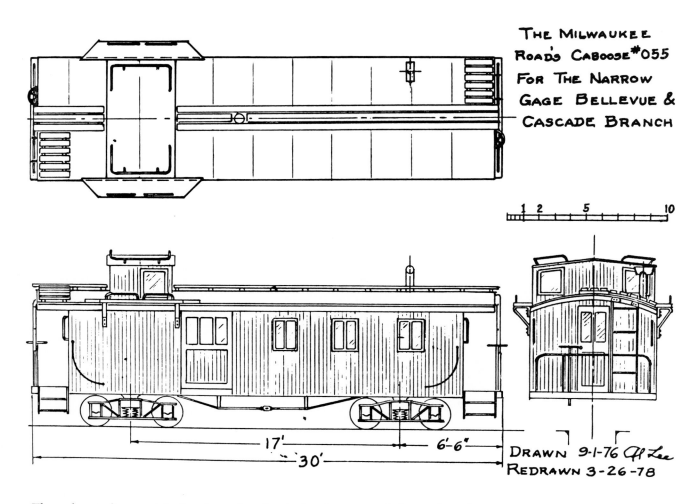

THE MILWAUKEE ROAD'S CABOOSE #055 FOR THE NARROW GAGE BELLEVUE & CASCADE BRANCH

17'   6'-6"

30'

DRAWN 9-1-76 *Al Lee*
REDRAWN 3-26-78

The only misalignment in the above drawing is the placement of the smoke jack, which should be between the third window and sliding door. Originally, the cupola was virtually all windows and did not have the interesting cat walk around it. Once the Milwaukee took over the gauge, the caboose was backshopped to its appearance above. The original No. 55 was designated No. 055 about the same time that the passenger equipment was repainted and renumbered.

Boxcars, wood body and underframe, capacity 20,000 lb., years built 1878-1913.

Numbers: 204, 254, 255, 256, 267, 275, 277, 280, 282, 283, 284, 285, 290, 294, 301, 302, 304, 305, 306, 307, 310, 311, 312, 314, 315, 318, 320, 327, 341, 343, 345, 367, 382, 395, 396, 412, 415, 416, 417, 418, 419, 420, 421, 422, 423, 424

Total boxcars: 46

Freight cars:

Flat cars, wood body and underframe, capacity 60,000 lb.

Number: 1

Flatcars, wood body and underframe, capacity 16,000 lb. built 1880-1882.

Numbers: 650, 678, 682

Flatcars, wood body and underframe, capacity 60,000 lb. built 1898.

Numbers: 685, 686, 687, 688, 689, 690, 691

Flatcars, wood body and underframe, capacity 20,000 lb.

Numbers: 694 (old 150)

Total flatcars: 12

Gondolas, wood body and underframe, capacity 50,000 lb. built 1903-1906.
Numbers: 900, 901, 902, 903, 904, 905

Gondolas, wood body and composite underframe, 60,000 lb. built 1930.
Numbers: 906, 907, 908, 909, 910, 911, 912, 913, 914, 915

Total gondolas: 16

Stockcars, wood body and underframe, capacity 16,000 lb. built 1879-1913.

Numbers: 104, 105, 108, 110, 111, 113, 114, 117, 120, 122, 128, 134, 139, 140, 141, 143, 145, 146, 147, 148, 149, 152, 153, 161, 163, 164, 165, 167, 168, 169, 171, 172, 173, 174, 175, 176

Total stockcars: 36

Caboose, wood body and underframe, capacity 20,000 lb. built 1880.

Numbers: 055 (old 55)

A good view of the cupola end of the caboose. Note the braces beneath the walkway around the cupola. Picture was taken during the winter of 1935-36, which finished the gauge.—*L. Deppe*

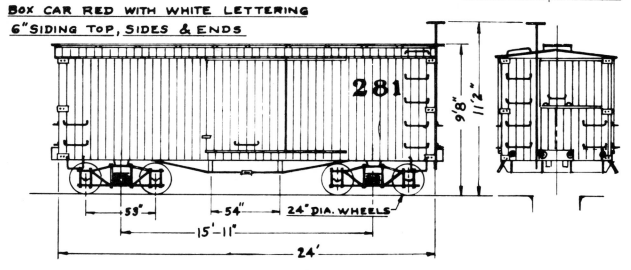

BOX CAR RED WITH WHITE LETTERING
6" SIDING TOP, SIDES & ENDS

281

9'8"
11'2"

53" 54" 24" DIA. WHEELS
15'—11"
24'

The twenty-four-foot boxcars came under fire from the shippers more than once because it took four or five boxcars on the gauge to haul enough to fill one standard car.—*A.L. Lee*

Two more views of the 1934 semi-truck/train accident that happened in Zwingle. Note the construction of the car roof and end detail in the one and the underside rigging of the air brake in the other.

In time the boxcars that had served for years on Iowa's Slim Princess would become tool sheds and storage sheds for many of the area's farmers.—*L. Deppe*

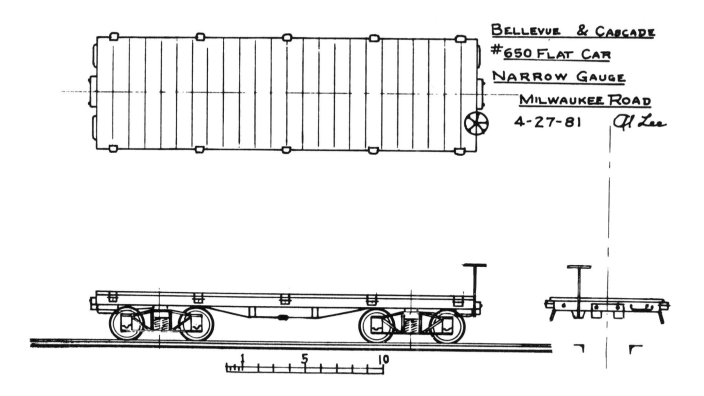

BELLEVUE & CASCADE
#650 FLAT CAR
NARROW GAUGE
MILWAUKEE ROAD
4-27-81   Al Lee

There were five types of flatcars, each with a different load capacity. Flatcar No. 1 and flatcars No. 685 through No. 691 had capacity of 60,000 pounds. No. X921053 and No. X921721 were used in maintenance of way service and were rated at 40,000- and 20,000-pound capacity respectively. No. 694 (old No. 150) was also rated at 20,000 pounds. No. 650 (as depicted above in A.L. Lee's drawing), and No. 678 and No. 682 were built with 16,000-pound capacity ratings.

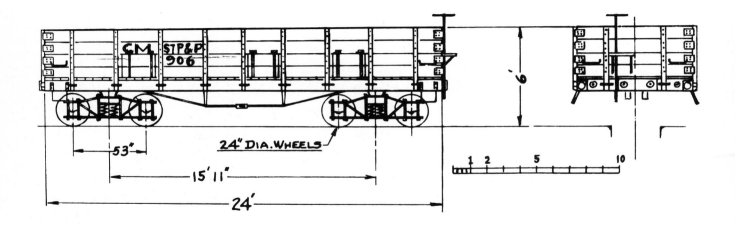

CM ST P&P 906

53"

24" DIA. WHEELS

15'11"

24'

6'

1 2   5   10

There were two sizes of gondolas. The smaller size could carry a maximum of 50,000 pounds and were constructed with a wood body and underframe. These were No. 900 through No. 905. The larger cars carried five tons more of weight, were constructed of wood but had a composite underframe and were built in 1930. According to Dick Sullivan, long time Milwaukee Road employee, the larger gondolas were almost as big as a standard car. The 1930 built cars carried No. 906 through No. 915.—*A.L. Lee*

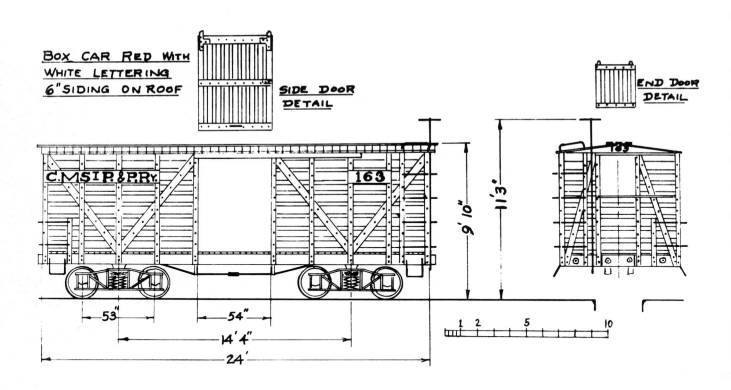

BOX CAR RED WITH WHITE LETTERING 6" SIDING ON ROOF

SIDE DOOR DETAIL

END DOOR DETAIL

C.M.ST.P.&P.Ry.   163

53"   54"

14'4"

24'

9'10"

11'3"

1 2   5   10

Naturally, the stockcars carried livestock, but the crews pressed them into service to carry bulk items as well. Shingles from Cascade and bags of cement being shipped inland were common freight items that could have been shipped in the stockcars. Note the small door at the end of the car. Boxcars as well had these doors, and allowed the transportation of longer items such as telephone poles. An idler car on either end of a boxcar or stockcar carrying such an item assured sufficient clearance.—*A.L. Lee*

The difference in size between the two different types of gondolas is clearly evident in this photo taken at Cascade.

Passenger cars, wood body and underframe, 4-wheeled truck, utilized as cabooses in later years and carried appropriate numbers.

Numbers: 02697 (old passenger#2), 02698 (old passenger #12), 02699 (old passenger #8)

Account #57 covered the maintenance-of-way and work equipment. Although the gauge did have a narrow gauge bunk and kitchen car at one time, it was destroyed in a fire in 1929. One or both of the following boxcars could have been converted to sleeping and eating quarters, but they are not so designated in this inventory. One sourse shows X911933 as a bunk and kitchen car.

Pile driver, wood body and underframe, capacity 60,000 lb.
  Number: X200 (old X900809)
Slope leveler, wood body and underframe, capacity 16,000 lb.
  Number: X246 (old X901224)
Snowplow, wood body and underframe, capacity 16,000 lb. built 1929.
  Number: X900104
Snow flanger, wood body and underframe, capacity 20,000 lb. built 1929.
  Number: X900351 (old freight car number 316)
Air dumps, wood body and composite underframe, capacity 8 cubic yards (probably built about 1930).
  Numbers: X905237, X905238

Boxcars, wood body and underframe, capacity 60,000 lb.
  Numbers: X911933, X914058 (These had three times the capacity of the twenty-four-foot "regular" narrow gauge boxcars and were conceivably older wide gauge cars with narrow gauge trucks.)
Flatcar, wood body and underframe, capacity 40,000 lb.
  Number: X921053
Flatcar, wood body and underframe, capacity 20,000 lb.
  Number: X921721

When the Bellevue and Cascade Railroad bought the gauge, it acquired 110 freight cars, four cabooses, and ten pieces of work equipment.

The two tank cars,[18] which had a capacity of five thousand gallons were leased from the Union Tank Lines and were numbered UTLX 40 and UTLX 41. They were not owned by either the Milwaukee or the Bellevue and Cascade.

A burrow crane, number X906007, was used from time to time on maintenance of the right-of-way. It was equipped with dual gauge wheels and was used more on the wide gauge track than the narrow. It was not considered a part of the narrow gauge rolling stock and was not part of the deal when the gauge was sold to the Bradley Company.

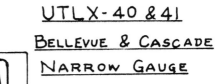

UTLX-40 & 41
BELLEVUE & CASCADE
NARROW GAUGE
MILWAUKEE ROAD
DRAWN FROM PHOTOS
4-27-81

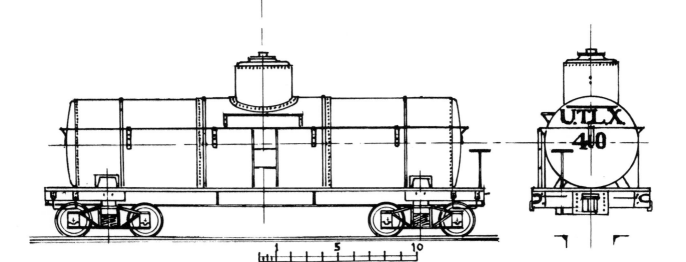

5   10

The two tank cars were leased by the Milwakee Road in 1916 from the Union Tank Line and stayed on the gauge until 1936 when the line was abandoned. The two tanks each carried 5,000 gallons of liquid.

Clear photo of one of the tank cars showing the detail necessary to build the model. Also note the detail of stockcar No. 148.

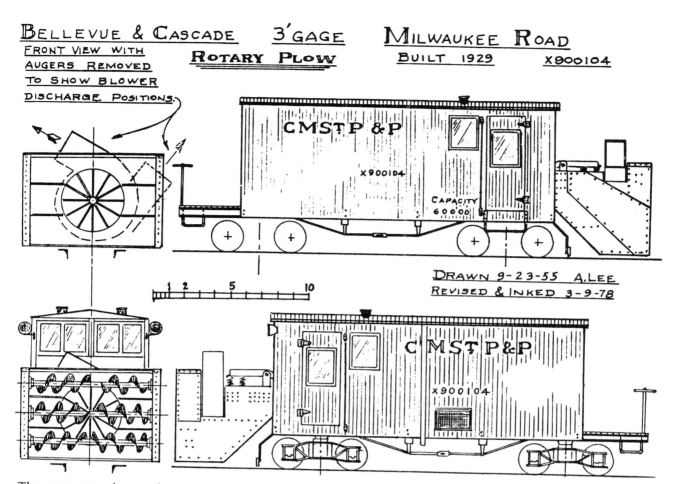

BELLEVUE & CASCADE   3' GAGE   MILWAUKEE ROAD
FRONT VIEW WITH ROTARY PLOW   BUILT 1929   X900104
AUGERS REMOVED
TO SHOW BLOWER
DISCHARGE POSITIONS.

CMSTP&P
X900104
CAPACITY
60000

DRAWN 9-23-55 A.LEE
REVISED & INKED 3-9-78

CMSTP&P
X900104

The most unusual piece of equipment on the gauge was the Klauer Sno-Go plow, which the Milwaukee commissioned in 1929. The same principle used then is still built into the much larger street plows being manufactured today.

Klauer Manufacturing Company bought the Sno-Go plow back from the B. &C. in 1936 and set it on a pedestal of ties as seen in this photo in the northeast corner of their factory lot. Nearby the C.G.W. tracks carried trains past everyday. In June 1972, after the trucks and coupler were donated to a museum, the scoop, blower, and augers were cut up for scrap metal.—*J. Kreuzberger*

Of all the pieces of equipment used on the gauge, the most unusual had to have been the Sno-Go plow, # X900104, which the Klauer Manufacturing Company built in 1929. It wasn't until the Ox was put to work pushing the plow that the full potential of the Sno-Go was realized. Because of the slow speed the Plymouth Switch Engine could maintain, the augers were able to eat away at the drifting snow. Once the six-cylinder Climax engine was taken out to power the disabled Ox, the moments of glory for the plow were finished. It never ran again. However, it did stimulate the interest of the Iowa Terminal Railroad Company. From June 2, 1936, when it was repurchased by the Klauer Company, until 1972, the plow sat on a pedestal of railroad ties in the northeast corner of Sno-Go yard close to Twenty-seventh and Elm streets. Within a

stone's throw, the Chicago, Great Western freight trains rumbled past toward Chicago or Oelwein, Iowa. In 1969, the Iowa Terminal Railroad inquired if the plow was for sale. The president, Wendell J. Dillinger, offered to report back the results achieved with the plow and in essence be a proving ground for Klauer. Nothing came of the offer and the narrow gauge plow continued rusting away.

Then, in May 1972, the trucks, couplers and other hardware were stripped and donated, by Klauer, to the Mid-Continent Railway Museum at North Freedom, Wisconsin. There, the cannabilized parts were mounted beneath a Chicago and North Western boxcar and they can be seen there today. The following month, June 1972, the augers, and blower were cut up and sold for scrap.

The last vestige was gone.

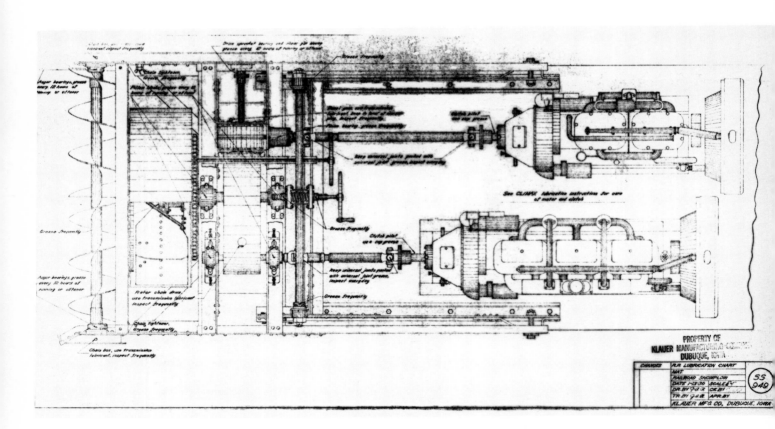

Overhead view showing the placement of the four-cylinder and six-cylinder Climax engines that operated the Sno-go's augers and blower.—*Courtesy, Klauer Manufacturing Co.*

216

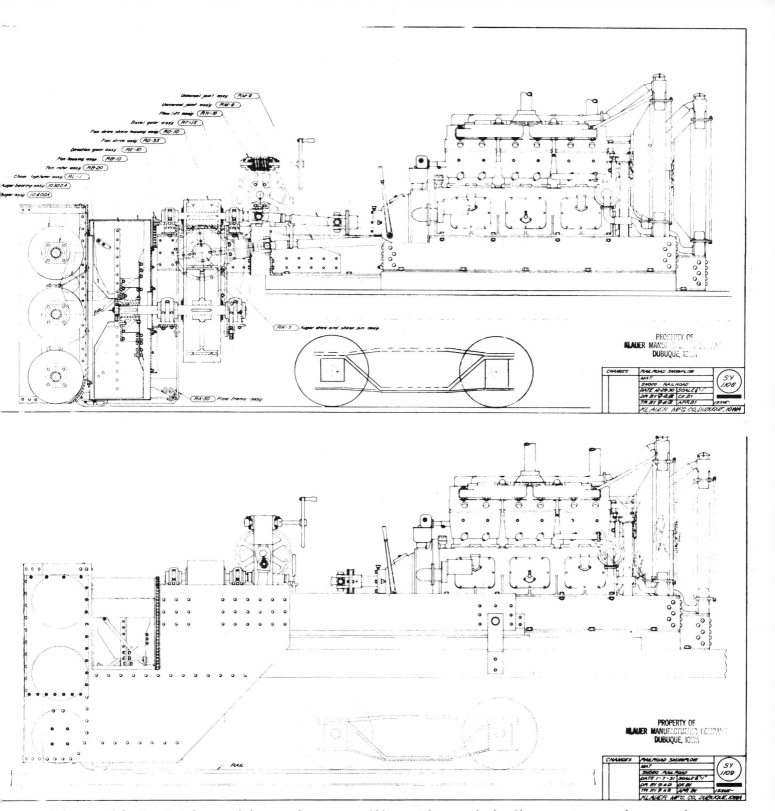

Universal joint assy RM-9
Universal joint assy RM-8
Plow lift assy RH-10
Bevel gear assy RF-15
Fan drive chain housing assy RD-10
Fan drive assy RD-35
Direction gear assy RE-10
Fan housing assy RB-10
Fan rotor assy RB-20
Chain tightener assy RL-1
Auger bearing assy 10300A
Auger assy 10400A

RK-5 Auger drive and shear pin assy

RA-50 Plow frame assy

PROPERTY OF
KLAUER MANUFACTURING COMPANY
DUBUQUE, IOWA

CHANGES	RAILROAD SNOWPLOW		SY 1106
	MAT.		
	SNOGO RAILROAD		
	DATE 12-29-30	SCALE ½"-1"	
	DR BY 9.2.B	CK BY	
	TR BY 9.2.B	APR BY	
	KLAUER MFG. CO. DUBUQUE, IOWA		ISSUE

PROPERTY OF
KLAUER MANUFACTURING COMPANY
DUBUQUE, IOWA

RAIL

CHANGES	RAILROAD SNOWPLOW		SY 1109
	MAT.		
	SNOGO RAILROAD		
	DATE 1-7-31	SCALE ½"-1"	
	DR BY 9.2.B	CK BY	
	TR BY 9.2.B	APR BY	ISSUE
	KLAUER MFG. CO. DUBUQUE, IOWA		

Side view of the Sno-Go's front end showing the augers and blower. The six-cylinder Climax engine was taken out and installed in the Ox.—*Courtesy, Klauer Manufacturing Co.*

Within a stone's throw of the Sno-Go plow, the Chicago Great Western freight trains and passenger trains passed on their way to Chicago or Oelwein, Iowa. In May 1972, the trucks and coupler were cannibalized and donated to the Mid-Continent Railway Museum at North Freedom, Wisconsin. Today, they support and grace one end of a Chicago and North Western narrow-gauge boxcar right outside the depot.—*Pregler*

217

⁴⁷ SNOGO — Date 12/2/29

KLAUER MFG. CO.

Order No. 60021	Model RR PLOW	Machine No. 57
Shipped to C. M. ST. P. & P. RY. CO. DUBUQUE SHOPS		Date. 12/2/29
Address DUBUQUE IOWA	Via	Car No. ON FLAT CAR

R16 - UNIT #915 - MOTOR 15049
R14 - UNIT No. 917 - MOTOR #14042

Engine, make CLIMAX	Model R14	Model R16		
Carburetor, make ZENITH	Model		No.	
Generator, make LEECE-NEVILLE		Volts 12	No.	
Starter, make LEECE-NEVILLE		Volts 12	No.	
Battery, make EXIDE		Volts 12	No.	
Radiator, make PERFEX			No.	
Flywheel, design				
Rear Axle, make NONE	Model	Ratio	No.	
Front Axle, make NONE	Model		No.	
Rear trans. make NONE	Model	Speeds	No.	
Front trans. make NONE	Model	Speeds	No.	
Tires, make NONE	Size front	Size rear		
No. L. F.	No. R. F.	No. L. R.	No. R. R.	
Rims, make NONE	Size	Size		
Cab, make MILWAUKEE SHOP	Model SPECIAL			
Steering gear, make N ONE	Model	Wheel size		
Light, make VICTOR	#654			
Rear springs, make NONE	No. Leaves	Length		
Front springs, make NONE	No. Leaves	Length		
Gas tank, make MORRISON	Capacity 250 GALLONS			
Univ. Joint, at flywheel, make NONE	Size			
Univ. Joint, drive TO FAN XXXXXXXXXXXX	Size B 5	O/A Length 30"		
Univ. Joint, TO AUGER DRIVE XXXXXXXXXXXX	Size B 5	O/A Length 60"		
Univ. Joint, propeller shaft, rear, make NONE	Size	O/A Length		
Univ. Joint, propeller shaft, front, make NONE	Size	O/A Length		
Fibre disc joint, make NONE	Size			
Fan clutch, make ON MOTORS				
Wheels, make NONE	Size	No. Spokes	Size spoke	
Number rear hub bolts NONE	Number front hub bolts			

Fan reduction Gear LINK BELT	Series	Ratio 3.72		
No. teeth in pinion 25	No. teeth in gear 93	R.P.M. fan 268.8		
Transfer gear NONE	Series	Step up ratio		
No. teeth in driver	Series	No. teeth in driven	R.P.M. clutch	
Auger drive sprocket R. P. M. 285.71	Pitch 1½	No. of teeth 19		
Auger sprocket R. P. M 271.42	Pitch 1½	No. of teeth 20		
Augers, make MOORE	Series FF-20 10400	O/A Length tubing 84		
Auger bearing SKF 230	Series FF-58 10300 / FE-58 10720 / FH-1	Size shear pins 2-3/8		
Shear pin unit	Series 1	Size shear pins 4-1/2		
Fan 60"	Series 1	Height of lift 4"		
Plow lifting gear	Series 1			
Housing tilting gear	Series 1			
Clutch housing NONE	Series			
Scraper blade NONE	Series 1			
Cab heater, make NONE	Model			
Loader NONE	Series			
Deflector NONE	Series			

BEVEL GEAR AUGER DRIVE   RATIO 3½ TO 1
PINION 16 T   BEVEL GEAR 14 T

FAN DRIVE SPECIAL 10" X 1" P LINK BELT
FAN SHAFT BEARINGS DODGE TIMKEN S 1 2-15/16
PINION SHAFT   "   "   S 1 1-15/16

S-72-Flat Car Wheels, etc. given to Mid Continent Rwy Museum...No Freedom

The specification sheets for the Sno-Go plow as provided by the Klauer Manufacturing Company at Dubuque, Iowa. The hand-written additions at the bottom of the second sheet concern the disposition of the plow from June 1936 to June 1972. An interesting fact about the Klauer firm is that the plow as provided for the C.M.&St.P. was only the fifty-seventh machine built in six years. Each one was and still is hand-built today. The total machines erected by 1981, most of which are still in service, numbered only 3,500 units.—*Courtesy, Klauer Manufacturing Company*

Burro crane photographed while clearing track ditch just east of the Cascade yards in September 1929. Also pictured is a mechanical dump car.

Carrying the number X-906007, the crane is equipped with dual-gauge trucks. Manufactured by the Cullen-Frestedt Co. of Chicago (now the Burro Crane Co.—1984), the crane carries the manufacturers model number CF 20.

According to crane company records, the model 20 was a full-revolving model with a 33' angle and lattice boom having a 10' radius. Powered with a four-cylinder Hercules engine and gear driven, this model was usually equipped with 24" wheels and had a 20-ton capacity.

However, according to Milwaukee records this crane's lifting capacity at 10' radius was 11,000 pounds, not 20 tons. It could handle a 1½ cubic yard clam bucket. Further Milwaukee specifications are as follows: self propelled with 60-horsepower engine; weight, 34,000 lbs.; top speed of 15 mph and capable of hauling two cars. The crane had two drums, 12" and 13", and has four special cast split wheels mounted on standard axles for 3' gauge track. The crane was serial number 38 with a body length of 12'8" and 8'8" wide.

The crane was purchased for the sum of $8,278 and was shipped May 11, 1929 and received at Bellevue on May 14. According to railroad records, the main reason for purchasing the crane was to transfer bulk materials at Bellevue and reduce labor costs.—*Milwaukee records—courtesy of Ted Schnepf*

Appendices

Marked "CM&StPRR," this lantern was purchased at a farm
auction near the old right-of-way of the B.&C. by Gerald
Volk of Cascade.—*Jon Jacobson*

Appendix I
Corporate History
of
The Chicago, Clinton, Dubuque
and
Minnesota Railroad Company
In Iowa

The North River Road

Dubuque & MacGregor Railway Company

Incorporated December 16, 1867.

Filed for record January 20, 1868.

Officers: Platt Smith, president; J.M. McKinley, secretary.

Name changed January 22, 1869, to Dubuque & Minnesota Railway Company.

Line of Road: From Dubuque northerly along the Mississippi River to Rome Junction, in Houston County, Minnesota.

Commenced construction in 1870.

Name changed January 4, 1871, to Chicago, Dubuque & Minnesota Railroad Company.

Chicago, Dubuque & Minnesota Railroad Company

Officers: J.K. Graves, president; Peter Kiene, Jr., secretary.

Completed from Dubuque to MacGregor in November 1871; to Harper's Ferry in March 1872; to La Crescent in October 1872; and from Turkey River Junction to Elkport in 1872.

Mortgage foreclosed and road conveyed to the Dubuque & Minnesota Railroad Company September 20, 1877.

Dubuque & Minnesota Railroad Company

Incorporated August 15, 1877.

Officers: James F. Joy, president; John N. Denison, secretary.

Acquired the railroad of the Chicago, Dubuque & Minnesota Railroad Company September 20, 1877.

Built from Elkport to Wadena, 29.60 miles in 1877.

Consolidated February 22, 1878 with the Clinton & Dubuque Railroad Company under the name of the Chicago, Clinton, Dubuque & Minnesota Railroad Company.

The South River Road

Dubuque, Bellevue & Mississippi
Railroad Company

Incorporated January 1, 1870.
Officers: William Vandever, president; Joseph Kelso, secretary.
Name changed to Chicago, Clinton & Dubuque Railroad Company,
    October 5, 1871.

Chicago, Clinton & Dubuque
Railroad Company

Officers: J.K. Graves, president; Peter Kiene, Jr., secretary.
Line of Road: From Dubuque southerly along the Mississippi River to
    Clinton, in Clinton County, 60 miles.
Construction commenced in 1871, completed to Midland Junction in 1872.
Mortgage foreclosed and the road conveyed to the Clinton & Dubuque
    Railroad Company on September 20, 1877.

Clinton & Dubuque Railroad Company

Incorporated August 15, 1877.
Filed for record September 8, 1877.
Officers: James F. Joy, president; John N. Denison, secretary.
Acquired property of the Chicago, Clinton & Dubuque Railroad
    Company, September 20, 1877.
Built no road.
Consolidated February 22, 1878, with the Dubuque & Minnesota Railroad
    Company under the name of the Chicago, Clinton, Dubuque &
    Minnesota Railroad Company.

Narrow Gauge Branch Lines

Waukon & Mississippi
Railroad Company

Incorporated in 1875.
Officers: C.D.Beeman, president; C.S. Stillwell, secretary.
Line of Road: Waukon to the Mississippi River, 23 miles.
At the last election of officers in May 1882, Alexander Mitchell was
    chosen president and P.M. Myers, secretary (Chicago, Milwaukee & St.
    Paul Railway Company).

Waukon & Mississippi
Railroad Guaranty Company

Incorporated September 26, 1876, to build road of the Waukon & Mississippi Railroad Company.

Officers: D.W. Adams, president, Martin Stone, secretary.

Date of commencement of construction unknown; completed to the Mississippi River in October 1877.

The property of the railroad company and the Railroad Guaranty Company was conveyed to the Chicago, Clinton, Dubuque & Minnesota Railroad Company, June 29, 1880.

At last election of officers, May 10, 1882, Alexander Mitchell was chosen president and P.M. Myers, secretary (Chicago, Milwaukee & St. Paul Railway Company).

Chicago, Bellevue, Cascade
&
Western Railway Company

Incorporated August 4, 1877.

Filed for record November 23, 1877.

Officers: Joseph Kelso, president; S.S. Simpson, secretary.

Line of Road: From Bellevue, in Jackson County, to Cascade, in Dubuque County, 35.6 miles.

Construction commenced in 1878 and completed by Chicago, Clinton, Dubuque & Minnesota Railroad Company, December 30, 1879.

Property conveyed to the Chicago, Clinton, Dubuque & Minnesota Railroad Company June 29, 1880.

At the last election of officers, November 23, 1881, Alexander Mitchell was chosen president and P.M. Myers, secretary (Chicago, Milwaukee & St. Paul Railway Company).

Chicago, Clinton, Dubuque
&
Minnesota Railroad Company

OFficers: James F. Joy, president; John N. Denison, secretary.

Consolidation March 1, 1878, of the Clinton & Dubuque (South River Road) and the Dubuque & Minnesota (North River Road) Railroad companies.

Line of Road: From Rome Junction, in Houston County, Minnesota, southerly along the Mississippi River to Midland Junction, Clinton County, Iowa, 170 miles; and branch from Turkey River Junction to Wadena, 43.9 miles.

Acquired Cascade Branch and Waukon Branch in Iowa and Preston Branch in Minnesota in June 1880 (purchased August 28, 1880); built from Midland Junction to Clinton in 1880; and on October 19, 1880, conveyed its railroad (the Chicago, Clinton, Dubuque & Minnesota Railroad Company) to the Chicago, Milwaukee & St. Paul Railway Company. Built from Wadena to West Union, 13.61 miles, in 1882 and conveyed to the St. Paul Company.

At last election of officers in May 1882, Alexander Mitchell was elected president and P.M. Myers, secretary (Chicago, Milwaukee & St. Paul Railway Company).

Appendix II

Letter Written
by
Reverend James Hill

(As it appeared in the October 3, 1877, issues of the Cascade *Pioneer* and the *Bellevue Leader*.)

Dear Sir:

Allow me through your valuable paper, to lay before our citizens of Cascade and Whitewater townships a few plain reasons why every voter should cheerfully vote a 3 per cent tax to secure a railroad from Bellevue to Cascade.

First. It is to the interest of every producer, consumer, and laboring man to have a railroad. A railroad would connect us with the commercial world and give us the highest daily cash price for our wheat, barley, oats, corn, pork, beef, butter, eggs, and everything we raise for sale. The farmer often loses more in one year than his railroad tax would amount to on the sale of his hogs and wheat not knowing the real market value. A railroad will remedy this evil by giving a telegraph price so that none need sell in the dark.

Second. It is to the interest of every farmer to vote a 3% tax. The saving on horses, wagons, and the great inconvenience of hauling our products from 12 to 26 miles would go far in one year towards paying a 3% tax.

Third. It would reduce our taxes in the aggregate: the railroad and all property there to is taxable and in addition to county and state tax, and railroad contributes a heavy school tax to each and every township through which it passes.

Fourth. It would build up manufacturing interests in our town and villages, increase the population, bring in capitalists, give employment to the laboring man and mechanic, improve our many water powers, convert our timber into implements that we now import for daily use, and give life and vitality to every enterprise.

Fifth. We cannot be humbugged or cheated out of our money. The 3% tax asked for is taken from the assessor's value of our real and personal property, last assessed by our township assessor, $3 on each $100 or $30 on each $1,000.

The law is wise and safe, because no railroad company can collect one dollar of our tax until such a road is built to such points or places named in the petition asking for the tax.

In event the said tax is voted and collected the county treasurer holds the same until the road is built to the place mentioned in the petition. And in the event the said railroad is not built, then the said tax is returned by the county treasurer to the original taxpayer.

The law is just, the said company constructing such roads are required to give back interest bearing bonds for every dollar of tax payer and should the road prove to be a paying road then the tax payer will receive back his money thus voted in addition to all the permanent advantages a railroad brings to any section of the country.

Many other good reasons may be given why all should vote said tax but our letter is already too long.

I am respectfully yours,

James Hill

Appendix III
Corporate History of the
Bellevue-Cascade Branch Line

The Chicago, Bellevue, Cascade
and
Western Railway Company

Incorporated August 4, 1877.

Filed for record November 23, 1877.

Officers: Judge Joseph Kelso, president; S.S. Simpson, secretary.

Line of Road: From Bellevue in Jackson County, westerly to Cascade in Dubuque County.

Company approved by the State of Iowa: January 30, 1878.

Change of officers, June 1878: John W. Tripp, president; Dr. W. H. Francis, secretary (both reelected at annual meeting September 4, 1878).

Commenced construction: September 19, 1878.

Construction completed by the Chicago, Clinton, Dubuque and Minnesota Railroad Company, December 20, 1879.

Property conveyed to the C.C.D.&M. Railroad Company June 29, 1880.

Property purchased by the C.C.D.&M. Railroad Company August 28, 1880. (See Appendix I for C.C.D.&M. officers.)

Property title conveyed to the Chicago, Milwaukee & St. Paul Railway Company October 19, 1880.

Chicago, Milwaukee & St. Paul Railway Company Board of Directors voted for receivership March 18, 1925.

C.M.& St.P. Railway reorganized and retitled Chicago, Milwaukee, St. Paul and Pacific Railroad Company March 31, 1927.

Property transferred to the Bellevue and Cascade Railroad Company July 22, 1933. Incorporated June 9, 1933.

Filed for record June 15, 1933.

Company approved by the State of Iowa (?).

Officers: Earl W. Bradley, president/treasurer; S.L. Goldish secretary.

Property and corporate name transferred to William G. Bell and Joseph Schoenthal, November 9, 1935.

Petition to abandon the property made February 25 (?), 1936.

Final run made March 14, 1936.

Appendix IV
Articles of Incorporation
for
The Chicago, Bellevue, Cascade
&
Western Railway Company

Articles of Incorporation
Chicago, Bellevue, Cascade,
& Western Railway Co.

Section One—In pursuance of the provisions of the General Incorporation laws of the State of Iowa, we whose names are hereto subscribed, do hereby form ourselves into a body corporate under the name and Style of the Chicago, Bellevue, Cascade and Western Railway Company of the Said corporation, and any who may hereafter become members of said company shall by said corporate name have perpetual succession, may sue and be sued, may have common seal, may make contracts, acquire and transfer property and exercise all the powers in such respects as natural persons enjoy.

Section Two—The objects of this corporation shall be to construct, maintain and operate a RailRoad from the town of Bellevue to the town of Cascade in the State of Iowa and to Extend the same by branch roads to connect with other points or with other lines of Rail Road within the State of Iowa or with Rail Roads of adjoining States.

Section Three—The Capital Stock of this Company shall be Two Hundred Thousand dollars divided into share(s) of fifty dollars each which shares shall be transferable by the holders thereof in the manner prescribed by the company. The highest amount of Indebtedness which this company at any one time is subject, shall not exceed one hundred and thirty thousand dollars. The capital stock may from time to time be increased, in which case the indebtedness to which the company at any one time is subject shall not exceed two thirds the amount of the capital stock.

Section Four—The affairs of this company shall be managed by a board of twenty seven (27) directors chosen from among the corporators or Stockholders—The Board of Directors may fill vacancies in their own number. Nine members of said Board Shall constitute a quorum for the transaction of business until the election of a new board by the stockholders. The following named persons shall manage the affairs of the company with full powers as a board of directors namely—John B. Sawyer, Frank May, James Hill, Thos. H. Davis, Joseph Kelso, A.J. Dorchester, G.G. Banghart, Daniel Seery, James Margargell, David Beaty, Thomas McMillon, T. Moore, Wm. H. Francis, T.E.L. Kasse (or Kane ?), James Conlin, William Jess, Dennis O'Brien, John Maloney, Joseph Hunter, James Dunne, C. Demlinger, James Hickson, Joseph Burke, John Wilson, C. Cort, Daniel Crowley.

Section Five—The principal place of business of this company shall be at Bellevue until otherwise determined—but in no case shall it be removed out of the State nor shall it be changed in the state until after thirty days notice by posting at the office of the company, along the line of the road and by publication in the newspaper of the vicinity.

Section Six—There shall be a President and vice President of said company chosen by the Board of Directors from among themselves who shall have the general management, control and oversight of the affairs of the company. There shall also be a secretary of said company chosen by the Board of Directors who shall hold his office at the pleasure of said board. The Secretary shall faithfully keep and preserve the books, papers and records of said company. He shall attend the meetings of the Board of Directors and record the proceedings of said board. The Board of Directors may also choose a Treasurer for said company whose duty it shall be to receive, safely keep and disburse the funds, and evidence of indebtedness of the company and report whenever called upon by the President or by the Board of Directors. The Treasurer shall give bond in such sum as the board may direct and he shall hold his office during the pleasure of the board.

Section Seven—The Board of Directors may establish Bylaws and make all rules and regulations deemed expedient for the management of the affairs of the company and the control of the officers and agents appointed by it: The Directors may at any time confer such special powers and duties upon the President of the Company and upon any of its officers or agents as the Board may deem for the interest or welfare of the company and best calculated to secure the objects of this Corporation.

Section Eight—The private property of the Stockholders shall be exempt from liability for the corporate debts.

Section Nine—This corporation shall commence August 4th A.D. 1877 and continue fifty years.

Bellevue Iowa August 4th 1877

J. Kelso
D.A. Wynkoop
Thos. H. Davis

Christian Kuchermann
S.S. Simpson
Frank Schlecht
W.A. Maginnis
John Bowen
G.G. Banghart

J.J. King

David Beatty
Thos. J. Chew
Robert Snowden
William H. Francis
John Taylor
Elon Rafferty
D.A. Dickinson
James Hill
Louis Benham

State of Iowa Jackson County—So Be it Remembered that in this 4th day of August A.D. 1877 personally appeared before the undersigned a notary public in and for said county, Joseph Kelso, T.H. Davis, D.A. Wynkoop, S.S. Simpson, Christian Kuchermann, Frank Schlecht, W.A. Maginnis, and John Bowen to me personally known to be the identical persons who executed the foregoing instrument and acknowledged the same to be their voluntary act and deed for the purposes therein mentioned.

Witness my hand notarial seal the day and year
above written

(seal)

W.H. Warren
Notary Public

State of Iowa Dubuque County—Be it Remembered that on this 10th day of August A.D. 1877 personally appeared before me the undersigned a notary public of Iowa in and for Dubuque County G.G. Banghart, J.M. King, David Beatty, Thos. J. Chew, Robert Snowden, John Taylor, Sen. Elon Rafferty, D.A. Dickinson, James Hill and Louis Benham to me personally known to be the identical persons who executed the foregoing instrument and acknowledged the same to be their voluntary act and deed for the purposes therein mentioned.

Witness my hand and notarial seal the day and year above
written

(seal)

William H. Francis
Notary Public

Dubuque County State of Iowa—Be it remembered that on this 10th day of August A.D. 1877 personally appeared before me the undersigned Justice of the Peace for Whitewater Township Dubuque County Iowa, William H. Francis to me personally known to be the identical person among others who executed the foregoing instrument and acknowledged the same to be his voluntary act and deed for the purposes therein stated.

Witness my hand the day and year above written.

Isaac H. Baldwin Justice of the Peace
in and for the township of Whitewater

Dubuque County

The foregoing instrument filed for record Aug. 23rd 1877 at 2/2 o'clock
P.M.

J.A. Griffin, Recorder

At a meeting of the Stockholders of the Chicago, Bellevue, Cascade & Western R.R. Co. at Bellevue the 4th day of September 1878 the following amendment was made to Section four of the Articles of Incorporation of said Company:

Resolved that Section Four -4- of the Articles of Incorporation of the Chicago, Bellevue, Cascade & Western R.R. Co. be amended so as to read as follows: The affairs of this company shall be managed by a Board of Thirteen Directors chosen from among the Stock-holders, the board of directors may fill vacancy in their own number, seven members of said board shall constitute a quorum for the transaction of business until the election of a new board at the next annual election meeting of the stockholders.

Signed—William H. Francis, Secty C.B.C.&W.R.R.Co. Filed for record 27th Day of Sept 1878 at 2-o'clock P.M. I hereby certify that at an annual meeting of the stockholders of the Chicago, Bellevue, Cascade and Western Railroad Company duly convened and held at the city of Bellevue Iowa on Wednesday the 7th day of September 1881 the following Resolutions were unanimously adopted—Resolved that Section Four of the Articles of Incorporation of this company be stricken out and in lieu thereof a new section be inserted to read as follows:

Section 4—The affairs of this company shall be managed by a board of seven directors who shall be elected annually by the stockholders and who shall hold office until their successors are elected and certified and Resolved that *Section Five* of the Articles of Incorporation of this company be stricken out and in leu thereof a new section be inserted to read as follows: *Section Five*—The principal place of business of this company shall be at Dubuque, Dubuque County, Iowa and resolved that the secretary be and he is hereby directed to cause the foregoing amendments to be duly recorded and established according to law In Witness Whereof I have hereunto set my hand and affixed the seal of the Company at Milwaukee, Wis this 13th Day of September 1881.

P.M. Myers, Secretary Chicago, Bellevue, Cascade & Western R.R. Co.

Filed—Sept. 19th 1881 at 10 o'clock A.M.

M.S. Dunn, Recorder

Appendix V
Annual Report
of the
Chicago, Bellevue, Cascade & Western
Railroad Company
For the Year Ending June 30, 1880
As Made To the
Iowa Railroad Commissioners

ANALYSIS OF EXPENSES.

Stationery and printing	$ 6.40
Contingencies and miscellaneous	2.70
Repairs of bridges (including culverts and cattle-guards)	799.67
Repairs of buildings	145.63
Repairs of fences, road-crossings and signs	2.75
Repairs of road-bed and track	6,749.56
Repairs of locomotives	698.18
Fuel for locomotives	857.58
Water supply	110.18
Oil and waste	21.55
Locomotive service, salaries and wages	1,645.00
Train service, salaries and wages	717.06
Passenger train supplies	.50
Repairs of freight cars	771.50
Telegraph expenses	210.37
Loss and damage, freight and baggage	.50
Loss and damage, property and cattle, including losses by fire	136.00
Personal injuries	38.00
Agents and station service, salaries and wages	1,172.96
Station supplies	92.46
Total operating expenses	$ 14,179.45

Class No. 1, maintenance of way	$ 7,697.61
Class No. 2, maintenance of motive power and cars	1,469.68
Class No. 3, conducting transportation	5,003.06
Class No. 4, general expenses	9.10
Total	$ 14,179.45

RECAPITULATION OF EXPENSES.

Total expenses in operating the road (*embraced in classes 1, 2, 3 and 4*)	$ 14,179.45
Per mile of road operated (37.67 miles)	$ 376.41
Per train mile for passenger, freight and mixed trains (15,666 miles), cents	90.5
Percentage of expenses to earnings	1.78

GENERAL RECAPITULATION.

Total earnings	$ 20,433.72
Total receipts during the year	$ 7,957.97
Total operating expenses	14,179.45
Total receipts above operating expenses	$ 6,254.27

REPORT

OF THE

CHICAGO, BELLEVUE, CASCADE & WESTERN

RAILROAD COMPANY,

FOR THE YEAR ENDING JUNE 30, 1880.

GENERAL EXHIBIT FOR THE YEAR.

Total income	$ 7,957.97
Total expense (including taxes)	14,179.45
Balance June 30, 1880 (deficit)	16,969.20

ANALYSIS OF EARNINGS.

From local passengers	$ 978.20
From through passengers	246.25
From express and extra baggage	14.91
Total earnings from passenger department	$ 1,239.36
From local freight	2,815.84
From through freight	4,241.51
Total earnings from freight department	$ 6,718.61
Total transportation earnings	7,957.97
Voluntary contributions	12,475.75
Total income from all sources	$ 20,433.72

Earnings per mile of road operated	$ 210.20
*Receipts from passenger trains per train mile run (15,666 miles)	
*Receipts from freight trains per train mile run (15,666 miles)	.51

*All trains run as mixed trains.

PROPERTY ACCOUNTS, CHARGES AND CREDITS BY WHICH THE CAPITAL AND DEBT HAVE BEEN INCREASED DURING THE YEAR.

Grading and masonry	$ 39,486.43
Bridging	13,424.08
Superstructure, including rails	103,581.69
Land, land damages and fences	1,984.95
Passenger and freight stations, coal-sheds and water-stations	6,460.87
Engine-houses, car-sheds and turn-tables	340.02
Engineering, agencies, salaries, and other expenses during construction	5,470.57
Total for construction	$ 170,749.21
Locomotives, 1	$ 5,212.64
Station and track outfit	957.47
Passenger, mail and baggage cars, 1	1,600.00
Freight and other cars (1 combination), 25	9,024.49
Total for equipment	$ 16,794.60
Total expenditures charged to property accounts	$ 187,543.81

BALANCE SHEET.

ASSETS.

Construction account		$ 350,899.21
Equipment account		16,794.60
Cash items (as follows:)		
Cash	$ 1,115.65	
Bills receivable	144,000.00	
Due from agents and companies	56.60	
		145,172.25
Total assets		$ 512,866.06

LIABILITIES.

Capital stock	$ 180,150.00
Funded debt	144,000.00
Unfunded debt (as follows):	
Vouchers and accounts	182,461.79
Profit and loss balance (if surplus)	6,254.27
Total liabilities	$ 512,866.06

MILEAGE, TRAFFIC, ETC.

Train mileage (mixed train)	15,666
Other train mileage	28,875
Total train mileage	44,541
Number of local passengers	1,144
Number of through passengers	288
Total number of passengers	1,432

Local passenger mileage (local passengers carried one mile)	25,643
Through passenger mileage (through passengers carried one mile)	
Number of tons of local freight carried in Iowa	7,394
Number of tons of local freight carried east in Iowa	1,618
Number of tons of local freight carried west in Iowa	262
Number of tons through freight carried in Iowa	1,356
Number of tons through freight carried east in Iowa	2,862
Number of tons through freight carried west in Iowa	2,797
Total number tons freight carried	65
Local freight mileage (tons local freight carried one mile)	4,480
Through freight mileage (tons through freight carried one mile)	45,745
	78,877
Rate of speed of passenger, express and freight trains, including stops, miles per hour	10

TONNAGE OF ARTICLES TRANSPORTED.

Grain	1,050
Flour	14
Provisions—beef, pork, lard, etc	3
Animals	1,557
Other agricultural products	96
Lumber and forest products	972
Coal	11
Salt	32
Merchandise, and other articles not enumerated above	745
Total tons carried	4,480

DESCRIPTION OF ROAD.

Length of main line of road from Bellevue to Cascade, miles	37.67
Length of main line of road in Iowa	37.67
Total length of road belonging to this company	37.67
Aggregate length of sidings and other tracks not above enumerated	1.15
Same in Iowa	1.15
Aggregate length of track, computed as single track	38.82
Same in Iowa	38.82
Weights per yard, iron, 30 pounds.	
Gauge of track	3 feet.

ROADS AND BRANCHES BELONGING TO OTHER COMPANIES, OPERATED BY THIS COMPANY UNDER LEASE OR CONTRACT.

Total miles of road operated by this company in Iowa	37.67
Total miles of road operated by this company	37.67
Number of stations in Iowa on all roads operated by this company	
Number of telegraph offices in same	7
Number of stations in same	5
Number of stations on all roads owned by this company	7
Same in Iowa	7

EMPLOYES.

Average number of persons regularly employed on all roads operated by this company	71

EQUIPMENT.

	OWNED.	TOTAL.
Number of locomotives	1	1
Number of passenger, baggage, mail and express cars (combination car)	1	1
	30	30
Number of freight cars (basis of eight wheels)		15
Maximum weight of locomotives in working order, tons		15
Average weight of locomotives in working order, tons		14
Maximum weight of tenders full of fuel and water, tons		14
Average weight of tenders full of fuel and water, tons		12
Maximum weight of passenger cars, tons		12
Average weight of passenger cars, tons		1
Number of passenger, mail and baggage cars, combined		1
Number of 8-wheel box freight cars		15
Number of 8-wheel stock cars		10
Number of 8-wheel platform cars		5
Length of heaviest engine and tender, from center of forward truck-wheel of engine to center of rear wheel of tender		35 ft. 6 in.
Total length of heaviest engine and tender over all		44 feet.

Are charges for the transportation of the company's supplies included in the earnings as reported for your road? No.

If any part of road was first opened for operation during the past year, state the date.

Ans. Entire line, January 1, 1880.

ADDITIONAL QUESTIONS.

EXPRESS COMPANIES.

American Express Company pays one and one-half first class freight rate per weight of articles carried; express package business, including packages of value, etc., also fruit and other perishable freight. Express company deliver their freight to trains and take it at trains.

U. S. MAIL.

Compensation not yet determined upon for transporting the mail.

LOCAL AID IN BUILDING ROAD.

Details not at hand to make up statement.

COST OF ROAD AND EQUIPMENT.

Total expended for construction	$ 350,899.21
Average cost of construction per mile of road, not including sidings (37.67 miles)	9,314.82

COST OF EQUIPMENT.

Locomotives	$ 5,212.64
Passenger, mail and baggage cars	1,600.00
Freight and other cars	9,024.49
Machinery and tools	957.47
Total for equipment	$ 16,794.60
Average cost of equipment *per mile of road operated* by company in the State	445.83

COST OF ROAD AND EQUIPMENT.

Total cost of road and equipment	$ 367,693.81
Average cost of same per mile	9,766.65

BRIDGES BUILT WITHIN THE YEAR IN IOWA.

	NO.	FEET.
Number of pile and trestle bridges and length in Iowa	71	6,282
Number of crossings of highways at grade	43	
Number of crossings of highways under railroad	5	

RATES OF FARE, ETC.

Average rate of fare per mile for passengers on roads operated by this company, in cents	3.8
Average rate of fare per mile *received* from passengers to and from other roads, in cents	3.3
Average rate of fare per mile *received* from *all* passengers, in cents	3.7
Average rate of local freight per ton per mile on roads operated by this company, in cents	6.15
Average rate of freight per ton per mile *received* from freight to and from other roads, in cents	8.90
Average rate per ton per mile received for all freight carried	7.90

CAPITAL STOCK.

Capital stock issued, number of shares	3,603
Total amount paid in as per books of the company	$ 180,150.00
Total number of stockholders	10
Number of stockholders in Iowa	9
Amount of stock held in Iowa	$ 550.00
Capital stock per mile	4,782.00

DEBT.

Funded debt as follows:

The $144,000 bonds turned over to the trustees, when settled for, will reduce the amount of floating debt the amount received for the bonds.

Unfunded indebtedness	$ 182,461.79
Total amount of debt liabilities	$ 182,461.79
Stock and debt	$ 362,611.79
Debt per mile	4,845.00
Stock per mile	4,782.00
Total stock and debt per mile	$ 9,627.00

ACCIDENTS TO PERSONS IN IOWA.

STATEMENT FOR THE YEAR ENDING JUNE 30, 1880, OF ALL ACCIDENTS RESULTING IN INJURIES TO PERSONS, GIVING EXTENT AND CAUSE THEREOF.

DATE.	NAME.	OCCUPATION.	PLACE.	INJURY.	REMARKS.
1880. April 16	H. Basel	Brakeman	Cascade	Legs and feet crushed.	While changing the link at the rear end of tender, while engine was in motion, walking backward, stumbled and fell between the rails and was caught by tender brake, crushing both feet and legs; he died from his injuries a few hours after the accident occurred. Occasioned by want of care on his part.
May 24	Peter Oans	Deaf mute	1 mile west of Zwingle	Killed	While walking on track was run over and killed by a gravel train; on account of a sharp curve he could not be seen in time to stop train to prevent accident.

RECAPITULATION OF ACCIDENTS.

Killed—Employes—from misconduct or want of caution............... 1
Others—trespassing, on track, etc................ 1

Total killed............... 2

OFFICERS OF THE COMPANY, WITH LOCATION OF OFFICES.

President—F. O. Wyatt.
Vice-President—W. S. Knight.
Secretary—C. M. Carter.
Treasurer—C. M. Carter.
General Superintendent—F. O. Wyatt.
Assistant Superintendent—S. A. Wolcott.
Chief Engineer—F. O. Wyatt.
Superintendent of Telegraph—E. P. Lyman.
Auditor—F. O. Wyatt.
General Passenger Agent—Jos. Chapman.
General Freight Agent—Jos. Chapman.

NAMES OF DIRECTORS, WITH RESIDENCE.

James F. Joy, Detroit, Michigan.
F. O. Wyatt, Dubuque, Iowa.
W. I. Knight, Dubuque, Iowa.
G. G. Banghart, Cascade, Iowa.
D. Beatty, Cascade, Iowa.
H. Bowers, Bellevue, Iowa.
A. J. Dorchester, Bellevue, Iowa.
J. H. Davis, Bellevue, Iowa.
N. Kilbourne, Bellevue, Iowa.
F. May, Cascade, Iowa.
W. H. Francis, Cascade, Iowa.
D. Cort, Zwingle, Iowa.
C. Denlinger, Zwingle, Iowa.

General offices at Dubuque, Iowa.
Fiscal year of the company, January 1st to December 31st, inclusive.

STATE OF IOWA, }
COUNTY OF JASPER. }

I, F. O. Wyatt, President and General Superintendent of the Chicago, Bellevue, Cascade & Western Railroad Company, being duly sworn, depose and say that I have caused the foregoing statements to be prepared by the proper officers and agents of this company, and having carefully examined the same, declare them to be a true, full, and correct statement of the condition and affairs of said company on the thirtieth day of June, A. D. 1880, to the best of my knowledge and belief.
(Signed)
F. O. WYATT,
General Superintendent.

Subscribed and sworn to before me this 4th day of October, A. D. 1880.
[L. s.]
M. P. DOUD, Notary Public.

Received and filed in the office of the Commissioners of Railroads this 5th day of October, 1880.
E. G. MORGAN,
Secretary of Board of Railroad Commissioners.

Appendix VI
Articles of Incorporation
for
The Bellevue & Cascade Railroad Company

(Abridged as indicated.)

The Bellevue & Cascade Railroad Co.
To Whom it may concern

Filed for record this 15th day
of June, A.D. 1933 at 9:45 A.M.
Ida M. McCarthy Recorder

Fee $2.80

Articles of Incorporation
of
The Bellevue and Cascade Railroad Company

We, whose names are hereafter subscribed, do hereby associate ourselves together into a body corporate under the provision of Chapter 384, Code of Iowa 1931, and amendments thereto, assuming all of the powers, rights and privileges granted bodies corporate and all the duties and obligations imposed by said chapter and amendments thereto, and do adopt the following articles of Incorporation, to-wit:

Article I

The name of this corporation shall be "The Bellevue and Cascade Railroad Company."

Article II

The principal place of business of this corporation shall be in the City of Bellevue, Jackson County, State of Iowa.

Article III

The object and purpose of this corporation and the general nature of the business to be transacted by it shall be, to do a general railroad business in all its branches, except the transportation of passengers. [The bulk of Article III spelled out specific objectives and purposes common to all railroads].

Article IV

The authorized capital of this corporation shall be Thirty Thousand Dollars ($30,000) divided into shares of stock as follows: Twenty five hundred (2,500) shares of preferred stock of the par value of Ten Dollars ($10.00) a share, and five thousand (5,000) shares of common stock of the par value of One Dollar ($1.00) a share, which capital stock may be issued at such time as may be determined upon by the Board of Directors and when issued shall be fully paid for in cash or property, provided, however, that when said stock is to be issued for anything other than money, such issuance shall be subject to the approval of the Executive Council of the State of Iowa as provided in Section 8413 of the Code of Iowa 1931. The corporation may commence business when qualifying shares have been issued to the directors provided for in these Articles. [The rest of Article IV defined series issues of Preferred Stock; annual dividends; the right of redemption; the right of conversion etc.]

Article V

The corporate period of this corporation shall begin on the date the Secretary of State issues a certificate of incorporation and shall terminate at the expiration of fifty (50) years from said date with the right of renewal and perpetual succession, as provided by law, unless the corporation be sooner dissolved by a two-thirds vote of the stockholders at an annual meeting or at a special meeting called for that purpose, or by unanimous consent as provided by law.

Article VI

The affairs of the corporation shall be managed by a board of three (3) directors who shall be elected by the stockholders at the annual stockholder's meeting as provided by Article VII hereof. The directors immediately following each annual stockholders' meeting, shall elect a president, a vice president, a treasurer and a secretary and such other officers as they may see fit or as may be provided for by the by-laws of the corporation...(abridgement)...Stockholders only shall be qualified to act as directors, and the disposition by sale or otherwise of all of the stock of any directors, in this corporation shall be equivalent to his resignation as such director and his office shall be considered vacant.

Article VII

The annual meeting of the stockholders of this corporation shall be held at the office of the corporation in Bellevue, Iowa, at 10:00 A.M. on the second Saturday after the first Monday of February of each year, beginning with the year 1934, at which time the stockholders shall elect a board of directors and shall transact such other business as may lawfully come before them.

Special meetings of the stockholders may be called at any time by the President upon giving ten (10) days notice in person or in writing to the stockholders, or such special meeting shall be called by the President at any time upon the request of stockholders representing twenty five per cent (25%) in interest of the shares of stock of the corporation outstanding.

Article VIII

Until the first annual stockholders' meeting of this corporation to be held on the second Saturday after the first Monday of February, 1934, the following persons shall be officers of the corporation, to-wit:

Name

Earl W. Bradley
V.R. Bradley*
S.L. Goldish
W.J. O'Brien

Residence

Duluth, Minnesota
Duluth, Minnesota
Duluth, Minnesota
Des Moines, Iowa

Office

President and Treasurer
Vice President
Secretary
Assistant Secretary

And the directors until said first annual meeting shall be:

Earl W. Bradley
V.R. Bradley*
S.L. Goldish

Duluth, Minnesota
Duluth, Minnesota
Duluth Minnesota

Director
Director
Director

[*V.R. Bradley was Mrs. Earl W. Bradley]

Article IX

The private property of each stockholder in this corporation shall be exempt from liability for the debts of the corporation or obligations created by it. This Article shall not be changed except by the unanimous consent of all stockholders in interest.

Article X

Stock of this corporation shall be transferred only on the books of the corporation. Certificates of stock shall be signed by the President and attested by the Secretary and have the corporate seal affixed thereto.

Article XI

The board of directors may make and adopt such by-laws for the management of the corporate business and the regulation of its affairs as they may deem necessary, the same not to be inconsistent or in conflict with the laws of the State of Iowa or these Articles of Incorporation, and said by-laws of the State of Iowa or these Articles of Incorporation, and said by-laws may be altered, changed or amended from time to time as the board of directors may desire.

Article XII

These Articles of Incorporation, except Article IX, may be amended at any regular meeting of the stockholders of this corporation or at any special stockholders' meeting called for that purpose by a two-thirds (2/3) vote of all holders of common stock voting on such amendments.

In WITNESS THEREOF we have hereunto set our hands this 9th day of June, A.D. 1933.

Incorporators:

Earl W. Bradley

Duluth, Minnesota

W.J. O'Brien

Des Moines, Iowa

Portions in Italics represent handwritten names and addresses.

State of Iowa   )

           (ss:

County of Polk   )

Be It Remembered, that on this 9th day of June, A.D. 1933, before me a Notary Public in and for said County and State, personally appeared Earl W. Bradley and W.J. O'Brien, each of said persons being personally known to me to be the identical person whose names are subscribed to the foregoing Articles of Incorporation and each for himself acknowledged the same to be his free and voluntary act and deed for the uses and purposes therein expressed.

Witness my hand and Notarial Seal at Des Moines, in the County of Polk, State of Iowa, this 9th day of June, A.D. 1933.

Gertrude Zigeler

(Seal)   Notary Public in and for Polk County, Io

Appendix VII
Annual Report
of the
Bellevue & Cascade
Railroad Company
For the Year 1936
As Made To the
Iowa Railroad Commissioners
[This is only a partial sampling showing the amount of track abandoned.]

TABLE 13—ROAD OPERATED AT CLOSE OF YEAR—ENTIRE LINE—1935

PART 1—MILEAGE OF ROAD OPERATED—SINGLE TRACK AND ALL TRACKS AND CHANGES DURING YEAR

Number	Railway Companies	Mileage Operated—Single Track							Mileage Operated—All Tracks								Changes during year
		Line Owned		Line of proprietary companies	Line Operated Under			Total	First main track	Second main track	Third main track	Fourth main track	All other main tracks	Industrial tracks	Yard tracks and sidings	Total	
		Main line	Branch lines		Lease	Contract, etc.	Trackage rights										
1	Atch., Top. & S. Fe	6,539.98	6,394.41	----	1.67	----	323.41	13,259.47	13,259.47	1,827.98	45.69	9.80	----	936.13	5,124.26	21,203.33	*29.00
2	Atlantic Northern	17.07	----				----	17.07	17.07							1.78	18.85	----
3	Bellevue & Cascade	----	----															*35.72
4	Chi., Bur. & Quincy	4,668.14	3,981.79	----	30.81	----	346.95	9,027.59	9,027.59	1,197.57	41.65	6.19	----	933.83	2,881.83	14,088.66	*56.74
5	Chi., Great Western	929.19	73.51	362.63	----	.26	147.15	1,512.74	1,512.74	106.23	11.80	11.80	----	28.61	584.27	2,255.45	*18.77
6	C., M., St. P. & P.	5,889.35	4,080.82	----	360.78	----	792.59	11,123.54	11,123.54	1,143.16	30.32	27.70	----	868.80	3,469.33	16,662.85	*72.25
7	Chi. & No. Western	3,347.94	4,873.55	----		----	133.93	8,355.42	8,355.42	919.55	98.42	83.11	----	764.99	3,192.10	13,413.59	*163.53
8	C., S. P., M. & O.	1,088.51	489.97	----		----	73.81	1,652.29	1,652.29	193.69	16.54	12.77	----	112.95	556.71	2,544.95	*9.32
9	Chi., Rock Isl & P.	3,282.08	1,982.37	34.92	1,826.19	----	448.92	7,574.48	7,574.48	585.21	22.60	10.80	----	440.94	2,514.69	11,148.72	*23.63
10	Great Northern	3,892.03	3,627.68	283.76	.08	----	447.25	8,250.80	8,250.80	653.30	12.76	12.76	----	345.68	2,513.72	11,789.02	*86.77
11	Illinois Central	1,518.67	707.26	1,016.10	1,526.32	----	212.36	4,980.71	4,980.71	886.97	73.44	33.29	196.89	450.49	2,593.19	9,214.98	*6.21
12	Manchester & Oneida	8.03	----			----	.12	8.15	8.15							.75	8.90	----
13	Minn. & St. Louis	1,069.03	456.89	----	.05	----	98.70	1,624.67	1,624.67	27.76			----	72.16	316.67	2,041.26	*42.45
14	Union Pacific	1,937.22	1,615.53	----		1.30	35.55	3,589.60	3,589.60	1,073.31	2.69	2.70	----	385.08	1,384.93	6,438.31	*188.01
15	Wabash	1,735.43	247.08	----	72.65	----	392.12	2,447.28	2,447.28	523.96	13.38		----	157.63	1,239.03	4,381.28	*27.55
	Total, 1935	35,922.67	28,530.86	1,697.41	3,818.55	1.56	3,452.86	73,423.81	73,423.81	9,138.69	369.29	210.92	196.89	5,497.29	26,373.26	115,210.15	*759.95
	Total, 1934	36,011.08	29,001.52	1,736.14	3,819.61	1.56	3,322.58	73,892.49	73,892.49	9,140.71	374.45	211.04	197.10	5,512.32	26,641.99	115,970.10	----
	Increase or decrease, 1935	*88.41	*470.66	*38.73	*1.06	----	130.28	*468.68	*468.68	*2.02	*5.16	*.12	*.21	*15.03	*268.73	*759.95	----

*Decrease.

TABLE 13—ROAD OPERATED AT CLOSE OF YEAR—ENTIRE LINE—1935—Continued

PART 2—MILEAGE OF ROAD OWNED SOLELY—ALL TRACKS AND CHANGES DURING YEAR

Number	Railway Companies	Mileage of								Changes During Year —All Tracks	Road Owned but Not Operated —All Tracks
		First Main Track	Second Main Track	Third Main Track	Fourth Main Track	Other Main Tracks	Industrial Tracks	Yard Tracks and Sidings	Total		
1	Atchison, Topeka & Santa Fe (System)	12,934.39	1,620.49	31.08	9.49		888.16	4,863.31	20,346.92	*67.97	55.94
2	Atlantic Northern Ry.	17.07						1.78	18.85		
3	Bellevue & Cascade R. R.									*35.72	
4	Chicago, Burlington & Quincy R. R.	8,648.19	1,070.93	40.89	5.43		767.82	2,599.58	13,132.84	*64.25	2.78
5	Chicago Great Western R. R.	1,365.33	58.86				28.61	484.76	1,937.56	*35.86	2.94
6	Chicago, Mil., St. Paul & Pac. R. R.	9,911.46	850.23	21.86	20.32		620.77	2,771.08	14,195.72	*110.58	40.01
7	Chicago & North Western Ry.	8,222.52	861.76	98.42	83.11		723.59	3,090.16	13,079.56	*170.99	178.94
8	Chicago, St. P., Minn. & Omaha Ry.	1,581.72	182.80	6.27	2.50		112.69	545.42	2,431.40	*10.22	.26
9	Chicago, Rock Island & Pacific Ry.	5,259.75	382.32	14.97	2.90		228.04	1,691.88	7,579.86	*18.55	34.13
10	St. Paul & Kansas City Short Line R. R.	417.27	2.50				20.38	90.12	530.27	.33	
11	Great Northern Ry.	7,530.53	414.81	11.69	11.60		310.14	2,206.63	10,485.40	*47.03	63.98
12	Illinois Central R. R.	2,230.91	454.78	73.44	33.29	102.71	218.74	1,303.17	4,417.04	*18.95	2.32
13	Dubuque & Sioux City R. R.	760.89	2.75		5.17		32.35	237.09	1,038.25	*.14	1,038.25
14	Manchester & Oneida Ry.	8.03						.75	8.78		
15	Minneapolis & St. Louis R. R.	1,525.92	9.54				72.16	286.68	1,894.30	*42.44	11.89
16	Union Pacific R. R.	3,551.18	1,068.97	2.69	2.70		369.46	1,336.54	6,331.54	*208.28	24.49
17	Wabash Railway	1,979.69	341.39				144.36	900.18	3,365.62	*40.01	9.05
	Total, 1935	65,944.85	7,322.13	301.31	176.51	102.71	4,537.27	22,409.13	100,793.91	*871.32	1,464.98
	Total, 1934	66,515.90	7,350.25	303.85	176.51	102.71	4,549.10	22,666.91	101,665.23		
	Increase or decrease, 1935	*571.05	*28.12	*2.54			*11.83	*257.78	*871.32		

*Decrease.

TABLE 13A—ROAD OPERATED AT CLOSE OF YEAR—WITHIN THE STATE—1935

PART 1—MILEAGE OPERATED, SINGLE TRACK AND ALL TRACKS, AND OWNED SOLELY, AND CHANGES DURING YEAR

Number	Railway Companies	Miles of Road Operated—Single Track						Total Mileage Owned Solely		Total Mileage Operated—All Tracks							Total Mileage Owned Solely	
		Line Owned		Line Operated Under						Miles of								
		Main line	Branches and spurs	Lease	Contract, etc.	Trackage rights	Total	Single track	Changes during year	First main track	Second main track	All other main tracks	Industrial tracks	Yard tracks and sidings	Total	Change during year	All tracks	Changes during year
1	Atch., Top. & Santa Fe	19.99					19.99	19.99		19.99	19.99		1.33	42.69	84.00		83.96	
2	Atlantic Northern	17.07					17.07	17.07		17.07				1.78	18.85		18.85	
3	Bellevue & Cascade								*35.72							*35.72		*35.72
4	Chi., Bur., & Quincy	372.80	846.64			81.75	1,301.19	1,218.60	*8.38	1,301.19	248.96		73.85	309.80	1,933.80	*14.50	1,800.50	*18.34
5	Chicago Great Western	728.57	29.42		.26	5.56	763.81	757.99		763.81	20.06		13.99	232.25	1,030.11	*3.22	1,017.25	*3.42
6	Chi., Mil., St. P. & P.	1,199.28	604.98	.03	.09	68.61	1,872.99	1,804.29		1,872.99	218.91		86.40	480.12	2,658.42	*2.21	2,508.70	*.40
7	Chicago & No. Western	360.79	1,171.90			40.72	1,573.41	1,610.72	*.02	1,573.41	361.31		49.04	463.65	2,447.41	*104.15	2,490.81	*2.69
8	Chi., St. P., M. & O.	56.82				27.50	84.32	56.82		84.32			4.27	47.30	135.89	.05	105.06	.05
9	Chi., Rock Isl. & Pac.	997.52	807.10	334.29	1.66	96.17	2,236.74	1,805.45		2,236.74	109.59		104.81	556.79	3,007.93	*4.08	2,432.45	*2.39
10	St. P. & K. C. S. L.							343.81	*1.46								437.66	.33
11	Great Northern		78.02				78.02	78.02		78.02			9.67	26.34	114.03		112.44	
12	Illinois Central				716.36	1.94	718.30	716.36		718.30	2.75	7.21	30.65	235.85	994.76	*.17	986.57	*.43
13	Dubuque & Sioux City	8.03				.12	8.15	8.03		8.15				.75	8.90		8.78	
14	Manchester & Oneida	8.03					8.03	8.03		8.03							978.56	*34.03
15	Minneapolis & St. Louis	562.76	239.96	.05		71.84	874.61	802.72	*22.95	874.61	4.75		38.99	141.36	1,059.71	*34.03		
16	Union Pacific	2.48					2.48	2.48		2.48	2.25		10.33	56.97	72.03		72.03	
17	Wabash	156.19	36.17			16.79	209.15	192.36	*10.95	209.15	2.20		8.80	62.83	282.98	1.48	232.76	*10.89
	Total, 1935	4,482.30	3,814.19	334.37	718.37	411.00	9,760.23	9,434.71	*79.48	9,760.23	990.77	7.21	432.13	2,658.48	13,848.82	*196.55	13,286.38	*109.59
	Total, 1934	4,551.92	3,877.59	335.83	718.37	390.42	9,874.13	9,514.19		9,874.13	990.77	7.21	463.24	2,710.02	14,045.37		13,395.97	
	Increase or decrease, 1935	*69.62	*63.40	*1.46		20.58	*113.90	*79.48		*113.90			*31.11	*51.54	*196.55		*109.59	

*Decrease.

Appendix VIII
Memorabilia

While the financially troubled Milwaukee Railroad still utilizes, to some extent, the freight yards at Dubuque, the buildings erected by the two River Roads and added to by the C.M.&St.P. still stand. Today most of the buildings are nothing more than warehouses. A far cry from the once prosperous railroad's activities.—*Jon Jacobson*

Zwingle depot, long since converted to residence, from the track side in this 1981 photo.—*Jon Jacobson*

The east end of the La Motte depot as seen through original headlamp lense from one of the steam engines on the branch. Stored for years at the Cascade drugstore and then sold at auction, the 24″ diameter lense was obtained from a Bellevue antique store.—*Jon Jacobson*

Looking northwest at La Motte depot in August 1980. The 20′ by 42′ depot was built after a fire destroyed the original depot in 1910. Residents of La Motte restored the exterior of depot for their centennial celebration in 1979. Tracks ran in the foreground.—*Jon Jacobson*

This electric lantern, used by Engineer Charlie Spielman, is 12" tall with the battery case being 3¾" in diameter. The base is 6¼" in diameter with a lense being suspended below the battery case. The top of the lantern is stamped "Electric Lantern GENESY CO. Kansas City-Missouri" and the handle is a composition material. Lantern now owned by Spielman's son Delbert.—*Jon Jacobson*

The wall lamp above once graced the wall of the La Motte depot. They have been completely restored and now adorn the living room wall of John Bissell's home in Dubuque. Bissell is a prominent commercial artist.—*Jon Jacobson*

Showing years of use, this spittoon rode the gauge on one of the combines. It was saved by Engineer Charlie Spielman and now belongs to his son Delbert.—*Jon Jacobson*

When the village of La Motte celebrated its one-hundredth birthday, specially designed beer cans were sold containing the brewer's art as rendered by Joseph Pickett, Iowa's only brewmaster at Pickett's Brewery in Dubuque. Thousands of the cans were snapped up by collectors of every type.—*Jon Jacobson*

Commemorative belt buckles graced many a waist during the centennial celebrations of La Motte in 1979 and Bernard in 1980.

Currently being used for hay storage, the remains of a B.&C. boxcar rests on a farm near Cascade. Dimension of car is 7' x 24'. The photo was taken in 1981.—*Jon Jacobson*

Remains of stockcar No. 163 behind feed store in Bernard. On the verge of collapse in this 1981 photo, the car had been used as shed for hogs.—*Jon Jacobson*

Jim Schroeder, a Bellevue, Iowa contractor, purchased the decaying remains of caboose No. 055 in 1979. Because the hulk of the waycar was too far rotted, he decided to build, with the help of his sons, an exact duplicate. Measurements of each item, board, opening, and piece of metal were made and the search for the right materials began. Today, it is displayed near Schroeder's home.—*Jon Jacobson*

Author John Tigges standing with the remains of a tank car still being used for diesel oil storage in La Motte in this 1982 photo. The current owner of the tank lists it's capacity as 4,500 gallons when filled to 5'6".

Measuring 25'4" long with a diameter of 66", the tank is marked "Harrisburg Car Manufacturing CO. Makers Harrisburg Pa. 1877" and carries the manufacturers number 6150. The dome is 35" in diameter and 31" tall.—*Jon Jacobson*

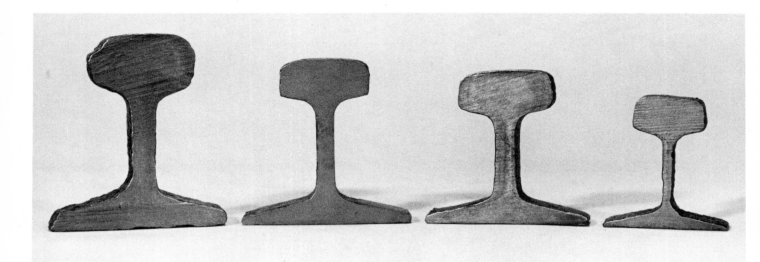

Cross sections of different rail sizes used on the gauge over the years. Left to right: 45-pound rail; 36-pound rail; 30-pound rail; 20-pound rail. The 60-pound rail used on the narrow gauge branch line was salvaged for scrap and use elsewhere on the Milwaukee Road.—*Jon Jacobson*

Typical narrow-gauge spikes found along the B.&C. right-of-way with standard gauge spike at far right. The narrow gauge spikes measure in length, from left, 4⅞", 5½", and 5⅜". The standard gauge spike measures 6½".—*Jon Jacobson*

Photographed with a Kennedy half dollar for scale, the 15-pound rail and the small spike measuring 2¾" long are so small that one has to be dubious that they were used on the Bellevue-Cascade branch.

The mine-sized rail pictured above was given to a Cascade resident by his now-deceased brother, a former B.&C. employee, who claimed the rail was used on the branch. The spike was found along the old right-of-way near Bernard by an area farmer. As the size and origin of these artifacts are at conflict, the authors leave the decision to the reader.—*Jon Jacobson*

Posing with the five-chime whistle from No. 3 (foreground) and a bell from one of the steamers on the B. &C. is Ray Kemerer, of Zwingle, Iowa. Paying the salvage value of scrap metal in 1936, Kemerer paid $1.50 for the whistle and $3.85 for the bell. Standing 22" tall, the whistle is 6" in diameter while the bell frame stands 33" tall with a diameter at the throat of 15".—*Jon Jacobson*

"Narrow Gauge" cigars were once manufactured by J.H. Gerlach in Bellevue. Boxes such as the one pictured are in demand by collectors of memorabilia concerning the gauge.—*Jon Jacobson*

Notes

1. There were steeper grades than the 2.8 percent average incline at the summit. For example: one four hundred-foot grade of 3 percent was not long enough to cause problems because of the relatively flat terrain on either side.

2. No one seems to know the correct spelling *or* pronunciation of this particular siding on the gauge. In most references it is "Sylva Switch;" people in the area pronounce it "Sylvie Switch" or "Sylvia Switch;" one railroad blueprint shows it as "Silver Switch Station." There was no station as such at this location. The book will refer to it as "Sylva Switch." You, the reader, are at liberty to make your own choice.

3. The exact elevation is 530 feet as per the Milwaukee Profile blueprint of 1905.

4. Most timetables, from the nineteenth century through the 1920s, show no stop at Paradise. Still, Timetable Number Four, dated February 26, 1933, shows Paradise located 7.2 miles from Bellevue and 25.7 miles from Cascade.

5. The average grade for the summit was 2.5 - 2.8 percent and had one stretch of 2.91 percent.

6. Bridges abounded on the gauge. According to the 1905 Milwaukee Road Profile Map, which was furnished by Ted Schnepf, seventy-nine bridges existed on the little railroad when the Milwaukee took over in 1880. However, the Iowa railroad commissioners report for the year ending June 30, 1880, shows seventy-one pile or trestle bridges and five locations where the rails passed over roads, for a total of seventy-six bridges. Take your choice.

7. The March 18, 1918, Milwaukee Road Right-of-Way Map (courtesy of Ted Schnepf) shows right-of-way specifications as narrow as twenty to thirty feet in Bellevue where the rails threaded their way between existing buildings to one hundred feet wide at most of the fills. Other individual widths are listed as: twenty-five feet, twenty-seven feet, forty-three feet, several stretches of fifty feet and one of sixty-three feet.

8. The actual height of this bridge (K-868) was thirty-eight feet and was built not only on a 2.09 percent grade but with a twelve-degree curvature.

9. As far as Ted Schnepf has been able to determine, the gauge may have been the only narrow gauge railroad to pick up mail on the fly. This provision allowed eastbound trains to keep their steam and momentum up for the grade between bridges K-870 and K868. The latter trestle curved twelve degrees and had a 2.09 percent grade.

10. For an in-depth explanation of James F. Joy's battle with the Chicago, Burlington and Quincy, how it affected the River Road and led to Joy's ouster from the C.B.&Q.'s board of directors, see *Burlington Route—A History of the Burlington Lines* by Richard Overton (Knopf, 1965), especially pp. 122-132, The Revolution; and p. 148, sale of the River Road to the C.M.&St.P.

11. This 268-foot siding at the top of the summit was La Motte Hill Switch and was located just east of La Motte. However La Motte Hill never caught on and the summit is still referred to as the summit today.

12. Although this method of communication was not unique to the gauge, it seemed to have been in use during the daylight hours as well as the nighttime since most of the pictures showing the rope in place were taken during the daytime. The Delaware and Hudson, for example, only used this method after dark.

13. Ted Schnepf maintains that he has uncovered information indicating the gauge leased three tank cars.

14. Because the U.S. Railroad Administration controlled all railroads during WWI, it ordered the Colorado and Southern to send to the Chicago, Milwaukee and Saint Paul Railway, a narrow gauge locomotive. The Milwaukee had to make extensive repairs before the 2-8-0 was operable. Since no price had been agreed upon, a considerable amount of time passed, once the USRA passed out of existence, before the C&S and the Milwaukee settled.

15. When the Milwaukee began operations in Indiana, it became the *only* Class A railroad ever to operate *through* Chicago.

16. The 1905 Milwaukee profile map shows Sylva Switch as a passing siding with access from the mainline at both ends. The siding was built on a nine-degree curve and 2.43 percent grade.

17. This inventory from the collection of Ted Schnepf.

18. Whether there were two or three tank cars is immaterial. However, one does still exist as a storage tank for an oil company at La Motte.

Photo Credits

Although many persons made photographs available to the authors, and many were available from more than one source, it is proper to credit, when known, only the original photographer. As one would expect with photographs being shared and copied by various parties over a number of years, the same photograph was occasionally attributed to more than one photographer (as well as differing locations and information as to what was pictured). In such cases the authors made every effort to determine the correct individual and information. When the originator could not be determined, no photo credit is given.

To add another bit of minor confusion, there were apparently two "J. Streusers," perhaps brothers, one of whom had a photography business in Bellevue, the other in Cascade. Photographs known to have been made by either of the J. Streusers is simply credited "Streuser" in the text.

We are particularly appreciative of the efforts of the early photographers such as the Streusers and Claude Wyrick, who made some high quality photos with equipment and under conditions that were not conducive to such results.

A special expression of thanks is due to the following individuals, who have been fans of the gauge for years and made their extensive photo collections available:

John Adney	Gerald Feeney
John Bissell	Ray Kemerer
Richard Bogue	Wm. Kell
Charles Conter	Albin Lee
Lester Deppe	Harry Roeder

Also deserving recognition, not only for sharing their photos and artifacts but for resisting the urge to throw out that "old stuff," are:

Adrian Aitchison	Wm. Dall	Geo. Rausch
Wm. Aitchison, Jr.	Ruth Ganfield	Jim Schroeder
Geo. Bevan	"Buck" Gross	Dick Sullivan
Vic Beringer	A.J. Hachmann	John Sullivan
"Slim" Boyle	Steve Knepper	Delbert Spielman
John E. Bradley	Adrian Kurt	Wm. Talbert
"Jack" Cannon	Mrs. Joe Merfeld, Sr.	Gerald Volk
Mr. & Mrs. Wm. Cook	Paul Neiers	
Robert W. Courtney	"Jack" Otting	

Philip Hastings, Ralph Otting, and Ted Schnepf—three railfans who made photos and provided additional invaluable information, also deserve a special thanks.

Bibliography

Arpy, Jim."The Railroad That Tried and Died." *Focus*, (June 2, 1972). pp. 4-5.

Bruce, Alfred W. *The Steam Locomotive in America*. W.W. Norton, New York, 1952.

Byam, P. *History of the Cascade Narrow Gauge Railroad*. Herald Publishing Company, Dubuque, 1880.

Cary, John W. *The Organization and History of the Chicago, Milwaukee & St. Paul Railway*. Milwaukee, 1893.

Corbin, Bernard G. and William F. Derka. *Steam Locomotives of the Burlington Route*. Bonanza Books, New York, 1978.

Daniels, Winthrop M. *American Railroads: Four Phases of Their History*. Princeton, 1932.

Derleth, August. *The Milwaukee Road: Its First Hundred Years*. New York, 1948.

Donovan, Frank P. "The Milwaukee Road in Iowa," *Palimpsest Magazine*, (1964). pp. 177-240.

Dorin, Patrick C. *Milwaukee Road East*. Superior Publishing Company, Seattle, 1978.

Fetters, Thomas. "A letter to the Editor." *Trains Magazine*, (December 1957), p. 58.

Fleming, Howard. *Narrow Gauge Railroads in America*. Grahame H. Hardy, 1949.

Goetzinger, James. *Cascade & The Narrow Gauge*. Loras College, Dubuque, 1963.

Hofsommer, Donovan L. "A Chronology of Iowa Railroads," *Railroad History, Bulletin #132*.

Holbrook, Stewart H. *The Story of the American Railroads*. Crown Publishers, New York, 1947.

Jensen, Oliver. *The American Heritage History of Railroads in America*. American Heritage Publishing Company, New York, 1975.

Kueter, Roger. *The C.B.C.&W. R.R. The Last Narrow Gauge East of the Rockies*. Loras College, Dubuque, 1964.

Larrabee, William. *The Railroad Question*. Chicago, 1895.

Lee. Albin L. "Narrow Gauge in the Hawkeye State." *Trains*, (April 1954).

———. "The Bellevue & Cascade Story" (Parts 1, 2, & 3). *Narrow Gauge Gazette*, (July/August, September/October, November/December, 1979.

Lewis, R.C. *Handbook of American Railroads*. Simmons-Boardman Publishing Company, 1951.

O'Connell, John. *Railroad Album*, Popular Mechanics Company, Chicago, 1954.

Overton, Richard. *Burlington Route—A History of the Burlington Lines*, Knopf, 1965.

———, *Burlington West*. Cambridge, Chicago, 1941.

Riegel, Robert E. *The Story of the Western Railroads*, University of Nebraska, 1964.

Stan, J.W. *One Hundred Years of American Railroading*, Dodd, 1928.

Turnipseed, John. *John Turnipseed Visits Dubuque Country, Prairie Farmers' Home and Country Directory for Dubuque Country*, The Prairie Farmer Publishing Company, Dubuque, 1924.

Wilson, Ben Hur. "Narrow Gauge in the Hawkeye State," *Palimpsest Magazine*, Iowa Historical Society, (April 1932).

Wood, Charles R., and Dorothy M. *Milwaukee Road West*, Superior Publishing Company, Seattle, 1972.

Board of Railroad Commissioners' Annual Report 1879
Board of Railroad Commissioners' Annual Report 1880
Board of Railroad Commissioners' Annual Report 1881
Board of Railroad Commissioners' Annual Report 1898
Board of Railroad Commissioners' Annual Report 1919
Board of Railroad Commissioners' Annual Report 1935
Board of Railroad Commissioners' Annual Report 1936
Railroad Commissioners' Report # 7670-1916

Iowa Journal of History and Politics—The Thirty-Fifth General Assembly—
   1913/1914
History of Dubuque County 1880, 1915, 1942
History of Jones County 1910
History of Jackson County 1879
Illustrated History Atlas of the State of Iowa, 1875
Portrait and Biographical Record of Dubuque, Jones and Clayton Counties, Iowa
   1894

Abstracts, Deeds, Titles: Dubuque County Courthouse
   Book T.T.-162
   Book S.S.-376
   Book T.L.-1
   Book 139M-172
   Book164M-429
   Book 130M-59
   Book 143M-110
   Book 130M-110
   Book 143M-583

Cascade *Pioneer*:

   June 23, 1876
   August 4, 1877
   July 4, 1879
   January 23, 1880
   March 13, 1885
   February 28, 1916

Bellevue *Leader:*

   April 28, 1875
   November 7, 1877
   January 9, 1878
   January 30, 1878
   February 20, 1878
   July 4, 1878
   July 18, 1878
   September 5, 1878
   October 3, 1878
   December 12, 1878
   March 6, 1879
   March 20, 1879
   July 3, 1879
   August 21, 1879
   September 25, 1879
   January 22, 1885
   September 22, 1887
   July 12, 1888
   February 28, 1907
   May 5, 1910
   May 19, 1910
   October 20, 1910
   January 26, 1911
   September 18, 1913
   November 20, 1913
   March 19, 1914
   May 4, 1916
   December 25, 1924
   March 25, 1926
   March 23, 1933
   June 15, 1933
   July 27, 1933
   March 21, 1935
   November 14, 1935
   February 20, 1936
   April 16, 1936

Dubuque *Herald:*

   April 5, 1877
   November 5, 1877
   December 30, 1877
   January 9, 1878
   January 20, 1878
   November 3, 1878
   January 25, 1879
   March 2, 1879
   May 18, 1879
   May 20, 1879
   January 1, 1880
   August 28, 1880
   August 29, 1880
   January 28, 1881

Dubuque Daily Herald:

   February 26, 1893
   March 8, 1893
   March 15, 1893
   March 25, 1893
   May 24, 1893
   May 26, 1893
   April 25, 1913

Dubuque *Telegraph Herald (Times-Journal)*:

   February 22, 1907
   February 23, 1907
   May 5, 1932
   March 26, 1933
   June 9, 1933
   December 12, 1933
   March 18, 1934
   May 21, 1979
   June 3, 1979
   April 11, 1980

Ralph Otting, who worked on the gauge as a teenager walks west up the "summit" in the spring of 1981, recalling the good days. Memories and a few artifacts are all that remain of Iowa's Slim Princess.—*Jon Jacobson*

254

INDEX